T0211660

Getting to Standard Work in Health Care

Getting to Standard Work in Health Care

Using TWI to Create a Foundation for Quality Care
Second Edition

Patrick Graupp and Martha Purrier, RN

Routledge
Taylor & Francis Group

A PRODUCTIVITY PRESS BOOK

First published 2012
2nd Edition published 2022
by Routledge
600 Broken Sound Parkway #300, Boca Raton FL, 33487

and by Routledge
2 Park Square, Milton Park, Abingdon, Oxon, OX14 4RN

Routledge is an imprint of the Taylor & Francis Group, an informa business

© 2022 Taylor & Francis

The right of Patrick Graupp and Martha Purrier to be identified as author of this work has been asserted by them in accordance with sections 77 and 78 of the Copyright, Designs and Patents Act 1988.

Library of Congress Cataloging-in-Publication Data

A catalog record for this title has been requested

ISBN: 9780367473938 (hbk)
ISBN: 9780367462673 (pbk)
ISBN: 9781003035305 (ebk)

Typeset in Garamond
by Deanta Global Publishing Services, Chennai, India

Patrick

To my daughter Emily, a nurse in Orange County, CA

who continually inspires me with her dedication and passion for life.

Martha

To my TWI Colleagues, it has been an honor to partake in your Fellowship and Camaraderie. And to Brian Knowles, the best Kaizen partner ever!

As Sensei Chihiro Nakao always says, "Keep trying."

Contents

Foreword to Second Edition

Integrated health care delivery systems are arguably among the most complex socio-technical systems that exist. Patients with highly variable physical conditions present in fragile physiological states with coexisting pain, discomfort, and emotional anxiety. These patients need health care workers to provide compassionate, prompt, efficient, effective, and defect-free care. Health care workers come to the hospital or clinic environments after years and even decades of advanced training at prestigious academic centers from around the world. Physicians, nurses, pharmacists, therapists, and technologists are trained under the tutelage of skilled professors and instructors. They were trained how best to perform their work. Owing to this instruction, trusted health care professionals have very particular perspectives on how best to perform their part of the health care work. Similarly, other critical team members that oversee the environment of care including housekeeping, dietary, and facilities maintenance workers all have their own specific background, training, and experiences that shape how they perform their crucial work. Unfortunately, most health care team members were not trained how to adapt their work patterns to the "standard" of their chosen health care organization. Furthermore, and possibly most importantly, most health care organizations have not developed clear detailed standards for the crucial value-added work performed for patients on the front lines.

I have spent a career in health care delivery as a cancer surgeon (gynecologic oncologist), a medical school and residency educator, a manager in operating room environments, a chief medical officer, and as the chief operating officer of a multi-state integrated health care delivery system. I have served in both academic and in community not-for-profit health systems. Through these experiences I have observed that health care workers are drawn to this field with a deep sense of altruism and empathy. However, I am convinced that health care delivery systems lag well behind other industries as it pertains to our collective ability to determine the standard to which any unit or department will perform work. In health care, policies and procedures are developed and embraced. But standard work is largely missing. Health care workers provide care to the best of their ability using knowledge gained from their training and their experience. However, without a defined unit-based organizational standard, great variation exists in the work and hence in the outcomes related to that work. This variability in work patterns leads to unnecessary variation in outcomes resulting in a negative impact on cost, quality, safety, and patient experience. This current condition in health care delivery systems sets the stage for low-reliability outcomes.

High-reliability industries around the world have learned that organizational excellence and operational excellence are dependent upon the systems they deploy and improve over time. These systems pull forward principle-based key behaviors that create a culture of safety, quality, efficiency, and service excellence. All industries are socio-technical by nature. These industries rely on people, processes, and technology to deliver desired products and outcomes. Some industries require more human-to-human interactions than others. Consider the automobile manufacturing industry compared to the airline industry. In the automobile manufacturing industry thousands of team members work seamlessly and cooperatively to create vehicles. The manufacturing team members do not have direct interaction with customers, though, and the vehicle itself will largely please or displease a customer. However, in the airline industry, thousands of team members must work seamlessly and in cooperation with customers to get them on the planes on-time and then safely delivered to their desired destinations. The latter is the more high-touch and complex socio-technical system which has improved dramatically over the last eight decades. Consider the safety and efficiency of flying today versus what it was like in 1940!

All things considered, health care may be the most complex and the most high-touch industry in the world today. Patients and family members present for highly variable care and support. These patients may desire an elective surgery to help them walk normally again or they may have had a life-threatening event, such as a heart attack, where they have no choice but to seek critical medical care. In each case, the health care system must be able to respond appropriately, assembling the correct resources and skilled team members to deliver both a high-quality health outcome and a satisfying experience. Not only do patients present with highly variable needs and conditions, but they also face the additional variation introduced by health care professionals with regard to their own work patterns. It is easy to see why health care outcomes are not consistently optimum. For instance, think of a patient who is being prepared to undergo an intense surgical procedure. Depending upon the physician preference the patient may be prescribed very different forms of pre-surgery anesthesia preparation. It does not stop there. Surgeons have different preferences regarding choices of instrumentation and implants utilized in the operating room. There may be varied practice patterns of the circulating nurses working in the operating room. Team members may vary on how well they adhere to the use of the time-out checklist. Consider also how the care team in the recovery room manages the early recuperation of the patient and so on, down the line to the ICU and finally to the acute care ward. This is an example of a complex series of activities that must be carefully orchestrated around a patient. The critical nature of this work and the impact this work can have on an individual and family make it even more important that we understand the significance of standard work and standardization of work processes and systems.

Leaders in health care delivery systems are called upon today to improve the efficiency, quality, safety, and patient experiences associated with the care they render. The leaders must focus on providing an optimal employee experience that will drive both engagement and retention. Where will leaders find tools that can help them create and manage the most complex socio-technical and high-touch system in the world? Well, in short, this book provides highly effective methods which will help. Herein the authors share their vast knowledge of Training Within Industry (TWI) as it can be applied to health care delivery organizations. TWI, which was first developed during World War II, was developed by industrial engineers and statisticians to help quickly train a new workforce who would be able to build planes, ships, tanks, and artillery. TWI had to help address not only the technical aspects of work instruction but also had to help deal with the human interactions required to produce worksite cooperation.

Fast forward eight decades. Today TWI offers health care leaders three powerful tools to help them deliver more reliable outcomes for patients and employees. These three skills are Job Instruction, Job Relations, and Job Methods. The authors show how these methods, when applied as part of an overarching management system, help leaders develop a standard, train to the standard, optimize interpersonal relations in the work areas, and provide for a better understanding of necessary unit-to-unit interdependence. This book will provide CEOs, operational directors, medical directors, managers, and frontline leaders with the novel application of TWI within health care.

Industry leaders have learned over the past eight decades that organizational and operational excellence are only achieved when leaders demonstrate respect for all people and when they lead with humility. These two principles are foundational to building a corporate culture and key behaviors that foster a productive work environment, while pulling forward the best thinking from all team members. All health care leaders, myself included, must be willing to throw out arrogance and be willing to learn from the lessons of other industries. Health care is a high calling, but it is not above or somehow better than other vocations or walks of life. Surgeons, nurses, pharmacists, and administrators can glean much from other industries about how best to deliver consistent results. With this book, the authors are giving health care leaders knowledge about skills which will assist them in their journey toward operational excellence and delivery of highly reliable outcomes.

Paul DePriest, MD
Executive Vice President and Chief Operating Officer
Baptist Memorial Health Care

Foreword to First Edition

In 1940, the United States faced perhaps the greatest crisis in its history. World War II was engulfing Europe and threatened to become even broader in its scope. In 1941, the United States was attacked at Pearl Harbor, triggering the Pacific War, and the United States subsequently entered the European Theatre of the war. The darkest days and most challenging times in our history were upon the nation. Many have studied this crisis as well as preceding and subsequent crises. It is clear that truly extraordinary times require new and different thinking. Old assumptions and mental models can no longer be relied upon. In 1941, that meant that new approaches to support manufacturing and to build infrastructure to support our war effort were necessary. New ways of engaging and training our workforce were required, the citizens rose to the occasion, and the result was truly remarkable.

Today, we again face a daunting crisis. Our healthcare system is in chaos as manifested by close to 50 million uninsured, suboptimal quality and safety, costs that are unsustainable and are overwhelming to both the public and private sectors, and a demoralized healthcare workforce within our clinics and hospitals. The American public, as well as the healthcare industry itself, is clamoring for solutions to healthcare's complex challenges. We know that our most valuable resource in these efforts is our people—the committed men and women who work every day to help keep patients healthy and reduce the burden of disease. In fact, 70% of the costs in the healthcare industry are related to labor or people costs. Our staff at all levels, including physicians, nurses, technicians, and front-line personnel, are doing great work, yet they are hampered by excessive complexity, waste-filled processes, lack of goal clarity, and inadequate or absent job-specific training.

In their book, *Getting to Standard Work in Health Care*, Graupp and Purrier share a major breakthrough in deepening our understanding of how we can best empower and equip our personnel to do their very best work on behalf of our patients and our communities. They show us a way forward that reflects the evolving understanding of how people learn and how best to train our most precious resource, our people. They also help us understand why we must discard our old ideas and assumptions to actually have our team members performing optimally. But what is perhaps most remarkable is that today's answers actually emerge from and build upon the solutions put in place during that time of crisis over 70 years ago!

Today's healthcare challenges are myriad in scope and complexity. Ensuring safety has been a significant emphasis, and despite concerted efforts, there is still a defect rate in health care that would never be tolerated in any other industry. Waste leading to excessive costs is a huge issue, with estimates ranging from 30% to 50% of all healthcare expenditures adding no value for patients. Workforce morale issues exist as mentioned, in part because we are asking our teams to work in waste-filled environments of chaos.

At Virginia Mason, where we employ the Virginia Mason Production System as our management method, we have learned that Standard Work eliminating non-value-added variation can greatly reduce errors and defects, improve quality, and reduce the burden of work for our staff. But this Standard Work is only as effective as our ability to put it into place and execute the many innovative initiatives underway across our country and around the world. Unfortunately, in many organizations, we are seeing the best intentions and ideas all too often becoming failures of execution because we have inadequately trained and prepared our workforce.

In *Getting to Standard Work in Health Care*, we are presented with Job Instruction Training, an approach that specifically addresses these issues and produces results in better execution and improved performance wherever it's been tried. In World War II, this meant that the Training within Industry methods resulted in successful production to sustain our existential war effort, and in health care we are seeing examples of superior execution, safer care, and a better experience for our patients. Proficiency and efficiency no longer must be dependent on "figuring it out," which has all too often been the case in health care. We now have a defined method that works reproducibly and in many ways more deeply embeds safety right into the work itself. The results of this approach are now predictable: Staff perform tasks without defects!

It is clear that the healthcare environment of today and the future must embrace rapidly developing new technology amid continuously increasing complexity. A trained, competent and engaged workforce has never been more essential. We are repeatedly finding that simplification and standardization where possible are precursors to higher reliability, better care, and an improved patient experience. In today's healthcare delivery world, a rejection of standard work and the perpetuation of a craft culture are no longer acceptable.

Graupp and Purrier have shown us a way forward that challenges many of our old assumptions and builds on our knowledge of learning theory. This approach demonstrates great respect for the worker and helps each of us ensure that our people have the resources, skills, and demonstrated proficiency that our patients have every right to expect. Our patients entrust us with their care at the most personal and intimate times in their lives. We must continue to strive to honor this sacred trust by ensuring each of us is as prepared as we can be to provide the very best care and caring. The important work of Graupp and Purrier will help us create this reality for patients everywhere.

Gary S. Kaplan, MD, FACP, FACMPE, FACPE
Chairman and CEO
Virginia Mason Health System

Preface

This book will introduce to you a method of training that was developed in the 1940s during World War II. Why, you will immediately ask, would anyone want to learn about a methodology from a bygone era, a time long before modern advances in both medicine and the understanding of human behavior? Certainly it would be more worthwhile, one would assume, to study the most advanced techniques and up-to-date theories of how we get people to perform their work in health care in the most efficient and correct manner without creating undue risk to patients as well as themselves. It turns out, though, that while science and technology have advanced dramatically in the past seven decades, people are still pretty much the same. It would not be far-fetched to say that people haven't changed all that much in the past several centuries, or even millennium. They still have all of their emotional frailties—pride, hope, despair, jealousy, love, fear, etc.—and, whether it is at work or at play, they still have to learn skills the "old fashioned" way, through practice and repetition. These things have not changed.

There are certain points in American history when society has been able to see more clearly various aspects of human nature that are authentic. In other words, the dynamics of the time forced people of the United States to cut through the petty grievances and disagreements of the era and reach deeply within and find their true, best selves. World War II was certainly one of those times. The threat to our way of life was severe. Moreover, the disruptions to the everyday running of the society and the needs placed on that society in order to win the war created incredible demands on it that had to be filled quickly and accurately. If our society could not find the true heart of the people and successfully unite, it would fail in this mission. We know how the story ends, so we can only marvel today at how well the people achieved what they needed to do. It is no small wonder that they have been labeled "the Greatest Generation."

In modern times, most lifestyles are generally more affluent and threats to our lifestyle exist, but not so immediate and pressing as the entire world at war. We tend to do just the opposite of what the World War II generation did—we make things difficult and complicated and we argue over small details to the point where the truth becomes obscured. Questions arise about how we behave and grow as human beings. We struggle to find the answers to overcome our problems and challenges and become frustrated when things fail to get better. Yes, life and work have grown more complicated since the 1940s, but what we are finding today, in industries across the United States and around the world, is that there is great wisdom in relearning and redeploying some of the timeless concepts that were utilized by those who came before us. What they sought, in fact, is just what we are seeking today and what countless generations before them sought as well, and that is how to achieve excellence in the work people do on a regular basis.

After the fall of France in June 1940, the United States knew that, whether we got into the war ourselves or not, we would play a vital role in supplying our allies with materiel to fight the war. This would mean rapidly ramping up defense production at a time when there were 8 million unemployed people in the country, most of whom had never before worked in a factory or shipyard. Later, when the United States ultimately did enter the conflict and millions of experienced workers left the country to fight in Europe and the Pacific, the demands on industry to develop the abilities and skills of its workforce only became more pressing. One report from that time described the situation like this:

> The nation's vocational education system could be geared to give them some schooling before they went to work, but not even the best school could bring them up to the level of productive proficiency that would be required by the demands being placed on the aircraft and automotive plants and the shipyards even in defense days.*

To meet these demands on production, the US Government War Production Board created the Training Within Industry Service to "assist defense industries to meet their manpower needs by training within industry

---

* War Production Board, Bureau of Training, Training within Industry Service (September 1945). *The Training within Industry Report: 1940–1945,* Washington, D.C.: US Government Printing Office, 3.

each worker to make the fullest use of his best skill up to the maximum of his individual ability."* It is interesting, although aggravating, to read the language of the era that always used a masculine pronoun for every person referenced. However, there is also a great deal of irony here considering that a large part of the workforce that went into the factories and shipyards were women—housewives who replaced all the men who went off to fight the war. This was the era of Rosie the Riveter, an iconic image of a woman who put a bandana over her hair, rolled up her sleeves, and went to work building B-29 bombers.

TWI drafted a national network of professionals, drawn largely from industry, to come up with an answer to a very simple question: "What can we do to make more people productively useful?" They responded by having their staffs collect, develop, and standardize three programs that came to be known as the "J" programs:

1. *Job Instruction (JI) Training:* Trains supervisors how to instruct employees so they can quickly remember to do a job correctly, safely, and conscientiously.
2. *Job Methods (JM) Training:* Trains supervisors how to improve job methods in order to produce greater quantities of quality products in less time by making the best use of the manpower, machines, and materials now available.
3. *Job Relations (JR) Training:* Trains supervisors how to lead people so that problems are prevented and gives them an analytical method to effectively resolve problems that do arise.

Notice that each of these programs was targeted at frontline supervisors to provide them with needed skills to succeed in their mission of producing quality goods at the proper cost. However, TWI defined "supervisor" as not only people in charge of others—the boss—but people who direct the work of others. In other words, if you were giving direction to other people and guiding their work, even though you might not necessarily be their boss, you were a target of the programs. The TWI founders realized that the person most influential in getting workers to learn and perform their duties with excellence and high morale is the person directly supervising their work. That is as true today as it was 80 years ago.

---

* ibid.

The secret to TWI's success during the war lay in the "multiplier effect" which was created to allow a minimum number of qualified trainers to reach a maximum number of people. They standardized each program and then trained people who then trained other people how to perform each method. By the end of the war, over 10 million people were trained under TWI. The huge success of the program is credited with helping win the war of production.* The TWI Service monitored 600 of its client companies from 1941 until it ceased operations in 1945 and the last survey, performed just after TWI had shut down field operations, detailed the following percentages of these firms reporting at least 25% improvement in each of the following areas[†]:

- Increased production: 86%
- Reduced training time: 100%
- Reduced labor hours: 88%
- Reduced scrap: 55%
- Reduced grievances: 100%

You may be thinking that this is all well and good for the manufacturing sector, but where does health care fit in? Guess what? The TWI methods were used in health care during World War II as well. Doctors and nurses were also sent off to the war and there was a shortage of hospital workers here in this country, just as there was a shortage of factory and shipyard workers. In the March 1944 edition of *The American Journal of Nursing*, Sister Mary Brigh, RN, of St. Mary's in Rochester, Minnesota, wrote about how TWI was being applied to nursing:

> To those outside the magic circle of hospital life, hospitals and nurses are synonyms for efficiency. Those inside the circle are only too conscious of the many weak pillars supporting it. Even a limited experience with the TWI programs indicates that the simple and practical methods presented in the three courses, Job

---

* Alan G. Robinson and Dean M. Schroeder, "Training, Continuous Improvement, and Human Relations: The U.S. TWI Programs and the Japanese Management Style," *California Management Review*, 1993, 35: 40.
[†] ibid. p. 44.

Instruction, Job Methods, and Job Relations, lead to increased efficiency and decreased strain.*

It is always the case in any human endeavor that when we find we are in need of improving ourselves, we must first go back to the basics. During World War II, the US government and corporations had to go back to the basics of good supervision and frontline leadership in order to develop a new workforce of people, including many women who had never worked outside the home before much less in traditional male-dominated sectors such as a factory or a shipyard. With this challenge, they could not hide behind poor precedents or bad habits that had buried themselves in the working culture. They had to cut to the truth about how people are led and taught. These truths do not change. It is only we who have to keep relearning them again and again. As mentioned previously, we have to keep going back to the basics.

There is again today a need, greater than we could have ever imagined, to lead workers effectively and to train them with a sure and reliable method. The COVID-19 pandemic has brought the world again to a "state of war" where all stops must be pulled out if our way of life is to survive. Health care organizations and facilities are being forced to provide accurate information just as fast as we can discover it. Places where care is given are being redesigned, workers are needing to perform new jobs that they have never before done, and equipment and supplies are changing regularly due to availability. Safety is literally a matter of life or death. TWI was made for times such as these.

This book will review all three of the original TWI methods as they are applied in health care. You will be shown how this program is as vital and applicable in the current era as it was when it was developed so long ago. In fact, with our emphasis on improvement and the creation of "perfect care," we will demonstrate how the TWI methods are indispensable to the achievement of what needs to be achieved in health care today. It is our hope that others will benefit from our experiences and can use what we have learned, taking the movement even farther. Once we have risen from this current crisis, let us not turn away from this method again, as we did after WWII, but continue to apply its teachings as we improve the safety and quality of health care for all.

---

* Sister Mary Brigh, R.N., "We Cannot Afford to Hurry: Training within Industry Applied to Nursing," *The American Journal of Nursing*, March 1944, pp. 223–226.

Acknowledgments

When we first started working together implementing TWI at Virginia Mason Medical Center (Virginia Mason) in 2009, we had no idea how appropriate and effective this method would prove in its health care application. We knew only that TWI's deep roots in the Toyota Production System would inevitably mesh with the incredible work the hospital was doing to implement the Lean philosophy. Since then, our extensive work at hospitals across the country, in particular, St. Joseph Health System (now Providence St. Joseph Health) and Baptist Memorial Health Care, propelled TWI forward and laid the groundwork for its application in the health care field. We feel privileged to be able to document these efforts in this book. We realize, however, that we could not have done it without the support of many other people who helped prepare the path for us.

We are deeply indebted to Linda Hebish from Virginia Mason Medical Center who saw TWI's potential early on and was instrumental in bringing it to Virginia Mason. Linda also proofread our finished manuscript for the first edition giving invaluable advice. Sarah Patterson and Charleen Tachibana of Virginia Mason were also strong sponsors and we greatly appreciate their tireless support as we continued to study, implement, and integrate TWI into our daily work.

We would like to thank Ellen Noel and Debbie Kelly from Virginia Mason, who helped us discover how and when to apply Job Instruction in order to get the very best results. Their willingness to try new things and then to reflect upon what we just learned made for a fantastic environment. Thanks to the Charge Nurse Team at Bailey-Boushay House who practiced over 23 versions of a daily management system integrating observations of standard work to achieve stability and continuous improvement.

We would like to thank Lili Bacon and Amber Gutman who were instrumental in introducing TWI at St. Joseph Health System and helped immensely with this book. Their early recognition of the value and use of TWI was a great inspiration in the pursuit of TWI in health care when we wondered if this was just a "niche" endeavor for select organizations.

Baptist Memorial Health Care rolled out, over several years, all three of the TWI modules across its 22 hospitals under the leadership of Skip Steward who was a tireless promoter, and trainer, of the program. There are too many true leaders to name at Baptist who played pivotal roles in promoting and sustaining TWI, but we send our thanks to Brad Parsons, Judy Mann, Ginger Purvis, Mary Ellen Sumrall, Sandy Holman, Brandy Waldrop, Kim Colbert, Susan Livengood, Melanie Edens, James Keller, Andrea Simpson, Kelly Tracy, Marci Wicker, Hannah Wilson, Nikki Griffin, Katie Parker, and Madison Rowan.

We would especially like to thank Scott Curtis and all of the people associated with the TWI Institute for their tireless efforts in promoting the TWI programs in health care. They continue to provide indispensable support for hospitals and health care organizations in the United States and around the world to implement this powerful program.

Finally, we would like to thank Kristine Mednansky from CRC Press for encouraging us to pursue this 2nd edition and her staff for their expertise, perseverance, and patience in helping us shepherd this book from concept to completion.

About the Authors

Patrick Graupp began his training career at the SANYO Electric Corporate Training Center in Kobe, Japan, after graduating with highest honors from Drexel University in 1980. There he learned to deliver TWI and other training to prepare employees for assignments outside of Japan. He was transferred to a compact disc fabrication plant in Indiana where he obtained manufacturing experience before returning to Japan to lead SANYO's global training effort. Graupp earned an MBA from Boston University during this time and was later promoted to the head of Human Resources for SANYO North America Corp. in San Diego, California, where he settled.

Graupp delivered a pilot project in 2001 to reintroduce TWI in the United States. The positive results encouraged him to leave SANYO in 2002 to deliver the TWI program on a wider scale throughout the United States in the same manner as he had been taught in Japan. He described this in his book *The TWI Workbook: Essential Skills for Supervisors*, a Shingo Research and Professional Publication Prize recipient for 2007. With colleagues in Syracuse, NY, he helped found the TWI Institute which has developed over 3,000 certified trainers who teach TWI on six continents in over 30 countries in 18 languages. He is the author of numerous books on TWI including *Creating an Effective Management System: Integrating Policy Deployment, TWI, and Kata*, which was published in 2020.

Martha Purrier is a registered nurse with over 30 years of experience in the health care setting. She earned a master's degree specializing in the clinical care of patients with cancer and in the training of nurses. During the past 20 years, she has worked at Virginia Mason Medical Center in Seattle, Washington, in a variety of positions: Oncology Clinical Nurse Specialist, Director of Inpatient Oncology and IV Services, Director of the Kaizen Promotion Office, and Director of Nursing Services at Bailey-Boushay House. Virginia Mason adopted Lean as a management methodology in 2001, and Purrier was certified in Rapid Process Improvement Workshops in 2006. During her work in IV therapy, the team won the Mary McClinton Patient Safety Award for the application of Lean methods, which produced increased safety for patients receiving central lines. In 2008, Purrier was appointed to the Kaizen Fellowship Program. She is a certified instructor of the TWI Job Instruction program and has spoken internationally on the application of TWI and Lean to health care.

CASE FOR STANDARD WORK IN HEALTH CARE

1

Chapter 1

When Clinical Best Practice Is Not Actual Practice

Introduction

Health care can be dangerous. In 1999, the Institute of Medicine first brought to the forefront the epidemic of medical errors. At that time, it was estimated that as many as 44,000 to even 90,000 Americans die each year as a result of medical error. Medical errors, incredibly, were statistically ahead of death due to motor vehicle accidents (43,458), breast cancer (42,297), or AIDS (16,616).* And while each of these other major causes of death is the target of concerted and continual efforts to reduce their totals through activism, fundraising, and research, deaths due to medical error seemingly fly under the nation's radar and go unnoticed—until you become the victim of an error.

Health Grades, Inc. released the 2nd Annual Patient Safety in American Hospitals Report in 2005. In this report, they noted that for every Medicare patient that experienced one or more safety incidents, what the Institute of Medicine (IOM) defines as an "accidental injury due to medical care, or medical errors," he or she had a one in four chance of dying.† Between 2001 and 2003, there were more than 1 million incidents associated with US$8.5

---

* Institute of Medicine of the National Academies, 1999. *To Err Is Human: Building a Safer Health System*. Online at: http://www.iom.edu/Reports/1999/To-Err-Is-Human-Building-A-Safer-Health-Sys tem.aspx.
† American Hospitals Report, 2005. Online at: http://www.healthgrades.com/business/img/PatientSa fetyInAmericanHospitalsReport2005.pdf.

DOI: 10.4324/9781003035305-1

billion of excess cost.* Hospital-acquired infection rates alone accounted for 9,552 deaths and US$2.6 billion in excess cost, almost 30% of the total excess costs related to patient safety incidents.†

In May 2016, the *British Medical Journal* published updated counts calculated by Marin Makary and Michael Daniel from John's Hopkins University, declaring the number of deaths from medical errors between 2008 and 2013 to be greater than 250,000.‡ This raises the incidence of dying from medical errors to the *third* leading cause of death in America. Great debate continues in the medical community regarding how to calculate this data and how to report deaths (data is currently gathered by review of death certificates, and there remains no ICD code for death caused by medical care givers); we will leave this for others to pursue.

For our work here, these numbers amount to nothing less than a health care epidemic that cannot, and must not, be ignored. When our goal is "one preventable medical error is one too many" and when our nation is being crushed by the high cost of health care, these tens of thousands of deaths and tens of billions in excess costs are simply not acceptable. What is more, medical errors are not limited to hospitals. In 2009, the *Journal of the American Medical Association* published an article comparing malpractice claims between inpatient and outpatient settings. They found that the number of claims reported to the National Practitioner Data Bank for events in the outpatient setting was similar to that reported for the inpatient settings.§

The Institute of Medicine and other reporting agencies have put real numbers to this critical issue, but it is sad to say this danger is not new. We have always known that errors do sometimes occur. Nevertheless, no one in health care wishes to be involved in harming a patient or in making any type of error. In fact, we are drawn to this profession by the desire to help, to relieve suffering, and to heal. So, it is devastating to be involved in an error. In the current system, everyone learns from their mistakes and adjusts their practice so that they never make the same error again. But there are too many types of errors and there are too many of us caregivers to cover every possible mistake that might happen. Most importantly, patients simply cannot afford the terrible burden of all of us learning from our individual mistakes.

---

* ibid.
† ibid.
‡ *British Medical Journal*, May 2016: https://www.bmj.com/content/353/bmj.i2139/rr-54.
§ T. Bishop, A. Ryan, and L. Casalino, "Paid Malpractice Claims for Adverse Events in Inpatient and Outpatient Settings," *Journal of the American Medical Association*, 2011, 305(23): 2427–2431.

Human Nature and System Design

Is medicine art or science? This is an age-old question, not unlike the chicken and egg dilemma. It is, of course, both. Science deals with a systematic understanding of our physical world, whereas art is the conscious use of human skill and, from a broader perspective, creative imagination. We advance in science through empirical study while we develop art through practice and experience and inspiration. But, in today's ever-expanding scientific world, we cannot deny the Art of Medicine. For all of our clinical studies, evidence of best practice recommendations, and outcome measurements to validate the effectiveness of our therapies, we are still dependent upon the human elements of critical thinking and judgment to deliver good health care.

The reality of medicine today is that there are many areas that have yet to be studied or recommended upon. To put it the other way around, we know what to do with absolute certainty in only a few areas. This means that health-care practitioners at all levels must use their experience and trust their judgment in order to make the right decisions and perform the correct procedures. This good thinking is the real Art of Medicine. With good reason, then, there is much skepticism over efforts to rationalize the work we do in health care to make it more efficient and productive, as if we were workers on an assembly line at a Toyota factory (Toyota factories around the world have become the benchmark in manufacturing efficiency) in Japan. While no one denies the overarching role of science when it comes to understanding human health and biology, we certainly must also recognize the unique human contribution that is added to each and every health care interaction and intervention.

Standard work is often criticized as just one such threat to the autonomy of practice, a threat to the practitioners' freedom to apply critical thinking and judgment to a specific patient care situation. Standard work is defined as doing a task in a defined way each and every time it is done. It is thought that standard work is in direct opposition to the customization and individualized care that is central to effective health care. The terms "cookie cutter medicine" and "one size fits all" are often used to counter and criticize the proposition of creating "standards" to health care practices. However, medically treating every patient with only one tool, such as one antibiotic or one surgical procedure, is not at all what is meant by standardization. Standard work is about creating reliability in the process and stability in the overall delivery of care. It is about *making routine the elements of care that we know to be beneficial so that we can create capacity for critical thinking and deduction where it is most needed.* By stabilizing part of the care, we create more room for good thinking. Reliability in our care, after all, is the only way that we will be certain that what we are doing is beneficial and not harmful to the patient.

In May 2011, *The New Yorker* posted Dr. Atul Gawande's commencement address to the graduates of the Harvard Medical School.* Dr. Gawande is a professor at Harvard Medical School and the Harvard T.H. Chan School of Public Health and is the bestselling author of *Better* (2007), *The Checklist Manifesto* (2011), and *Being Mortal: Medicine and What Matters in the End* (2014). In his address, Dr. Gawande contrasted medicine of the past with today's challenges. He described how we now have treatments for nearly all of the tens of thousands of diagnoses and conditions afflicting human beings, whereas just 60 years ago "there were only a few." We have more than 6,000 drugs and 4,000 medical and surgical procedures. Moreover, these advances have come to us within one generation of training professionals. It is no longer possible for any one person to possibly hold all of the knowledge and technical skills needed to care for a patient, he explained, and yet our medical schools still train in the style of the craftsman. Medical training is still designed to prize autonomy, independence, and self-sufficiency among its highest values.

Dr. Gawande points out that "medicine's complexity has exceeded our individual capabilities as doctors." In actuality, every individual contributes only a piece of the total care for a patient, so if we continue with a structure that prizes autonomy and independence, it will be difficult to achieve great care. We need to understand what each individual contributes and how each contribution adds value to the care provided. And, Dr. Gawande believes, if we want to be able to function on this wide of a scale, we need discipline, "the belief that standardization, doing certain things the same way every time, can reduce your failures." That is the theme of this book and the Training Within Industry (TWI) skills described here gives us the means to demonstrate the exact value that each job contributes.

It is no longer possible for any one doctor to hold all the information and to possess all the skills needed to manage everything themselves. The public's experience is that we have amazing individual clinicians and the most advanced medical technologies, but these do not consistently come together

* Atul Gawande. *The New Yorker*, May 26, 2011. Cowboys and Pit Crews. Online at: http://www. newyorker.com/online/blogs/newsdesk/2011/05/atul-gawande-harvard-medical-school-comme ncement-address.html.

to provide a complete and consistent system of care. "We train, hire, and pay doctors to be cowboys, but it's pit crews that people need," according to Dr. Gawande. In a NASCAR pit crew, for example, you have individuals assigned to specific tasks, namely jacking up the car, changing the front tires, changing the rear tires, carrying the tires, and putting fuel into the car. There is also a utility person who attends to the driver and cleans the windshield. Working in perfect, well-trained harmony, this team can change four tires and refuel a racecar in 12 to 16 seconds. And, depending on the always unique and differing conditions of the race and the racecar at the time of the pit stop, each member of the pit crew will help the other with their tasks: the gas man will help pull away old tires if the car doesn't need full refueling and the jack man will watch to be sure the tire changers have secured all the lug nuts.

Our responsibilities extend beyond the competency of our own professional contributions, just as any one person on the pit crew, while performing a specific and highly defined role, is responsible for the overall success of the race. They extend to understanding all the critical parts needed and the sequencing of these contributions to achieve the most optimal outcome for the patient. Imagine an outpatient clinic visit where there is no waiting because your health care team is expecting you and has each step of the process choreographed right from the minute you walk in. Imagine a system of health care where the right screening and detection procedures are followed at the right time in your life based upon your health risks. Your history and medication information follow you no matter which specialist you see in a coordinated system where each piece picks up right where the last one left off. Each provider understands the contribution of the other toward optimizing your health.

Reaching these kinds of results will not be easy, but it is possible. As Dr. Gawande explains:

> And, the pattern seems to be that the places that function most like a system are most successful. By a system, I mean that the diverse people actually work together to direct their specialized capabilities toward common goals for patients. They are coordinated by design. They are pit crews. To function this way, however, you must cultivate certain skills, which are uncommon in practice and not often taught.*

---

* Ibid.

To get colleagues along the entire continuum of care to function together like a pit crew will require humility, an understanding that no matter who you are, how experienced or smart, if you rely only on yourself, you will fail. It will require discipline in order to standardize care, performing certain tasks the same way every time in order to reduce errors. And it will require teamwork, the recognition that others can save you from failure no matter who they are in the hierarchy.

As we stated above, the discipline required to standardize our work is no easy task. On the surface, it appears to be a grand, noble, and even obvious work; it is a philosophy that most of us can readily recognize as beneficial given the potential gains. But to act on this vision requires a commitment to the details. A commitment to do *all* of the small things right *all* of the time. Believing in this philosophy and doing it, however, are two different things.

Throughout the health care industry, good clinical practices are already established for many simple procedure recommendations, practices that are backed by the strongest evidence. In these cases, we no longer question the strength of the science behind the guidelines. Yet, contrary to all reason, we do not follow these standards consistently. We "override" the recommendations with our own logic and rationale. Hand hygiene, where people do not wash their hands when they know they are supposed to, is the classic case, but there are others. For example, health care workers oftentimes override recommendations in the application of a complete set of personal protective equipment (PPE) (gown, gloves, and a mask) when entering the room of a patient in isolation. We may say, "I'm not planning on touching anything, and this is for contact precautions, therefore, I do not need to wear any protection." Or we may say, "I'm just going in there for a second; no need to gown, I'll just hold a mask up to my face."

Labeling a specimen is another such case. Here a prescribed sequence of actions is designed to minimize the risk of unlabeled or mislabeled specimens from reaching the lab. This process includes matching the label to the patient's armband for verification, collecting the specimen, and attaching the label right there on the spot. Yet, we still have unlabeled and mislabeled specimens that reach the lab. How does this possibly happen with such a specifically prescribed process? One organization discovered that the printer for the patient labels was located in one area of the department, the lab collection materials in another, and the patient in a third area—their room. Because the staff member had to round up the needed supplies from two different areas before entering the patient's room, they sometimes made the decision to override the standard by taking a shortcut, dropping the step of obtaining the label before entering the patient's room. The rationale used was, "I'll label it when I get back to the nurses' station. I have to come back anyway in order to drop off the specimen for transport to the lab." By rationalizing the omission of the critical safety check of comparing the label to the patient's armband, mislabeled specimens creep into the process.

Other examples of not following our own practice guidelines include both simple everyday practice shortcuts as well as more personal practices that keep us safe and healthy even as we work around sick people. We fail to follow procedures, such as how long to swab an intravenous port before injecting a medication or a catheter lock before accessing it. We fail to follow health maintenance screenings or even, amazingly, schedules for getting an influenza vaccination for ourselves. When we investigate the root cause of an error, we often find a "failure to follow the procedure/protocol." Is this really the root cause? If we continue to ask why ("Why was the protocol not followed?"), we start to get more specific and useful answers:

It was too far to walk; I was trying to save time.
I did not understand the details and why they were important.
I thought that my way would be easier.

Knowing the right thing to do does not seem to be enough to influence practice. We will not achieve reliability, and thus great outcomes, if only some of us follow the standards some of the time, or even if most of us follow the standards most of the time. To achieve reliability, it must be all of us, all of the time. We will need to work together to discover the best sequence and the best way to deliver care.

In the years since the IOM report, the best minds in our industry have worked to identify the factors that contribute to the risk and the opportunity for making errors. For example, we are moving away from excessively long mandatory hours of work, standardizing abbreviations for medications, and eliminating needles wherever possible. Perhaps most importantly, we are eliminating the culture of blame. Blame does nothing to improve safety. In a culture of blame, no one speaks up, no one calls out the potential for an error, and few report actual errors. The problem in health care is not "bad workers"—the problem is "bad systems." Dr. Paul Batalden, an expert in quality improvement in health care and founder of Health Care Improvement Leadership Development at Dartmouth, has said that "our systems are designed perfectly to give us the results that we are getting." If we believe this, we can move forward. There are three things that we must do in order to correct and improve our systems:

1. We must systematically engineer safety into our care.
2. We must provide more effective training for new caregivers in the profession.
3. We must continually update our training for veteran employees and move clinical best practice from research studies into actual daily practice.

Engineering Safety into Our Care

In all facets of our culture there has long been the notion that "accidents will happen," which implies that these tragedies "can't be helped" or that they are "the cost of doing business." This way of thinking, of course, provides very little solace to the victims of these accidents and, as we have pointed out, they are equally as devastating to those who commit them. The truth of the matter is that accidents have causes and, if these causes are eliminated, then the accidents can be prevented. This takes an incredible amount of effort to achieve, but when the result is nothing less than possibly saving a human life, there should be no limit to the energy we put into this endeavor.

The good news is that the work of providing safer care has begun. For example, we know that there is a high risk for errors prior to surgery or procedures and that these errors can be catastrophic. In the past, there was oftentimes a culture of intimidation contributed to by the authority asserted by the proceduralist as well as the urgency created by a very busy schedule. With individual team members busily preparing and performing their own duties, no one member of the team had the opportunity to keep the whole picture in view and this narrow-mindedness of vision and purpose allowed for mistakes to slip in. There is no shortage of horror stories about incorrect limbs being amputated and patients being treated for illnesses they didn't have. By engineering a "pause" into the process and using a checklist of critical elements in surgical and procedural areas, this culture is changing. Everyone involved with the care of a patient, regardless of his or her role, is now required to speak up and concur with the proposed plan for care. The checklist provides the structure for everyone to follow and assures that every important item is reviewed by the entire team prior to caring for the patient—by slowing down, the team reduces errors and rework (Figure 1.1).

BEFORE PATIENT LEAVES ADMIT AREA

ADMIT NURSE: _____
- ☐ Identify Patient ("It takes Two")
- ☐ Patient is NPO   ☐ Patient has a ride home
- ☐ Contact Precautions   N   Y _____
- ☐ Allergies   N   Y (Arm band on)
- ☐ H&P within 30 days (available)
- ☐ Necessary labs drawn and results reviewed :

Date	HGB:	HCT:	PLT:
Date:	INR:	PT:	PTT:
Date:	Creat:	Other:	

- ☐ Medications reviewed (Updated in Cerner)
- ☐ Anticoagulants : (See IR Guidelines)   ☐ None or N/A
  ASA – stop date: _____   Ibuprofen – stop date: _____
  Plavix – stop date: _____   Coumadin –stop date: _____
  Lovenox – stop date: _____
  Anticoag Clinic _____
- ☐ Nursing assessment completed
- ☐ Verify consent is accurate and signed

🛑

PROCEDURALIST or RESIDENT: _____
- ☐ Identify Patient, Procedure and Site/Side
- ☐ Verify side with green armband with patient involved to the degree possible
- ☐ N/A
- ☐ Review relevant documentation and match to the patient
- ☐ Complete Procedural and Moderate Sedation Physician Report
- ☐ Relevant images and/or diagnostic tests are labeled and available

CIRCULATING RAD TECH: _____
(Confirms before the Time-Out)
- ☐ Required supplies/equipment available

ANESTHESIA PROVIDER: _____
- ☐ Anesthesia Assessment completed
  Difficult airway/aspiration risk
      ☐ Yes   ☐ No
- ☐ Anesthesia plan of care discussed with Proceduralist
  - Duration of intended procedure
  - Special Needs identified
  - Type & technique of anesthesia required

(a)

IN PROCEDURE ROOM – BEFORE LIDOCAINE
- ☐ Proceduralist calls for all-team stop for Time-Out

PROCEDURAL RN: _____

🛑

- ☐ Identify self: first name and role
- ☐ Identify patient using two identifiers
  - Patient states full name and Date of Birth when possible
- ☐ Confirm consented procedure
- ☐ Review
  - Allergies
  - Labs
  - Medications
- ☐ Procedural Time Out Board has been updated

SCRUB RAD TECH: _____
- ☐ Identify self: first name and role
- ☐ Verify special equipment availability

CIRCULATOR: _____
- ☐ Identify self: first name and role
- ☐ Confirm that correct patient's information is on imaging equipment
- ☐ Confirm that correct MD's information is on imaging equipment
- ☐ Confirm site mark visible and marked with yes, if applicable

ANESTHESIA PROVIDER: _____
- ☐ Identify self: first name and role
- ☐ Concerns, co-morbidities and hemodynamics
- ☐ Antibiotics – ordered/administered/re-dosing plan
- ☐ Plan for post-procedure pain management

PROCEDURALIST or RESIDENT: _____
- ☐ Identify self: first name and role
- ☐ Site/side confirmed with imaging   ☐ N/A
- ☐ Verify planned procedure
- ☐ State relevant patient clinical history
- ☐ State anticipated difficulties/ significant co-morbidities
- ☐ Post op plan
- ☐ Solicit any others in room to identify self & role
- ☐ Encourage – any Additional Input or Safety Concerns
- ☐ **All team agree verbally (individually)**

(b)

Figure 1.1   Procedural safety checklist. (2010 Virginia Mason Medical Center. All rights reserved.)

Ten years since the World Health Organization developed the checklist as part of its Global Patient Safety Challenge, the Department of Clinical Surgery at the University of Edinburgh reported "a 47% reduction in mortality and a 36% reduction in complications in a cohort of nearly 8,000 patients from 8 different countries."*

To counter the stigma associated with being involved in an error, and to reverse the culture of blame, we must work toward transparency and more open and honest communication. We can demonstrate this by reporting actual and *potential* errors and openly discussing these in team meetings where everyone is given the opportunity to express their concern without fear of reprisal or condemnation. During these discussions, the emphasis is not on who is to blame, but on what contributed to the event, how we counter those factors, and what will be done to implement and sustain the countermeasures. Most of all, recognition is given for the reporting of these

* Published online 17 May 2018 in Wiley Online Library (www.bjs.co.uk): https://bjssjournals.onli nelibrary.wiley.com/doi/10.1002/bjs.10907.

problems so that people are encouraged to continue the practice. An example of talking points to assist a leader in facilitating this type of discussion is included in Figure 1.2.

Another way that hospitals and health care centers are trying to engineer safety into their processes is the way in which we use technology to purposely prevent errors. With electronic medical records, for example, a patient's medical allergies are stored in the database and if any provider prescribes that medication, the program will alert the provider to the risk of adverse reaction. Also, the electronic medical record eliminates the need to interpret handwriting and puts the patient's past medical history right at the fingertips of the team. As we learn more about the systems that we have designed, we are actually seeing more and more opportunities; the momentum is all around us.

The more we understand the contributing factors to medical errors and mistakes, the more successful we will be at eliminating risk. As we eliminate risk, we eliminate errors. Therefore, the need to engineer safety into our care is one of our greatest needs. We must rethink and redesign our processes, both human and mechanical, so that they provide safety as the overarching and uncompromising goal. In order to achieve that goal, though, we must also have *a mechanism that ensures these redesigned processes actually become a regular part of our daily work.* As we will see in this book, the Training Within Industry (TWI) program provides a specific and learnable skillset that allows us to both analyze our work methods finding opportunities to make them easier and safer to do as well as to take these improved processes, both hard and soft, and make them our standard way of working through effective training and leadership. This brings us to our next two goals of providing more effective training for new caregivers and training veteran employees in the best clinical practices to date.

More Effective Training for New Caregivers

The second need for our industry is the need to train new caregivers into the profession. In years past, training was seen as a sort of rite of passage or initiation. Newcomers had to earn the respect of their peers and knowledge was acquired individually, over time, with the burden and responsibility of being trained placed on the learners themselves. Competency, which was coveted above all, was elusive. "Experts" enjoyed the status and exclusivity

Yellow PSA Investigation

A Guide for Managers: PSA Arrival to Report Out

Getting a weekly report

Many managers inspect a high volume of Patient Safety Alerts. To ease this review, VM Patient Safety will e-mail these managers a weekly report of Yellow Patient Safety Alerts (PSAs) assigned to them or related to their area/department.

Weekly report

What is a Yellow PSA?

A Yellow PSA is a "low priority" PSA as determined by VM Patient Safety using the **PSA Sorting Tool** below. A Yellow PSA must have a total score between 2 and 4 using the tool.

	Add top score of each risk
Potential for harm	No risk = 0
	Minor to Moderate = 2
	Major or death = 3
Occurrence of Care Process	Infrequent = 1
	Weekly or Monthly = 2
	Hourly or Daily = 3
Resources needed to resolve	Single manager = 1
	Multiple depts. = 2
	Hospital-wide = 3
Liability exposure	None = 0
	Moderate = 2
	Major = 3

Overview of key tasks for managers

1. Review PSAs listed in weekly report.
2. Send e-mail of acknowledgement to staff reporting the PSAs.
3. Determine if the PSA can be resolved alone or if additional assistance is required.
4. Investigate details of PSAs from involved staff.
5. Report findings and solutions to your own staff.

1. Review PSAs

Managers are expected to inspect the PSAs listed in their weekly report. If a report contains no PSAs, that means no PSAs were either assigned to them, or were related to their area/department.

2. Acknowledge reporting staff

Provide positive feedback to staff reporting PSAs to you, thanking them for their concerns. Do this even if you think the PSA should not have been assigned to you, for the front-line staff were not responsible for the assignment.

3. Do you need help?

VM Patient Safety made its best attempt to assign the PSA the appropriate risk priority and manager based on the available information.

Consult your supervisor first if you feel you need help. Your supervisor may be able to offer you guidance and allocate resources to ease your work load.

If you feel a PSA should not have been assigned to you, tell VM Patient Safety. You can suggest an alternate manager.

If you feel you need help resolving the PSA, this may mean it should have been sorted as an Orange or Red PSA. Tell VM Patient how you would have scored the PSA using the PSA Sorting Tool listed in the left-hand column.

4. Investigate the PSA

- **Interview staff** involved in the PSA to determine a course of action.
- **Ask "why" 5 times and explore contributing factors** get to the root cause of a defect or problem.
- **Keep notes!** Your supervisor may also receive this PSA as part of a monthly round-up of PSAs assigned to direct reports and might ask you about it.

5. Report findings and solutions

Engage your staff at PeopleLink to discuss the safety events you received.

- **Encourage reporting PSAs** so you are kept informed of all safety issues. The PSA System isn't punitive. PSAs identify defects and are how leadership learns about safety concerns and fixes them. Staff are empowered to report.
- **Ask for staff input.** Has your staff encountered these situations before? Pass around blank Everyday Lean Idea forms.
- **Discuss your solutions.** Ask if the solutions are clear.
- **Encourage reporting follow-up PSAs** to see if the solutions are working.

Share your solutions.

- Talk with your peers and supervisor.
- Notify VM Patient Safety of your solutions that have cross service use.
- Post to VM's Idea Supermarket.

VM Patient Safety Department, 206-583-6057 (x 30000 in the hospital)
VMMC.VM_Patient_Safety_Alert@vmmc.org
V-Net > Patient Safety

Edited July 29, 2011

Figure 1.2   Guide for Managers. (2011 Virginia Mason Medical Center. All rights reserved.)

of the title and were not forthcoming with sharing their "hard-earned secrets of the trade." A successful new staff member was one who remained vigilant in order to recognize and collect the best practices from among his or her peers who operated under the cultural principle of "do as I do." Over time, then, by watching numerous experts, asking the right questions, and trying out practices, good students became proficient caregivers.

TWI refers to this training method as "showing alone." Eventually, the learner may understand how to do the job, but only being shown how leaves to chance the learner's understanding of the importance of the job, the right sequence of steps, and the critical factors that make for the success of doing the job correctly. Another popular phrase has been, "see one, do one, teach one" implying that the learner ought to "jump in" and get it quickly (no time for proper training!) and that proficiency is gained by doing the task/skill a single time, or "close enough." These methods do not include information that might make the job safer or easier. By leaving it up to the learner to "figure out" how to do the job, the result is that patients become the guinea pigs of this learning by trial and error. No one should have to experience this ineffective approach and it goes without saying that this is exactly where many of the medical errors we discussed earlier occur.

The industry has long understood the problems with this approach, though it is still, unfortunately, deeply entrenched in the culture of how things get done in health care. Today training models based on mentorship, where learners are assigned to a competent worker (a preceptor or buddy) to instruct them, are becoming the norm. While this is an improvement from our previous random instructor model, there are still many deficiencies. First of all, not every competent worker makes for a great instructor. A person may be skillful at doing a job, but that is different from being skillful at instructing that job; these are two separate and distinct skillsets. A willingness to learn themselves and a genuine caring and concern for others are just two qualities identified by Liker and Meier in their book, *Toyota Talent* (McGraw-Hill, 2007), where people are not assigned to be mentors based solely on their job skills and availability, but on their aptitude to be good trainers. Figure 1.3 is an example of how information from Toyota's experience might be incorporated into an assessment tool helping to identify the potential for great trainers.

Second, and perhaps most importantly, even if we assign people with the right qualities to train our new caregivers, they need a strong method by which to perform that training. In other words, they need a sure and

Trainer Capability Evaluation Sheet		
Name: _____		
Department: _____		
	Score	Notes

		Score	Notes
Intuitive ability/personal characteristics	Willingness to learn		
	Adaptability and flexibility		
	Caring and concerns for others		
	Patience		
	Taking responsibility		
	Confidence		
	Questioning nature		
	Average for personal characteristics		
Fundamental/ learnable skills	Observation and analysis ability		
	Communication skills		
	Attention to detail		
	Job knowledge		
	Respect of fellow employees		
	Average for fundamental skills		

Scoring

0–1 = Intermittently Demonstrates   2–3 = Generally Demonstrates   4 = Consistently Demonstrates

Willing and Able to Learn – the true Master Trainer is a Master Student. A trainer must have the desire and ability to continually learn and grow and to reinvest his or her own learning into the teaching. People with this trait make efforts to learn on their own initiative and accept new challenges.

Adaptable and Flexible – every training circumstance will be different: work conditions, ability of the student, time available, etc. The trainer must be adaptable and not rigid in their teaching methodology.

Genuine Caring and Concern for Others – trainers must want the student to become successful in the task and as a person overall. They respect others and can be empathetic of a person's situation as a student. They demonstrate genuine interest in the individual and naturally make efforts to help others learn- without being asked to do so.

Patience – Conditions for the ideal training situation rarely occur, and challenges are plentiful. Some students will need lots of practice to master the job. If the trainer is easily frustrated, they will not be able to put the learner at ease so that they can concentrate on the task.

Persistence – a trainer must stick with the process until the outcome is achieved. They must be "ok" that everyone has a different capacity for learning new skills and that not everyone will learn at the pace that they have mastered a skill. Persistence should not be confused with belligerence or doggedness- relentless pestering of the student leads to resentment.

Taking Responsibility – The responsibility for a successful outcome rests with the trainer. If the student hasn't learned, the trainer hasn't taught. They must continue to adapt the training plan until the desired outcome is reached.

Confidence and Leadership – Trainers should be confident and self-assured; viewed as the content expert. They must be able to handle having their capability challenged, their rationale questioned and should come across as an authority without being seen as an autocrat.

Questioning Nature – trainers should question the content of a job and fully understand why each step is important. They have already asked all of the questions that students come up. They have sought out the answers on their own and are willing to share this insight.

Figure 1.3   Trainer capability evaluation sheet. (Adapted from J. K. Liker and D. P. Meier. 2007. *Toyota talent: Developing your people the Toyota way*. New York: McGraw-Hill. With permission.)

dependable method that will work every time when applied in order to ensure that learners are fully capable of doing their jobs and adhere to the best practices for doing them. This training method should not be left to chance or to the whim and individual preferences of different trainers. In effect, what we need is a *standard for training*, just like we need a standard for any other process or task, so that every time training is performed it follows a defined method that ensures success. We will present this method, TWI Job Instruction, in this book.

In some facilities, the process by which we learn a clinical practice is moving toward incorporating skills labs and the chance to practice best practice procedures in a controlled setting. This removes the patient from the first trial performances while simulating a real clinical setting. Instructors show and tell how to do procedures and the TWI method works just as well in this setting. The constraints for this method of training, however, are the resources of space, the cost of the technology and equipment, freeing caregivers up from current assignments of providing direct care, and the limited number of clinical situations that can be set up in the skills lab.

Training Veteran Employees in Clinical Best Practices

There is an urgent need to move clinical advances "from the bench to the bedside" or from research studies into actual daily practice. We always need to update our practice and, as professional clinicians, we must actively pursue the advancement of our craft. We are trained in the scientific method where hypotheses are tested and statistical rigor is applied and retested. Once assured that the new process is an improvement over the current process, we publish the findings. This is done via numerous modalities: papers in journals, books, presentations at conferences, and via the Internet. The method of information dissemination is well established and expanding with new technologies. Access to these new findings is readily available. Our professional training and the need to maintain accreditation by obtaining continuing education drive us to seek out these new practice findings so we read articles, attend conferences and webinars, discuss and debate the new findings, and incorporate them into our own practice.

The reality of this process, though, is that it is very slow moving. It may take up to ten years or more for a known best practice to make its way into daily practice with a critical mass of caregivers. Why does it take so long if we have a reliable process for assuring the recommended change is warranted and we maintain a reliable and diverse means of "getting the word out"? Why don't we adopt the new recommendations immediately?

One explanation, and there are several change management factors to consider, is found when we critique the method by which we update practice within our organizations. Again, it is the way in which we design our systems that holds us back. We typically assign an expert clinician to write or rewrite a procedure document depicting the way in which specific care ought to be carried out. These experts have access to the best and latest research publications and they are trained to interpret and translate the findings into actual practice instructions. This is important and good work that has a well-established history across nearly every organization. *The problem is how we next use these documents with our staff.*

How do we train everyone in this new technique of delivering care? How do we motivate them to use the new method regularly? Everyone is busy and the entire staff is never completely together in one location "off-line," so we come up with novel and creative ways to try and change regular routines and behavior of the staff. Popular methods include physically posting or electronically sending the new procedure document for staff to review when they have time. The document might be lost among other emails or visually not accessible given the large number of other important postings in a department. Staff may be assigned numerous electronic training "modules" that they work through on their own which may even include a quiz to "verify" knowledge learned. Another common method is to present the information at a short "huddle" or at a meeting where staff pauses from their work with patients to hear announcements. All of these strategies fall back on a less effective method known in TWI as "telling alone," where an instructor tells the learners the critical information and expects them to organize and filter the information correctly if they hope to recall it at a later time. Even if they can do this effectively, there is still no guarantee that they understood it correctly or can actually put it into their own practice.

Another drawback to the procedure update process is that we commission this work in batches, usually once a year, or, even more likely, every three to four years, usually in sync with an outside accreditation visit. There may be a dozen or more updated procedure documents for staff to review. We may even strategize a half-day training session to run everyone through stations to quickly cover all of the new material with a large number of staff to get it all done "in one shot." This method of training will usually produce nothing more than a completed checklist. Staff will be signed off and we may be tempted to symbolically wipe our hands of this task, declaring that we have trained everyone necessary in the new best practices when we know, realistically, that these practices, in fact, will not become the norm.

Yet another drawback to the procedure update is that research findings for new practices, which confidently declare themselves to be a "Best Practice," give an abundance of technical information but very little, if any, practical directions on how to actually perform the practice. For example, when using a specific type of personal protective device against a particular organism, the research does not include such practical logistics as the sequence in which to don (put on) the protective equipment and how to safely doff (remove) the equipment with the least amount of risk for contamination or exposure. A review of one medical center's policy for personal protection equipment (PPE) use revealed a ten-page document containing 16 links for additional information.

One useful attachment to this larger document is shown in Figure 1.4. This is the summary of what ought to be worn for the potential of different exposures. This table summarizes the information for the worker and can be pulled up at the point of use in the clinical area as a reference when needed. This is an example of a practical tool that is useful to manage a large amount of complex information. What is missing here, though, are hands-on instructions for how to don and doff the equipment prescribed in the guidelines. Figure 1.5 is a TWI job breakdown used to train staff. It depicts exactly how to put on the protective equipment most used. This breakdown is used in conjunction with the table identifying which equipment to use in which situation. Both tools are important in achieving the results that we are after: protection and prevention of the spread of diseases. (Section II of this book will describe how this breakdown is made and used to effectively teach the job.)

As with the training of new health care providers we looked at in the previous section, if we want clinical best practices to be adopted by our veteran workers and to become the standard way we do work, then we need a sure and dependable method of training them in these practices. The TWI instruction method not only ensures that learners will be able to perform the new procedures, but it also does this in a way that deploys these best practices into the health care units quickly and effectively. Moreover, TWI creates strong job relations skill that helps to ensure staff are motivated to follow the standards and cooperate in their sustained usage. If we want to improve our practice and reduce errors and inefficiencies, then we must employ better methods of introducing and locking in the best practices we

Transmission-Based Precautions

Contact Precautions:
- Risk Zone: Patient and anything attached to or frequently touched by the patient.
- PPE: Gown and gloves to enter zone. Visitors if providing care or visiting more than one patient.
- Hand hygiene: Gel in and out of room and from dirty to clean.
- Patient out of room: Contain drainage, clean patient hands, cover patient with clean gown/cover linens.

Enteric Precautions:
- Risk Zone: Patient and anything in the patient room.
- PPE: Gown and gloves to enter room. Visitors only if providing care or visiting more than one patient.
- Hand hygiene: Gel into room and from dirty to clean. Soap & water out of room.
- Patient out of room: Same as above for Contact Precautions.

Droplet Precautions:
- Risk Zone: Unmasked patient and three (3) feet around unmasked patient.
- PPE: Staff and visitors wear mask with eye protection to enter zone.
- Hand Hygiene: Gel in and out of room and from dirty to clean.
- Patient out of room: Patient wears plain mask. No mask for others if patient masked.

Special Droplet Precautions:
- Risk Zone: Unmasked patient and three (3) feet around unmasked patient.
- PPE: Staff and visitors wear mask with eye protection to enter zone. During aerosolizing procedures wear PAPR or respirator with eye protection.
- Hand Hygiene: Gel in and out of room and from dirty to clean.
- Patient out of room: Patient wears plain mask. No mask for others if patient masked.

Airborne Respirator Precautions:
- Risk Zone: Unmasked patient and air shared with patient.
- PPE: Staff and visitors wear PAPR or respirator to enter patient room.
- Hand Hygiene: Gel in and out of room and from dirty to clean.
- Patient out of room: Patient wears plain mask. No mask for others if patient masked.

Airborne Contact Precautions: DO NOT ENTER UNLESS IMMUNE
- Risk Zone: Patient and air shared with patient and anything attached to or touched by the patient.
- PPE: Gown and gloves to enter patient room. Visitors only if providing care or visiting another patient.
- Hand Hygiene: Gel in and out of room and from dirty to clean.
- Patient out of room: Patient wears plain mask. No mask for others if patient masked.

Diseases/Symptom	Contact	Enteric	Droplet	Special Droplet	Airborne Contact	Airborne Respirator
Chicken Pox/Disseminated Shingles					X	
C. difficile Suspected or confirmed		X				
Severe Cough				X		
Diarrhea		X				
Influenza			X			
Measles					X	
Meningitis				X		
MRSA Infected or colonized	X					
Multidrug-Resistant Gram Negative Organisms e.g. ESBL Infected or colonized	X					
Norovirus (Norwalk)		X				
Pertussis or uncontrolled cough			X			
RSV	X					
Scabies/Lice	X					
Shingles – localized herpes zoster	X					
TB, Pulmonary						X
VRE Infected or colonized	X					
Wound drainage that cannot be contained	X					

Questions? Call Infection Prevention 223-6699 Final 6/7/11

(a)

Standard Precautions – "Every Patient, Every Time"

Standard Precautions:
- A group of infection prevention practices used for all patients regardless of diagnosis.
- These practices reduce or prevent contact with patient body fluids or substances.
- Hand hygiene, personal protective equipment (PPE), safe injection practices, and environmental cleaning are essential elements of standard precautions.

Hand Hygiene:
- Hand cleaning using soap and water or an alcohol product.
- Required before and after all common tasks to protect patient and HCW.

Gowns:
- Used to protect arms and body from contact with patient body fluids or substances. Usually needed when large amounts of blood or body fluids are expected or when blood is likely to spray or splatter.
- If a gown is needed, gloves are also needed. Consider need for facial protection.

Facial Protection:
- A fluid-resistant mask worn with goggles or eye shield.
- Used to protect the eyes, nose, and mouth from contact with patient body fluids or substances, including vomitus, which can spray or splatter into the face of the healthcare worker.
- If facial protection is needed, gloves are also needed. Consider need for gown.

Safe Injection Practices:
- Always use a sterile single-use needle and syringe for each injection.
- Do not reinsert a used needle into multiple dose vials or solutions.
- Do not reuse a single needle or syringe to administer IV medication to multiple patients.

Environmental Cleaning:
- Clean and disinfect all patient care equipment between each patient use.

* Use of sterile gloves and sterile technique not addressed. Refer to policies or physician orders regarding use of sterile gloves and sterile technique.
** Reasonable anticipation; may not apply to every situation.

Common Task*	Potential Exposure**	Gloves	Gown	Facial Protection	Hand Hygiene Before & After
Insert peripheral IV (PIV)	Blood	X			X
Access PIV line	Blood	X			X
Change PIV dressing	Blood	X			X
Change central line (CL) dressing	Blood	X			X
Access CL	Blood	X			X
Remove CL	Blood	X	X		X
Insert urinary catheter (UC)	Urine & mucous membrane	X			X
Access/drain UC	Urine	X			X
Remove UC	Urine/mucous membrane	X			X
Change surgical dressing	Blood/serous exudate	X			X
Empty JP/other drain	Blood/serous exudate	X	X		X
Give oral med	None				X
Give IM/SQ Injection	Blood	X			X
Give IV med	Blood	X			X
Check BP/pulse	None				X
Check Temp, rectal/oral	Mucous membrane	X			X
Give bed bath	Non-intact skin/mucous membranes	X			X
Brush teeth/tongue	Saliva, mucous membrane	X			X
Give peri care, handle bedpan/urinal	Urine/stool/mucous membrane contact	X			X
Assist to ambulate	None				X
Turn/lift	None				X
Dirty/infected wound care	Wound exudate	X			X
Trach care	Mucous/sputum	X	X		X
Suctioning, oral or trach	Saliva/sputum/drainage	X	X		X
Handling emesis basin	Stomach contents, saliva	X			X

(b)

Figure 1.4 Precautions against infection. (2011 Virginia Mason Medical Center. All rights reserved.)

JOB INSTRUCTION BREAKDOWN SHEET

Task: <u>**Application of PPE**</u>
Supplies: (gown, gloves, mask, mask with eye shield)
Instruments & Equipment: None
<u>**(Perform H.H. before this job)**</u>

IMPORTANT STEPS	KEY POINTS	REASONS
A logical segment of the operation when something happens to advance the work	Anything in a step that might – 1. Make or break the job 2. Injure the worker 3. Make the job easier to do, i.e. "knack", "trick", special timing, bit of special information.	Reasons for key points
1.Put on gown	1. Unfold carefully 2. Tie back 3. Fasten Neck (Tuck in hair if needed)	1. Not to disturb air 2. Fasten secure in place 3. Prevent contamination
2. Put on mask	1. Pinch nose 2. Over ears 3. Fit chin	1. Creates seal 2. Hold securely in place 3. Creates seal
3. Put on gloves	1. Cuff over cuff 2. Inspect	1. Prevent contamination 2. Possible glove damage

Figure 1.5 TWI Job Instruction breakdown for PPE application.

develop. The need to continually update our training, then, is the third need for health care.

Where We Go from Here

Many of our success stories around improved clinical outcomes come from establishing reliability, doing what we know to be the best clinical practice every time—no editing, no workarounds, no shortcuts, and no additions of "my way is better" edits. The best examples of this good work come from what is known as *Bundled Care*. Care bundles, in general, are group-ings of best-known practices with respect to a disease process that when applied together confer substantially better outcomes. The science support-ing the bundle components is sufficiently established that the bundle is now

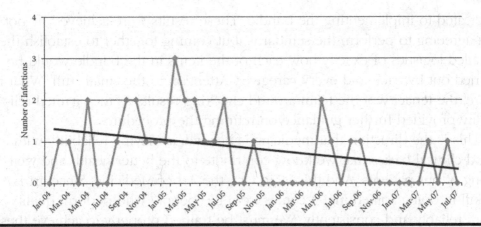

Figure 1.6 Central line infection rates in critical care units.

considered the "standard of care." The key component moving forward, then, is to practice the standards correctly and consistently.

A classic example of bundled care is the Central Line Infection Bundle. According to the Institute of Healthcare Improvement, 48% of ICU (intensive care unit) patients have central lines accounting for 15 million central venous catheter days per year in ICUs.* Studies of central line-associated bloodstream infections (CLABSI) that control for the underlying severity of illness suggest that attributable mortality for these infections is 4–20%. Thus, it is estimated that between 500 and 4,000 US patients die annually due to bloodstream infections.† The cost of care is estimated to be between US$3,700 and US$29,000 per infection occurrence.‡ The essential elements of the central line bundle include:

- Hand hygiene
- Maximum barrier precautions upon insertion
- Chlorhexidine skin antisepsis
- Optimal catheter site selection
- Daily review of line necessity and prompt removal of unnecessary lines

By identifying the key components of care, and establishing reliability in the Central Line Infection Bundle, practitioners at the Virginia Mason Medical Center were able to bring these dangerous infection rates down. Figure 1.6 shows the rates of infection before and after a team of caregivers was

---

* Institute for Healthcare Improvement. *Implement the IHI Central Line Bundle*. Online at: http://www.ihi.org/knowledge/Pages/Changes/ImplementtheCentralLineBundle.aspx.
† ibid.
‡ ibid.

dedicated to implementing the bundle. These results were achieved by not just agreeing to perform the standards, but coming together to establish the detailed logistics of exactly how each of the items in the bundle would be carried out by each and every caregiver. Attention to the small stuff. What is more, the tenacity of the team around checking results as they gained reliability provided further guidance on refining the procedures.

This is the direction that medicine is headed: achieving reliability with good clinical basics that we know contribute to the better health and well-being of our patients. And this is, in fact, the Art of Medicine. Since art is a skill in doing something, it comes from the people who perform quality work reliably and consistently. We must be trained properly to achieve these needed skills and no health care facility should rely on a long process of "trial and error" to obtain good results from the work their people do on a regular basis. Science gives us the technical details of what it takes to heal the sick, but it is still people who must learn to perform the needed tasks to carry out this work. Technology can help us here, but it can never become the substitute for the skillful hands of the people who actually touch the patients.

As we stated at the beginning of the chapter, there is much misunderstanding and resistance to standard work in health care. A neurosurgeon, commenting in *The New Yorker* on the Harvard commencement speech, called Dr. Gawande's analogy to health care workers as pit crews "pure drivel."* Because people are human beings, he claimed, their diseases do not affect them like they would machines. "Doctors are not simply mechanics that can choose a protocol that produces the same result by working on the same problem every time. Medicine is an art as much as a science and requires dedicated professionals who use their mind, training, and experience to provide customized, compassionate care each patient needs." Well said. But the surgeon's implication here is that the protocols we enact do not allow for customization depending on patient needs and based on a doctor's experience and judgment. Just the opposite. Because we identify and take care of the basic things, just like a pilot takes care of all the fundamental things on the takeoff checklist before "flying the plane," we create the capacity to use our "mind, training, and experience" to address the *truly unique* aspects of each individual patient's needs.

---

* Atul Gawande. *The New Yorker,* May 26, 2011. "Cowboys and Pit Crews." Online at: http://www
  .newyorker.com/online/blogs/newsdesk/2011/05/atul-gawande-harvard-medical-school-comme
  ncement-address.html.

This work is an excellent match with the methods of TWI. As we shall see in Section II of this book, training a person in the "knack" of doing a job or how to perform the "tricks of the trade" is all about understanding the intricacies of responding to the many subtleties and variations we encounter in each iteration of performing a job. Knowing what to look for in a medical procedure or how to approach a patient who is nervous and afraid are things that we can define and learn. Following a defined protocol does not take away from delivering unique services any more than scheduling your appointments takes away from your ability to be spontaneous. When you have a well-made schedule you have a good handle on what your needs are for that day; then, and only then, can you respond appropriately to the unique situations that arise without failing in your overall duties and responsibilities.

A dependable means to achieving consistency of practice is to apply the TWI concepts of Job Methods (JM) and Job Instruction (JI) to the design of standard work. When analyzing the JM breakdown for lab specimen labeling, for example, the authors went to the workplace and walked through each detail of the task, questioning whether they were necessary or performed in a productive sequence. By doing it at the work site, discoveries could be made, such as the long distance between where critical supplies are stored or the discovery that the labels were stored at the specimen drop-off location instead of near the clean specimen containers. When creating the JI breakdown for teaching the task, by asking themselves what "makes or breaks the job" or "makes it safer or easier," Key Points were discovered that could help learners understand the details of why it is important to do this job exactly this way. We uncovered the best way to do the job in the safest, easiest manner. Then, by teaching this "one best way of doing the job" in an effective manner that not only shows the learners what to do but motivates them to do it that way each time, we can ensure that this part of our daily work is completed correctly each time it is performed.

However, even when people are properly taught best practices, there will inevitably be resistance to change and they, especially experienced workers, will naturally rebel against "being told what to do." Many supervisors and trainers say, "Even if I had an effective instruction method, they still wouldn't listen to me." This is not a problem of instruction but of leadership. As we shall see in Section III of this book, in order to develop and sustain standard work we also need skill in leadership which means the ability to build strong relationships based on trust. Leaders are people who have followers and if no one is following your instructions, we cannot say you are a leader. For example, even if we effectively teach a person why a job needs to be performed a certain way, if the learner does not trust our motives and feels strongly that we never appreciate the good work they do each day, then no amount of reasoning will convince him or her to "follow the standard." There are basic foundations for good relations, like giving people credit when due, that can be learned and practiced thus building these good relationships that lead to good results.

Long ago, Taiichi Ohno, who was the founder of the Toyota Production System (TPS), observed that "without standards there can be no improvement." We find this to still be true today and we find that it applies as equally to health care as it does to manufacturing. Standards provide reliability, reliability provides visibility, and visibility provides our next opportunity to improve. If we truly want to get better in health care, we must get back to the basics and that starts with creating and maintaining standards for the good work we do each day.

Conclusion

Training Within Industry's Job Methods, Job Instruction, and Job Relations programs meet three identified needs in health care: engineering safety into our care, providing more effective training for new caregivers, and continually updating best practices for veteran employees. The four-step method of Job Methods Improvement gives us the means to generate ideas for eliminating waste and inefficiencies in our work making them easier and safer to do. The Job Instruction breakdown tool allows us to combine the evidence-determined best practice with the logistical tips and tricks of our most seasoned workers. We can engineer safety to the exact point in the process where there is a risk, thereby eliminating that chance for error. The four-step method of Job Instruction provides a practical method for layering information into right-sized pieces so that the learner can "digest" the content combining the showing with the telling. And the four-step method of Job Relations provides a practical method for building relationships that matches up with our commitment and pursuit of a supportive environment.

If we want to turn best practices into actual practices, then we must learn to train more effectively and to lead people in a way that brings out cooperation and dedication. Just because we say we have a standard and document it accordingly, doesn't ensure that people are actually practicing that standard. Changing people's behavior and actions is the most difficult task of all. It takes real skill to make and enforce that change. For the safety of our patients, and the long-term viability of our health care organizations, this effort is just what is needed.

Chapter 2

The Challenge of Designing Standard Work

Introduction

Standard work is a verb and not a noun. While there are certainly documents we can call "Standard Work," the concept of standard work is not a formal document preserved in the archives of the organization, shown to surveyors and orienting new staff. Standard work is meant to be a hypothesis to test the results of everyone doing something in the same way all the time. Reliability. In that sense, it is much like a clinical trial where we test out a procedure, treatment, or medication to see if this new way is better than the old way. By having everyone do something the same way numerous times, we can now see the outcome results of that standard. We can also see what problems the new way addresses, and what issues still remain. The more often the new standard is used, the faster we will be able to determine the results or effect the new way has on the process. Standard work, therefore, is not the destination itself but simply a *tool* we use along the way in our endless quest to find the best, safest, and easiest way to deliver patient care.

PDSA Cycles—Forming and Testing Your Hypothesis

Many readers will be familiar with the term PDSA (Plan, Do, Study, Act) as the abbreviation describing incremental improvement cycles (see Figure 2.1).

DOI: 10.4324/9781003035305-2

Figure 2.1   The Plan-Do-Study-Act (PDSA) Cycle.

While the PDSA model was conceived in the 1920s by Walter Shewart, it is most famously attributed to Edward Deming who introduced his concepts of quality control and continuous improvement to the Japanese after WWII, the same period in which TWI went to Japan, and these models were the foundation for the revival of the Japanese economy after the war. Continuous improvement requires the pursuit of continuous cycles of trying new and better ways of doing the work. How we do the work requires the vigilance of constant tinkering. Creating the standard work, training our staff in those standards, and then establishing reliability in the process all fall under the term "Do" in the PDSA cycle.

PLAN

- Observe the process
- Measure the outcomes
- Understand the defects

DO

- Propose a hypothesis of new standard work
- Train everyone
- Establish reliability

STUDY

- Evaluate the results of the new standards
- Compare against results of the old way
- Understand the remaining defects

ACT

- Propose the next hypothesis in the form of standard work addressing the next target (defects)

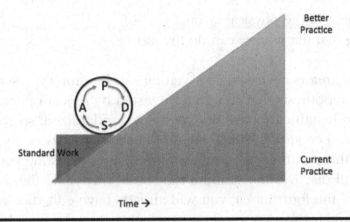

Figure 2.2 Standard work is a "placeholder" or wedge in our pursuit of perfection.

While there are a multitude of *kaizen* tools available to measure and more fully understand a process in the "Plan" and "Study" phases of the PDSA cycle, including TWI's Job Methods Improvement plan introduced in Chapter 11 of this book, TWI Job Instruction is perfectly designed for both phases of "Do" and "Act" when good instruction is needed to teach everyone the most current way to do the job which, as we have stated, is our current hypothesis. Put another way, standard work can be seen and used as a *placeholder* in our pursuit of perfection. Imagine an incline representing the journey of improvement in which we seek to climb to better performance. Standard work helps us "hold the gains," like a wedge, until we design the next better way to do the work (see Figure 2.2).

In his blog post in January 2016, Mike Stocklein noted that standard work that remains static and documented as a permanent process may act to *prevent* innovation and improvement.* Imagine the wedge in the diagram moved to a position above the PDSA cycle! If we assume the standard is "written in stone," then we cut off ideas and efforts to find a better way than what we are doing now. Just like any great journey, you can't reach your destination with just one or two steps. The same is true when you are pursuing the perfect patient experience—many, many trials of standard work, in an endless cycle of improvement, will be needed as you get better and better.

The creation of standard work requires the consideration of four areas:

1. Review of the clinical literature
2. Understanding of the supply chain within our system

---

* Stocklein, Mike in: gembawalkabout.wordpress.com. *Standard Work and PDSA*. Posted January 26, 2016.

3. Assessment of the physical layout
4. Assuring that the worker can do the job

Work in each area is necessary for "vetting" and refining the standard work as the hypothesis that can then be tested by repeat operations. Most of our jobs in health care have not yet been standardized, so we must start somewhere and create our initial attempt at standardization. By proceeding sequentially through these four areas, refining and adjusting your standard work, you will discover much about the "best" way to do the work. By the completion of the fourth area, you will already have edited or changed your draft standard work several times which will make for a better roll out when the team adapts the standard work as "our current best-known way to do this job." It is more respectful to the team to have worked through a few versions of the standard before you implement it on a larger scale.

Clinical Practice Guidelines—the Place to Start

In health care, we are familiar with clinical practice guidelines or the term "evidence-based practice." These recommendations are born out of clinical trial results and the experience of clinical experts. These are the guidelines advancing the science and the practice of medicine. Health care workers constantly look to these guidelines and seek to contribute to the body of findings from which we all draw upon to update our own practice. These recommendations are presented through publications in respected journals and textbooks, at conferences, and on online websites designed to be the repositories of such information. Access to this treasure of general and specialty information is increasingly easy in part due to Internet publications and free specialty websites. Examples of such websites include PubMed.gov, the CochraneLibrary.com, NCCN Cancer Guidelines, and the Oncology Nursing Society (ONS.org).

Although this fundamental clinical information is readily more available than ever, there continues to be the need to both understand the findings (often written in jargon and language full of scientific medical terminology) and determine their influence in actual practice (findings often lack specific details for implementation). Involving and including clinicians to assist in the interpretation of the literature is encouraged in this initial and foundational step to the development of standard work.

Review of Current Supply Chain

The second area in developing standard work is to become familiar with the exact materials and supplies that your organization possesses to complete the job. The literature review done earlier may provide guidelines as to the agent best suited to clean the skin prior to a procedure, for example, but it most likely will not provide the details of the exact product that should be used. There may be numerous products, all designed differently, with the same cleansing agent in them:

- Small, individually wrapped sponges
- A packet of three large swab sticks
- Entire bottles of the cleaning agent and separate gauze packets

We must understand the clinical function or purpose of the material to be used for each specific job. Purchasing contracts, the manufacturer's ability to produce the products, and demand all influence what might be available to any one organization. There is therefore a need to observe the job being performed using the exact materials, supplies, and equipment that are actually available.

Assessment of the Physical Layout

A keen understanding of the physical space will be the next step in determining where and how the work will take place. Consideration may need to be given to the movement of the patient into and out of the space, lighting, location of outlets, or the storage needs for shelving or countertops. There may be the need to maintain a sterile field or separate "clean" and "dirty" areas. The workplace will need to be laid out in a way that promotes the worker having what they need, where they need it, and when they need it to do the job efficiently.

This special understanding of the physical layout of the working space is not gained by merely reviewing a map or blueprints of the workplace alone. We must go and see the location in person creating a mockup in the area where the work will be completed and trying out the job. Rearrange the space and materials used and then try it again. Creating diagrams of the space as it relates to the specific job will help you understand and see more clearly the rationale of what is placed where and how people and material flow through the space. This knowledge becomes invaluable when plans for usage of space change, as they inevitably will, due to need or opportunity.

Assuring the Worker Can Do the Job

The final area for the development of standard work is to assure that the job can be performed by the worker as designed and this starts by ensuring that the job can be *physically and actually* performed. Our goal is nothing less than an elegant design! Make adjustments to the layout of supplies, instruments, tools, and equipment; the sequence of work steps and motions; and the material amounts on hand until the work "flows" with ease of movement by the worker and the appropriate clinical outcomes are achieved. The Job Methods skill of TWI will assist here and is described in detail in Chapter 11. Now you are ready to document the process and, as we stated at the beginning of this chapter, there are many tools you can utilize here, like process flow mapping or standard work sheets (see Chapter 12), which are not in the scope of this book.

Also needed in this step is the determination of *who* should do the job. Identifying the clinical expertise, skill level and licensure credentials (scope of practice) that are required for the job is a necessary step to assure safety, quality, and job satisfaction. The final element of this step, then, is to *train* the worker to the job and *motivate* them to following the set standard. The Job Instruction and Job Relations skills of TWI will be invaluable in this endeavor and are explained in detail in Sections II and III of this book.

Rising to the Challenges of a Global Pandemic

All of our skill and knowledge would be put to the test in early January of 2020 when news of a new respiratory virus in China came to our attention. At the time, this author was working in Seattle, Washington, at Bailey-Boushay House, a skilled nursing facility, operated by Virginia Mason Medical Center and designed to care for people with HIV, Huntington's Disease, ALS and other conditions requiring acute care for chronic, terminal illnesses. As the Director of Nursing Services, I was in a leadership position responsible for the care of the patients and the safety of our staff. Our team went into hyper-alertness when the first case of SARS-CoV-2 was diagnosed in Snohomish, Washington, just north of Seattle, and, soon after, several cases were identified in a nursing home in Kirkland, Washington, less than

10 miles away! All of a sudden, our local colleagues were on the national news. Very little was known at this point including how it was spreading and why the elderly seemed to be at such high risk. As early as mid-February, we understood that our work was going to change rapidly and dramatically. We were literally at "ground zero" for what would become a global pandemic.

All four of our developmental areas for standard work would be impacted (and still are, as of this writing), requiring us to rapidly rethink and retool our practices.

Clinical Practice Guidelines—the Place to Start

The first challenge we faced was the rapid pace of changing information from our *clinical guideline recommendations*. Long acknowledged as the undisputed best sources of information, recommendations from the World Health Organization (WHO) and the Centers for Disease Control and Prevention (CDC) were suddenly in conflict with each other. Worse still, the national government recommendations were in conflict with local public health organizations and local experts of infectious diseases. For example, early information reported that the transmission was not suspected to be from person to person, but from animal to person. Within 10 days, this information was changed to confirm that person-to-person transmission was not only possible but widespread.

The WHO recommendations for health care workers were initially for contact and droplet precautions when caring for persons known to be positive for the virus. Airborne precautions, they stated, were only necessary when performing respiratory procedures such as nebulizers or intubation when droplets would have a greater chance of traveling. This was changed weeks later to airborne precautions for all contact. The CDC and the US Surgeon General initially stated that healthy members of the public should not wear masks as these should be reserved for health care workers directly caring for patients who had the virus. In addition, it was thought that individuals might actually increase their risk of contracting the virus by touching and constantly adjusting the outside of the contaminated mask, transmitting virus directly to their nose, mouth, and eyes. By April, both had reversed their guidelines and by June, the WHO also recommended masks to be worn by the general public at all times.

Early efforts at screening focused on restricting travel or identifying people who had recently traveled from China to the US, but as cases continued to be identified in more and more states, this recommendation was dropped and patients coming into the facility were no longer screened with this question. The people we allowed into our facilities evolved as well, moving from all volunteers and visitors who appeared healthy to one visitor per day per patient and, finally, to only essential staff.

Guidelines to clinical practice were issued from numerous organizations, and our experience in Seattle was that we found ourselves accountable to the following organizations:

- World Health Organization
- Centers for Disease Control and Prevention
- The Department of Social and Human Services
- King County Public Health Department
- The Department of Infection Prevention within our own organization

The rapid changes in the clinical recommendations shook our team to the core, causing anxiety and fear—how deadly was this virus? Because of the changes and inconsistencies, it appeared the information was not reliable and that we could not trust the very organizations we had always relied upon. Alice Park, in her article for TIME Magazine, noted that the normal scientific process was pressured to speed up due to demand for information. She stated,

> Research is normally a plodding, tedious process. Scientists check
> and recheck their data; review and re-review their conclusions,
> then submit their hard work to a scientific journal for publication,
> where their peers put it through further scrutiny. But a viral pan-
> demic doesn't adhere to a cautious timeline. We are in a scramble
> for information.*

She noted that there was a tension between the vetting of facts, being reputable and reliable, and the global urgent need for information. The result was confusion and contradictory messaging.

Tom Frieden, former Director for the CDC, has said that when experts change their advice, they draw criticism. Although some changes reflect

---

* Park, Alice. TIME Magazine. "Pressure on Good Science during a Pandemic Is Leading to Confusing and Conflicting Advice on COVID-19." June 22, 2020. Appearing online June 11, 2020, 0634 AM.

errors, many are responses to new and better information. For example, the early recommendations for wearing masks were driven by our basic knowledge of viruses but, as we learned from the evidence that what was really happening was asymptomatic spread, more masking recommendations came out. The change in recommendations was *progress*, not correction of a *mistake*.

Understanding that we were on the very edge of rapidly evolving information, along with the discovery of new findings, helped us reframe the way we looked at these changes to recommendations. By being diligent and continually reviewing a broad range of literature, we were able to recognize the emerging science and spot the trends toward any new recommendations. This understanding enabled us to quickly make fundamental changes to our existing standards and to present these changes to staff with the "very latest" findings which contained little to no "lag time" between the publication of a new recommendation and "putting it into practice." When training staff, we included and shared the most current literature source that was guiding our practice changes and this transparency helped to improve confidence that we were doing the right things to prevent disease and to protect our teams. The result was that trust was restored.

Review of Current Supply Chain

The next significant challenge that we faced was to our *supply chain*, especially for Personal Protective Equipment (PPE) such as masks, gowns, and eye protection. Equipment that was familiar and comfortable to staff suddenly became harder to obtain, with some items being delivered in inconsistent quantities at inconsistent delivery times, right when we needed them the most.

Many previously disposable or single-use items were replaced with multi-use items which created the need for each job instruction sheet to be updated (see Figure 2.3). While similarities existed in the use of these items, there was always just enough difference between them to warrant a need to create a unique instruction sheet. Measures were taken to balance the need between conserving supplies and using them when the protection was truly necessary. Inventories were counted closely on a daily basis and critical supplies were even more closely controlled. Some items had to be stored under lock and key.

Our understanding of TWI Job Instruction and how to make breakdown sheets for training allowed us to continuously update our training materials

Disposable equipment and materials	Reusable
Paper towel-type wipes for disinfecting surfaces	Cloths and spray bottles
N95 masks	Cleaning process for N95 Mask
Masks with face shields attached	Mask with goggles, then face shields
Surgical masks	KN95 Masks worn all shift
Gowns-made of treated paper	Treated cloth gowns, laundered
Specific types/size gloves	Double glove with any type/size
Specific brand of hand sanitizer	Any approved brand of sanitizer

Figure 2.3 Replacement list for disposable items.

keeping staff current with the changes and assuring that staff and patients were safe and well protected. By making and applying separate breakdown sheets for each of the different supplies, staff could get a sense of how similar the processes were while, at the same time, knowing exactly what they needed to change with each different supply. For our storage area, we chose a seldom used lounge area that had large windows in the door and on the side so that kitted stores of equipment were highly visible and ready to use when needed. Every Charge Nurse had access to these additional supplies. Each type of supply had the job instruction breakdown sheet to go with it so that as inventories changed, the correct directions for that particular supply were always handy at the point of use.

The need continues to this day, even as the pandemic persists and supplies become more stable, for staff to know how to do their jobs in the best way possible, using a variety of products and materials. The responsibility falls on us to assure that we understand the differences in products, and how to use them, so that we properly pass on this knowledge. Figures 2.4 through 2.7 show some of the tools and checklists we used to manage proper storage and use of supplies.

Assessment of the Physical Layout

We were challenged to dramatically change the way we thought about our *spaces*. This came to us in phases, requiring more innovation with each round of problems we had to solve. Early on, the challenge was *where* to set up screening of people entering the facility—ideally, this would be outside of the building to prevent any contagious person from ever being allowed inside and exposing others. We found that this was not practical given the weather in January and February in the Pacific Northwest, so, instead, we set up a screening station in the main lobby as you entered the front door

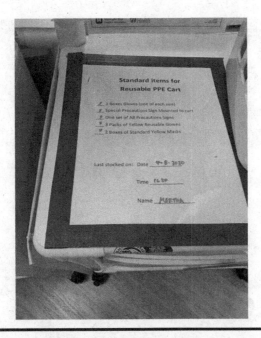

Figure 2.4   Checklist for resupply of an isolation cart.

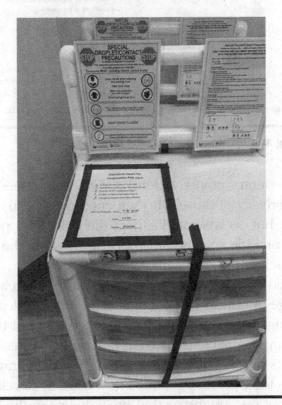

Figure 2.5   Precautions and PPE requirements specific to SARS-CoV-2 in early February 2020. Later guidelines included Airborne Precautions.

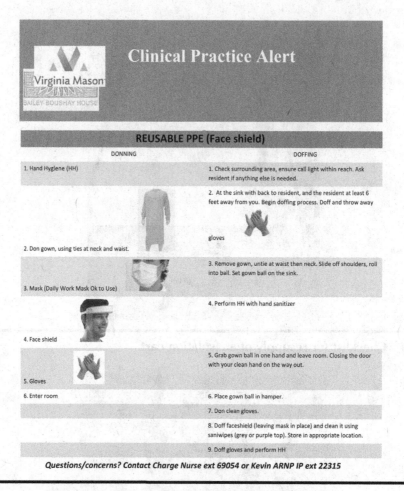

Clinical Practice Alert

Virginia Mason
BAILEY-BOUSHAY HOUSE

REUSABLE PPE (Face shield)

DONNING	DOFFING
1. Hand Hyglene (HH)	1. Check surrounding area, ensure call light within reach. Ask resident if anything else is needed.
2. Don gown, using ties at neck and waist.	2. At the sink with back to resident, and the resident at least 6 feet away from you. Begin doffing process. Doff and throw away gloves
3. Mask (Daily Work Mask Ok to Use)	3. Remove gown, untie at waist then neck. Slide off shoulders, roll into ball. Set gown ball on the sink.
4. Face shield	4. Perform HH with hand sanitizer
5. Gloves	5. Grab gown ball in one hand and leave room. Closing the door with your clean hand on the way out.
6. Enter room	6. Place gown ball in hamper.
	7. Don clean gloves.
	8. Doff faceshield (leaving mask in place) and clean it using saniwipes (grey or purple top). Store in appropriate location.
	9. Doff gloves and perform HH

Questions/concerns? Contact Charge Nurse ext 69054 or Kevin ARNP IP ext 22315

Figure 2.6 Donning and doffing checklist for reusable PPE.

and closed all other entry points. Careful consideration needed to be given to the safety and privacy of those who screened positive and required further evaluation. But, as we noted earlier, the guidelines published for screening did not provide specific directions for triaging those who replied affirmative to the screening questions.

As the pandemic entered a more dynamic phase of spread and infection, caring for the surge of critically ill patients caused our colleagues in health care facilities throughout the region to experience some of the greatest challenges of all: the unimaginable expansion of care units outside of the hospital facility into tents on play fields and even in parking garages. Regardless of where the crisis took us, though, our knowledge of developing standard work and testing out our job instruction breakdowns in the actual place that the work is done allowed us to very quickly identify what we needed and where for our staff to continue to perform their work.

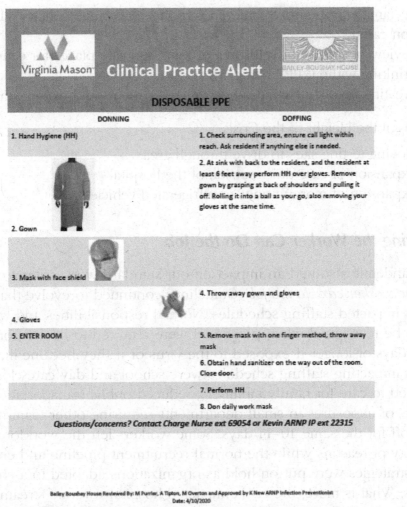

Figure 2.7   Donning and doffing checklist for disposable PPE.

PHASES OF SPACE ALLOCATION

Initial Actions

- Reduction of in-person meetings
- Reallocation of common areas (previously used by inpatients)
- Reduction of people entering our spaces: vendors, visitors, volunteers, interdepartmental meetings

Actions Taken as Crisis Expanded

- Changing services in outpatient areas from in-person visits to telemedicine
- Screener location and control of entry points

- Reclamation of empty conference rooms for storage centers (PPE, isolation carts)
- Review of spaces for staff break rooms and safe places for eating/drinking without PPE being worn
- Creating capacity for more hospitalized patients and expansion of ICU

Actions at the Height of the Crisis

- Moving testing sites to drive through areas
- Expansion of care units outside of the hospital
- Expansion of morgue units to refrigerated vehicles

Assuring the Worker Can Do the Job

The pandemic also had an impact on our standard work criteria of *assure that the worker can do the job*. Guidelines continued to evolve that immediately impacted staffing schedules. Normal responsibilities and work roles had to be reassigned when personnel were required to be off from work 10–14 days or longer if exposed to the virus or if they became ill. Other factors impacting staffing schedules were school and day care closures, the need to care for family members, reduced public transportation, and clusters of exposures in small departments requiring other team members to be off for the same 10–14 days. Some workers left the workforce for a variety of reasons while the normal recruitment pipeline and employment strategies were put on hold as organizations adapted to a changing census. What is more, the crisis impacted hospital revenue streams, for example, the reduction in elective procedures to free up space for COVID patients.

The need to cross train and shift workers from one area of the organization to another became a huge challenge. At an all-staff training session, we posted a list of jobs from all departments that resembled a Job Instruction Training Timetable (explained in Chapter 7) and allowed staff to voluntarily record their willingness to being cross trained in order to help in a different department from their own. We were amazed and proud that approximately 80% of them signed on to the list and nearly all were willing to move to *any* department that needed their help. We attributed this spirit of enthusiastic collaboration to our willingness to be honest, straightforward, and transparent with the facts and what we understood our situation to be and the challenges that we faced. We were reminded of the inspiring campaigns using images of "Rosie the Riveter" and others who "jumped in to help" during the war effort in the 1940s when our TWI training was born. A slogan of "Everyone Can Clean" was quickly adopted.

In other organizations, there was a shift from outpatient visits to virtual, telemedicine visits. Some hospitals closed selected areas for a period of time, which freed up staff to be trained in rapidly expanding areas like employee health, public screening, and inpatient care areas. These changes created a need for clarity and preparation in how required duties were carried out. Figure 2.8 shows a flow chart of job duties to care for a patient with COVID-19 symptoms which was clearly displayed showing everyone's contributions and providing direction for leaders to be fully prepared in all areas of the patient's care. The greatest challenge to persons knowing how to do the jobs is when the surge of patients requiring critical care or inpatient hospitalization grows beyond the capacity of the current workforce. More work is needed to "offload" any tasks that can be done by others to continue to redistribute the burden of this work.

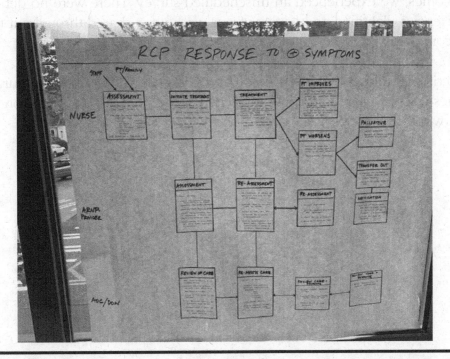

Figure 2.8 Diagraming out the flow and job duties for the care of a patient with symptoms of COVID-19, creating clarity of everyone's contribution and capacity for leaders to be "ready" before things actually occur.

Summary

The COVID-19 global pandemic has been the greatest health care challenge of our careers. This challenge has brought further to the forefront the need that we already understood: standard work in health care will save lives. By following our "formula" for developing standard work, working through the four areas, and by having a sure and reliable means to train and motivate staff, we experienced the following outcomes early in the pandemic:

- We were able to support staff during frightening and tumultuous times by giving real answers on how to protect themselves and care for their patients.
- We created capacity for leaders to "look ahead" in preparation for the next complex problem to solve.
- By having a method by which we could document practice, we were able to translate guidelines into practice quickly. Exactly 10 days after DSHS issued 23 pages of national practice guidelines for nursing homes, we experienced an unscheduled survey. There were no deficiencies identified and copies of our work were shared throughout the community.

This crisis is still upon us as of this writing. We have no doubts that our colleagues in health care will continue to rise to the occasion and carry on this good work. In fact, we are counting on them.

Chapter 3

Hand Hygiene Training Case Study

Introduction

Virginia Mason Medical Center (Virginia Mason) is one of three major hospitals in Seattle with a staff of more than 500 employed physicians and a total of more than 5,500 employees. The hospital, which includes a main campus in the "Pill Hill" neighborhood overlooking Puget Sound and nine regional centers, has 336 beds and generated just over US$1.1 trillion in total revenue in 2019. In 2001, Virginia Mason began studying and applying the Toyota Production System (TPS) to its work and has made dramatic strides in improving the quality and cost of its health care delivery. After more than a year of study and some initial successes, Virginia Mason sent the entire top level of management, over 30 people in total, on a 13-day study tour of Toyota in Japan in June 2002. During the study, this group of executives actually experienced hands-on work in the assembly lines in order to understand the concepts and application of standard work.

Following these initial steps, the hospital began implementing TPS principles and tools including Takt time, 5S (sort, set in order, shine, standardize, sustain), *heijunka* (leveling or smoothing), and the *kanban* (signboard) system, and in the first four years of the application saved US$6 million in planned capital investment, freed up 13,000 square feet of space, reduced inventory costs by US$360,000, cut walking distances, shortened bill-collection time, slashed infection rates, and, most importantly, improved

DOI: 10.4324/9781003035305-3

patient satisfaction.* By the end of 2009, those results increased to US$11 million saved in planned capital investment, 25,000 square feet of space freed up, US$1 million saved in inventory, and staff walking distances reduced by 60 miles per day.† What is more, they were able to cut down by 85% the time it takes to get lab results reported back to patients while reducing labor expenses (overtime and temporary labor) by US$500,000 in just one year.‡

In 2007, as part of their ongoing and energetic effort to replicate the Toyota system, they read Jeffrey Liker's *Toyota Talent: Developing Your People the Toyota Way* (McGraw-Hill, 2007) and realized for the first time that there was a method they could learn that would help them promote their efforts at standard work. This method, called Training Within Industry, or TWI, had been adopted by Toyota in the early 1950s and is still used by the company today. Virginia Mason staff immediately began putting the concepts they learned from *Toyota Talent* into action, making breakdowns of jobs, such as Hand Hygiene in Compliance with CDC and WHO Hand Hygiene Guidelines and Time Out Prior to Surgery or Invasive Procedures. They found out, though, that their breakdowns (Figure 3.1) were too detailed and learners were confused by the process, just the opposite of what they expected to find from this time-tested method so effectively used by Toyota. What happened, in fact, was that they didn't use the method properly, thinking that breaking down the job was all there was to it. They simply took their 10-page policy and reorganized all of the content to fit onto one page using the TWI format. They rolled this out per the usual method—they posted it and told people it was there and this was the new way.

The head of the Kaizen Promotion Office (KPO) of Virginia Mason at the time, Linda Hebish, attended a workshop given by the TWI Institute at an Association for Manufacturing Excellence (AME) conference in San Diego in June 2008. There, she learned that the TWI program was traditionally trained following a well-defined plan that ensured proper learning and use of the methods. Moreover, she found out these training courses were packaged and ready to teach and could be initiated literally at a moment's notice. She became convinced that TWI could help advance the ongoing *kaizen* efforts at Virginia Mason but needed an enthusiastic promoter who could lead this part of the effort. When she got back to Seattle, she engaged one

---

* "Toyota Assembly Line Inspires Improvements at Hospital," *The Washington Post*, June 3, 2005, p. A1.
† Virginia Mason Medical Center, *2009 VMPS Facts*. Online at: www.virginiamason.org/home/work-files/pdfdocs/press/vmps_fastfacts.pdf.
‡ Ibid.

JOB BREAKDOWN SHEET		
DATE: January 21, 2008	TEAM LEADER: Debbie S., Beverly A., Jenny C.	SPONSOR: Debbie S., MD
AREA: All areas providing direct pt care or in contact with pt care supplies, equipment or food	JOB: Hand Hygiene in compliance with CDC & WHO hand hygiene guidelines	WRITTEN BY: Jenny C.
MAJOR STEPS	**KEY POINTS**	**REASONS FOR KEY POINTS**
Step #1: Identify the need for clean hands	Remove artificial fingernails or extenders when in direct contact with pts or their environment	Artificial nails house germs that can be passed on when you touch pts
	Clean hands whether or not you use gloves (i.e. before putting on gloves & after removing gloves)	Gloves are not a substitute for cleaning hands because gloves don't completely prevent germ transmission
	Before direct contact with pt, pt's environment or equipment	Protect the pt against harmful germs carried on your hands
	After direct contact with pt, pt's environment or equipment	Protect yourself & the health-care environment from harmful pt germs
Step #2: Inspect your hands to determine best cleaning method	If not visibly soiled, use alcohol-based gel	Cleaning with gel is faster, more effective, and better tolerated by your hands
	Visibly soiled hands or hand with fecal contamination require washing with soap & water	Dirt, blood, feces or other body fluids are best removed with soap & water (C. diff spores are not killed with alcohol-based gel)
Step #3: Use enough product to cover all hand surfaces & fingers	GEL: Cover all surfaces with a thumb nail-sized amount	Friction & skin contact are required to remove germs
	WASH: Wet hands with water, wash with enough soap to cover all hand/finger surfaces	
Step #4: Spend enough time cleaning your hands	GEL: Vigorously rub until product dries on your hands	Antiseptic action is not complete until fully dried (approx 15 sec.)
	WASH: A minimum of 15 sec. (the length of singing "Happy Birthday to You")	As least 15 sec. is needed to ensure complete coverage of hand surfaces
	Use paper towel to turn off water faucet	Prevent transfer of germs from faucet onto clean hands
Step #5: Let your hands completely dry	Moisturize hands with lotion available through Central Supply	To minimize contact dermatitis without interfering with antimicrobial action
	Put on gloves after hands are dry	Skin irritation may occur if moist hands come in contact with glove material
Step #6: Perform task with clean hands	Task is done immediately after cleaning hands	You may be distracted & touch unclean surface with clean hands

Figure 3.1 Original job breakdown sheet for hand hygiene. (From P. Graupp and R. J. Wrona. 2011. *Implementing TWI: Creating and Managing a Skills-Based Culture.* **Boca Raton, FL: Taylor & Francis Group/CRC Press. With permission.)**

of the hospital's oncology nurses, Martha Purrier, to lead the effort to bring these training programs to Virginia Mason. (*Ed*.: As an author of this book, I will refer to myself and colleagues as "we." This case study took place before I moved to the Bailey-Boushay House described in the last chapter.)

We immediately began consulting with the TWI Institute on good strategies for getting the true value out of a TWI introduction and began benchmarking with other successful company rollouts. We organized the first TWI

10-hour sessions to be held in March 2009 and decided to select an initial group of 10 who would take both the Job Instruction (JI) and Job Relations (JR) modules in the same week. These 10 people included 3 people from the KPO, 2 staff members from the clinical education office, 2 nurses, and 3 nursing assistants.

Our first strategic move, then, was to begin implementation at the assistant nurse level with assistance from the clinical education office whose mandate was to be sure all hospital personnel were well trained in their jobs. This move would prove extremely effective because, once the actual training of jobs began, nurses saw the positive effects of what the assistant nurses were doing and came to us asking how they could receive the same training. Notably, the head of nursing and senior vice president at the hospital, Charleen Tachibana, saw the power of the training method and quickly became a vocal advocate for its use throughout.

Initial Training and Insights

In preparation for our first TWI training, we instructed the 10 participants to read *Toyota Talent* and review the TWI Institute website, which explained the different facets and history of the TWI program. We also had them read articles by Art Smalley on "Basic Stability" and Jim Huntzinger on "Why Standard Work Is Not Standard." We had been given an introductory letter on how to prepare for the TWI training, which included bringing in a real job to practice in the class. Thus, we required them to observe key jobs in their areas and review the relevant standards.

As we approached the training, we were still not sure which hospital jobs would be appropriate for the training or for use with the JI method. Just about this time, as we were doing a purposeful literature search on the subject going back deep into the nursing archives, we discovered a copy of an article from *The American Journal of Nursing* dated June 1946. It was written by Olive White, RN, who had worked at King County Harborview Hospital, which was just a few blocks down the street from Virginia Mason in Seattle. In the article, which explained how TWI was brought to hospitals during the critical years of the war when the training of "auxiliary workers" was vital to compensate for the decrease in nurses, was a long list of trainable duties divided into four categories: (1) housekeeping duties, (2) transportation and communication, (3) patient care, and (4) clerical duties. The jobs on the list, such as clean sterilizers, get supplies, assist with patient transfers, dress and undress patients, pass bedpans, test urines for sugar, give bed baths, chart stools, and fill in admissions and discharges, were not all that different from our current tasks in spite of the passage of over six decades. We felt invigorated to get this help from the past and to be able to "stand on the shoulders" of the nurses who came before us.

For the 10-hour JI class, then, we were instructed to bring in "small jobs" that could be done in the training room. The 10 members decided on the following tasks:

- Hand hygiene
- Handwashing
- Six-point hourly rounding
- Collecting a specimen
- Blood glucose monitoring
- Removing a saline lock
- Donning and doffing of gown, gloves, mask (personal protection equipment [PPE])
- Placement of patient ID band
- Stool occult blood testing
- Emptying an ostomy bag

During the 10 hours of training, we found out that not only did these jobs seamlessly fit into the JI format for training, but they could indeed be trained more effectively than the way they were presently being taught. We also learned a method of analyzing the jobs to be taught by breaking them down into their fundamental elements: Important Steps and Key Points. The breakdown sheets that came out of this analysis were then used as notes by the trainers when training the jobs.

Once the class was complete, we took the list of 10 jobs we had drafted on and presented it to the managers of the two inpatient departments that participated in the training. These managers felt that 10 jobs were too many to begin with and suggested the list be slimmed down to just two or three jobs that were the most critical or would have the most impact. These jobs could then be taught as an initial pilot of the TWI program to demonstrate the value of the method. They helped reduce the number of jobs down to three: (1) hand hygiene soap/water, (2) hand hygiene gel, and (3) hourly rounding.

Even after the 10 hours of training, we felt that the group still needed practice and that the breakdowns we made in the class could be improved further. So we divided the members into groups of three and had each group work on one of the jobs, with the author being the fourth member of each group. The groups practiced doing the jobs and refined their breakdowns. Once this work was complete, we set up a room with stations for each job and hung the breakdown for each job on a wall nearby for easy viewing. A member of each group then taught the job to a member of the other two groups and we went around the room from job to job until everyone was trained in the jobs of their fellow groups. When issues or insights came up during these practice rounds, they were written down on the breakdowns on the wall, further refining our breakdown sheets. We were able to evaluate how smoothly the training went, and, when it was all over, all members of the team were trained in and able to do all three of the jobs.

Now we were ready to begin showing the hospital the power of this new training method.

Hand Hygiene: The Right Place to Start

From the very beginning of this effort when we began reading *Toyota Talent* and found the TWI training program, the Virginia Mason staff knew that hand hygiene would be an area we wanted to pursue. In fact, throughout the world, it is common knowledge that washing your hands, and washing them well, is one of the most effective ways of staying healthy. This is true in the public at large, but much more important for the working people of hospitals and health care facilities, where infections can be transmitted from one patient to another. At Virginia Mason, the slogan is, "The single most important thing we can do to keep patients and ourselves safe is handwashing."

Typically, the way to address this issue has been to create a hand hygiene campaign that promotes frequent and consistent handwashing using speeches, PowerPoint® presentations, posters depicting germy hands, clear directions, and individual buttons declaring that "I wash my paws" in either Washington State Cougar red or University of Washington Husky purple. At Virginia Mason, we followed directives from the World Health Organization (WHO) that offered detailed instructions on how to wash hands, including simple diagrams of hands being washed (Figure 3.2), and directives on when they were to be washed:

- Before patient contact
- Before aseptic (infection prevention) task

How to Handwash?

WASH HANDS WHEN VISIBLY SOILED! OTHERWISE, USE HANDRUB

Duration of the entire procedure: 40-60 seconds

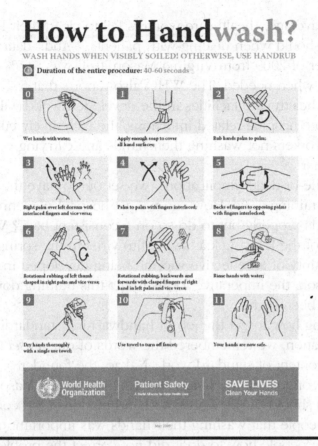

Figure 3.2 World Health Organization handwashing instructions.

- After body fluid exposure risk
- After patient contact
- After contact with patient surroundings

We even adopted the WHO pledge of: "We will clean our hands before and after each patient contact and remind others to do so as well."

In spite of these valiant and sincere efforts at Virginia Mason and health care everywhere, audits of hospitals nationwide show that health care workers and professionals are not adhering to these important guidelines and when measured they consistently come in at less than 50% compliance. The Centers for Disease Control and Prevention, in its *Guideline for Hand Hygiene in Health Care Setting*, reported in 2002 that there was an overall adherence to just 40%.* More recent data from the WHO also claim that

---

* Centers for Disease Control, MMWR, Oct 25, 2002/51 (RR 16): 1–44.

worldwide, on average, "healthcare workers fail to clean their hands 60% of the times they should when dealing with patients."* Audit data up through the third quarter of 2009 from Virginia Mason itself was 83.5% of staff washing their hands when needed. The WHO also reports that 5–10% of patients in modern-day health care facilities in the developed world will come down with one or more hospital-related infections, the most likely culprit of which is health care workers not washing their hands and carrying germs from one patient to another.[†]

With these life-or-death implications, we set out to have the group tackle this important training issue: How can we get hospital personnel to not only wash their hands properly but to do so on a consistent basis? What is more, with the onset of the H1N1 (a.k.a. swine flu) virus in the spring of 2009 and the uncertainty of an effective vaccine being developed in time for the coming flu season, the imperative for us to get this training done effectively could not have been higher.

In considering how to get the job of handwashing standardized throughout the organization, we remembered the words of our *sensei* Chihiro Nakao on the content of standard work. Nakao, the founder of Shingijutsu USA, who was conducting the *kaizen* training at Virginia Mason, had said the instructions should be "down to the hand motions." We considered how simply telling people that washing their hands was important or putting up posters showing people how to do it did not correct the problem to the levels needed. Here would be the true test of good job instruction technique, to both show and tell people how to do the job on a one-on-one basis in a way that would explain why they had to do the job as instructed. By getting "down to the hand motions" we would try to instill a deep understanding of each step of the process.

Having failed earlier in trying to use JI before we took the formal TWI Institute training, we now realized how our original breakdowns were too complicated and cumbersome for effective training (Figure 3.1). We had to make them clearer and more concise. So, we began by splitting the hand hygiene task into two separate jobs: one for washing with soap and water and the other for cleansing with gel. The two tasks were similar but contained distinct differences—gel is to be used when the hands are not visibly

---

* World Health Organization, *SAVE LIVES: Clean Your Hands, A Briefing Kit to Advocate for Action on 5 May 2010.* Online at: www.who.int/gpsc/5may/resources/slcyh_briefing-kit_website.pdf.

[†] World Health Organization, *Health Care-Associated Infection and Hand Hygiene Improvement: Slides for the Hand Hygiene Co-ordinator,* WHO presentation, slide 6. August 2009. Online at: www.who.int/gpsc/5may/tools/training_education/slides/en/index.html.

soiled with dirt, blood, feces, or other body fluids, while soap and water is needed to clean these contaminants.

Then, upon deeper reflection, we realized that our original breakdown was more a generalized set of "work instructions" that tried to describe everything that happened in the process. In the JI training class, we learned that we should stick to short and simple terms as we demonstrated the job, focusing on just those Key Points that were not readily seen in the demonstration (Figure 3.3). More significantly, we found that by looking intensively at "the hand motions" of the job, we were actually able to explain the process in more detail even as we reduced the breakdown to just a handful of words.

For example, our original breakdown described the process of washing as: "Wet hands with water, wash with enough soap to cover all hand/finger

JOB BREAKDOWN SHEET

Task: _____ Hand Hygiene-Washing _____

Supplies: __Soap, Running Water, Disposable Towel_____

Instruments & Equipment: _____

IMPORTANT STEPS	KEY POINTS	REASONS
A logical segment of the operation when something happens to advance the work.	Anything in a step that might— 1. Make or break the job 2. Injure the worker 3. Make the work easier to do, i.e. "knack", "trick", special timing, bit of special information	Reasons for the key points
1. Wet hands	1. Thoroughly without soap	Rinses away with water; soap naturally lathers when put onto water
2. Apply soap	1. Enough to cover all surfaces	Fail to kill all germs
3. Rub hands	1. Palm to palm 2. Palm to backs	1. Clean the entire surface 2. Clean the entire surface
4. Rub fingers	1. Interlocking 2. Backs of fingers to palm 3. Tips to palm 4. Thumbs	1. Sides of fingers cleaned at one time 2. Corners and creases of cuticles and knuckles 3. Under fingernails 4. Most active part of hand
5. Rinse & Dry	1. Use towel to turn water off	Prevent recontamination of hands

Figure 3.3 New job breakdown sheet for hand hygiene. (From Graupp and Wrona, 2011. With permission.)

surfaces," and then to continue: "a minimum of 20 seconds (the length of singing 'Happy Birthday to You')." After doing the job and studying the process referring to the WHO diagrams, we got into more specific detail with the procedure. First, we made it clear what should be put on the hands first, the soap or the water. This was a source of considerable variation as many people found it more efficient to put soap on their hands first and to begin washing with water directly. However, soap lathers more completely when put on top of water and will tend to rinse away when applied the other way around. Thus, the "efficient" way of washing hands was actually diminishing the effect and quality of the work. The hands should be thoroughly wet before applying soap and this was clearly taught in the new breakdown:

Step 1. Wet hands.
Step 2. Apply soap.

Next, our original breakdown simply specified that "all hand surfaces and fingers" needed to be covered with soap because "friction and skin contact are required to remove germs"—the reason for the Key Point. This was clearly not "down to the hand motions" and left too much ambiguity over how to make sure all germs on the hands were cleaned off. The next two steps of the new breakdown specifically pointed out how to "rub hands"—(1) palm to palm and (2) palm to backs; and how to "rub fingers"—(1) thumbs, (2) interlocking, (3) backs of fingers to palm, and (4) tips to palm. Only these few words are needed because learners are watching the instructor perform the job of handwashing as they point out these Important Steps and Key Points. By practicing the proper procedure while remembering these critical factors, learners would be able to perform the job correctly each time they did it from then on out.

Once this was accomplished, we then felt that the total time of the handwashing, the time it takes to sing "Happy Birthday," was really not significant anymore. The original idea of 20 seconds was an attempt to make sure that proper time was taken to get to every part of the hands and fingers. However, there was no guarantee of this happening, even if you sang the song, especially when people were never made aware of the proper technique or if they felt they could shortcut the process. Knowing the proper procedure would ensure a correct practice every time without specifying a minimum time to wash.

The team got confirmation very soon that the procedure we were teaching was indeed the correct practice. One of the nursing assistants who had

been trained early in the pilot just happened to be taking phlebotomy training, where she was learning how to draw blood so that she could do some
extra work in the lab. In the class, the first thing the instructor did was to
show the importance of clean hands by having everyone put fluorescent gel
on their hands, wash them, and then see what gel was still left, usually in
the cracks of the fingers or along the edges of the fingernails, under a black
light. The nursing assistant who had been trained how to wash her hands
with JI was the only person in the class to pass the test. In fact, the instructor said he had never seen anyone get all of the fluorescent gel off and
asked her to do it again thinking it was a fluke. When her hands came back
completely clean again, they spent the rest of the session having the nursing
assistant teach everyone in the class how to wash their hands properly.

There were many compelling reasons for us to challenge hand hygiene as
an appropriate task to teach hospital personnel. Because it was such a univer-
sal and visible function of the entire facility, success here could propel the use
of TWI as a standard practice for the training of jobs throughout the hospital.

Training Rollout

Now that we had a good process to teach, the next challenge was to roll
out the training to eight nursing units—467 RNs and nursing assistants—
over a nine-week period (Figure 3.4). We were determined to teach each of
these people individually using the JI four-step method on three jobs: the
two hand-hygiene jobs (the job of washing hands with gel was basically the
same as with soap and water, but without the wetting, rinsing, and drying of
the hands) and hourly rounding (described in Chapter 6). Moreover, we also
planned to do follow-up checks with each person trained, up to five meetings depending on the person, to make sure they were using the methods
taught. With the typical hectic nature of a hospital ward, where nurses and
other staff take care of patients on an ongoing basis, we felt that it would
be difficult to pull people off the floor for training. And we didn't want to
do the training as overtime because of the expense and because the nurses,
who worked 12-hour shifts, would not be focused on training at the end of
a long day. We also thought that since training was part of their required
work it ought to be completed on the job, not after already putting in a full
shift. The task seemed daunting.

We started by looking for downtime during the day that would be best
for doing training. Looking at it the other way around, we tried to identify

JOB INSTRUCTION TRAINING TIMETABLE - Healthcare

Job Name: Depart(s): 17, 16, 15, 14, 10, 9, 8, 7 Date: Summer 2009 1. Hand Hygiene - Soap & Water 2. Hand Hygiene - Gel 3. Hourly Rounding	July 26th - Aug 1st	Aug 2nd - 8th	Aug 9th - 15th	Aug 16th - 22nd	Aug 23rd - 29th	Aug 30th - Sept 5th	Sept 6th - 12th	Sept 13th - 19th	Sept 20th - 26th	Changes in Schedule
Level 9	X	X	X							
Level 14	X	X	X							
Level 8			X	X	X					
Level 7			X	X	X					
Level 17					X	X	X			
Level 16					X	X	X			
Level 15							X	X	X	
Level 10							X	X	X	
Turnover **Work Performance**										

Figure 3.4 Training timetable for nine-week rollout. (From Graupp and Wrona, 2011. With permission.)

when there were flurries of work time each day when training would not be practical. From 7 to 10 in the morning was just one of these times. This is when the shift change occurs, so nurses coming on shift are busy transitioning care from one caregiver to the next, rounding on patients, and prioritizing their duties. Patients are also waking up and need to go to the bathroom, be served breakfast, get their medications, and so on. Also, this is typically the time when deliveries are being made, so there is a lot of commotion sorting through incoming materials and getting them arranged and put away. We found, then, that 10 AM to 2 PM was a good time as well as 5 to 9 PM in the later shift. Therefore, we blocked off four-hour chunks of time for training and made a daily schedule for when members of the JI training team would visit the various units (Figure 3.5).

Even with this schedule, we still had to maintain a high level of flexibility. Within each two-hour spot we would shoot to train four people, one at a time, in all three jobs. A week before going into any area, we would go over the schedule with the charge nurse, being respectful of the unit's unique situation and looking for bits of downtime. We would try to preplan who would be trained, but if we found that the area was slammed the day

This Weeks Focus Units: 7, 8, 16, and 17						
AUGUST						
	Sunday	Monday	Tuesday	Wednesday	Thursday	Friday	Saturday
	23	24	25	26	27	28	29
12:00 AM							Jennie C.
1:00 AM							
2:00 AM							
3:00 AM							
4:00 AM							
5:00 AM							
6:00 AM							
7:00 AM							
8:00 AM							
9:00 AM							
10:00 AM		Martha P.	Martha P.		Beth W.		
11:00 AM							
12:00 PM							
1:00 PM				Kathy T.			
2:00 PM			Kathy T.				
3:00 PM							
4:00 PM		Beth W.		Averie V.			Annie G.
5:00 PM							
6:00 PM					Martha P.	Dora K.	
7:00 PM							
8:00 PM							
9:00 PM						Jennie C.	
10:00 PM							
11:00 PM							

Figure 3.5 TWI training schedule. (From Graupp and Wrona, 2011. With permission.)

of the training and there were no individuals available to train, we would move to another area to continue the training. The rule was to always move backward on the schedule and do follow-ups or pick up people who had missed the training in previous sessions. We wanted to maintain good communication and support with the units, so we tried not to jump ahead on the schedule to areas before it was their turn and they were expecting to be trained. The key was to partner with the areas so they didn't feel like this was "*us* coming to do *this* to *them*."

Before we began, we looked at the overall schedule and made a running count of how many people needed to be trained each day in order to meet our deadline. Preparing a standard Takt Time Calculation Sheet, a tool we had learned to use in our study of the Toyota Production System, we figured we needed to stay on a pace of seven people trained per day. We continued doing the calculation on a weekly basis as the training moved forward, adjusting the daily total to be trained; sometimes the total would go up to as many as nine people per day. The team tried to stay on track even as we struggled with the daily challenges of getting people into the training.

			Hand Hygiene Soap/Water						Hand Hygiene Gel						Hourly Rounding					
Name	Training Minutes Left	Breakdown #	Training	F/U #1	F/U #2	F/U #3	F/U #4	F/U #5	Training	F/U #1	F/U #2	F/U #3	F/U #4	F/U #5	Training	F/U #1	F/U #2	F/U #3	F/U #4	F/U #5
R., Beth																				
M., Taki																				
S., Ariel																				
G., Artie																				
B., Karisa																				
F., Erika																				
A., Tevya																				
D., Alma																				
G., Mary																				
L., Lidia																				
P., George																				
F., Carly																				
B., Madison																				
M., Martha																				
B., Marty																				
J., Dwayne																				
P., Maggy																				
E., Dean																				
T., Alex																				
C., Solina																				
C., Larry																				
A., Aman																				
A., Lee																				
W., Loma																				
J., Annabelle																				
Changes In Schedule																				

Name: Abolafya
Group: PCT
Dept: ACE
Date: June/July 2009

Job Instruction Training Timetable – Healthcare

Unit Training Minutes Left: 1500

Figure 3.6   Detailed training timetable. (From Graupp and Wrona, 2011. With permission.)

Our trainers were instructed to "resist the temptation to group train." When going to a unit, we would first check the training timetable for that area (Figure 3.6) and deliver the training to people on the list one at a time. It was a common practice, especially for nontechnical tasks, to batch train people and send them directly out to the floors. But the results were always spotty, at best. The JI technique taught them the need to train "*a* person how to quickly remember to do *a* job correctly, safely, and conscientiously," meaning that this was one-on-one training. This was a huge commitment, but we were confident that the results would prove it to be a smart investment.

Nevertheless, for the small group of initial JI trainers, getting through 467 training sessions one at a time was a heavy lift. And, to get them all done in nine weeks meant we had to encourage them and maintain high enthusiasm. A July 30, 2009 memo to the training team exemplifies this effort:

> ITEM 2. Apparently, there is a limit to how many consecutive staff one is able to train before one can't remember his/her own name. If this happens to you, fear not! Your brain will remember the jobs

perfectly … no need for you to be present. Also, you will be wearing a name tag, and a nice member of our staff will assist you.

When a training session was completed, we would write the date in the
appropriate box of the timetable. We also would conduct follow-ups where
we viewed the jobs being done in the flow of actual work. These could
be conducted "as early as the same day as the training as long as the staff
member has had a chance to get some real-time practice." During these
follow-up visits, we would not only watch them do the job, but also ask
them how the training had gone, if they had had a chance to try out doing
the job, how were things going with the job itself, and if they felt there was
anything missing. There were five slots allotted for follow-ups on the timetable (see Figure 3.6), but that didn't mean we had to do all five. Our instructions were to continue conducting follow-ups until we felt the person had
mastered the technique and successfully integrated it into his or her daily
routine. If we felt the person needed more follow-ups, we would circle the
date. Otherwise, we would write "done" next to the date.

We learned one thing at the outset when we began doing the training
in front of the patients. Although patients at Virginia Mason are oftentimes
invited to participate in process improvement efforts, and usually do so with
great enthusiasm, in this case, they became very concerned while watching a staff person learn to wash his or her hands. They could not grasp that
the learners already knew how to wash their hands and were just learning
a more standardized method of doing it. Patients began complaining that
they did not want a nurse caring for them who was so inexperienced that
she did not know how to wash her hands. So the team immediately made
the adjustment to have all the training done in an empty room, and locat-
ing this space became the first task of the trainers when we went to the
floors to teach. As the training started making progress, though, these very
same patients began noticing the improved technique of the staff and started
making comments about staff washing their hands "like they were going
into surgery!" The effect was so large and immediate that head of nursing, Tachibana, already a big proponent of TWI, began assisting with the JI
follow-up checks to make sure nurses were using the proper handwashing
technique.

One other benefit of giving the training to the nursing assistants, who
normally would not have received this level of intensive training with this
much detail, was providing the reasons why. Until TWI, few people had

taken the time to explain to them the reasons they should do their jobs in certain ways. This more respectful way of training via TWI, providing the reasons why, created greater motivation, and a more pleasant working environment. During the training process, the nursing assistants asked many questions on other aspects of infection control, which never came up before, and their overall level of expertise grew dramatically.

The initial training rollout was completed on schedule in nine weeks. In Section II of this book, we will explain the details of the Job Instruction method our group used along with the tools we have referenced here. But, for now, let's look at the results that were gained through these efforts.

Results of the Initial Rollout

The first signs that the training pilot was having a positive impact came from comments the staff began hearing from the patients themselves who, as the hospital's "customers," are always auditing the performance of the care they receive at Virginia Mason. Ellen Noel, a med-surg clinical nurse specialist, made this observation:

> Recently, I entered a patient's room on Level 10. From her bed, this patient watched me wash my hands. The patient remarked, "That is so interesting! *Everybody* coming in here washes their hands the exact same way. I've never seen anything like it!"

Even outside of the hospital, people were noticing. One of the nurses trained in handwashing was using the restroom before going into a theater to see a movie and, while washing her hands, another patron noticed her method and commented that she must work for Virginia Mason because "that's the way everyone washes their hands there." Then the person asked if she would show her how to do it correctly and, before she knew it, several other women in the restroom were observing and learning how to wash their hands correctly.

With the rounding procedure as well, patients were noticing the standardization and reliability of the service they were getting. This procedure, which will be explained in detail in Chapter 6, was designed to help minimize inpatient falls, especially when ambulating to the bathroom. The following conversation was overheard between a patient being discharged and his nurse in the Telemetry Unit:

You know ... you all must go through some kind of special training because *everyone* asked me if I was comfortable, offered the
bathroom, made sure that I had my call light and phone, and then
asked if there was anything else I needed. I've never seen such
great customer service while in a hospital.

Incredibly, the patient here was able to recite the job procedure, completely
and in proper sequence, simply by watching it being performed exactly that
way each time. This demonstrates that the procedure has, in fact, become
the *standard* way it is done by everyone on the floor. Notice also that, from
the patient's perspective, this procedure was all about "great customer service" and not fall prevention. Thus, the hospital was able to obtain a significant benefit over and above the gains realized by reducing falls.

The steadiness and reliability of the processes could be locked in through
the JI training process—through learning properly how to do the jobs—and
this proved more effective than simply telling people how important it is to
do these tasks. Rowena Ponischil, director of Levels 7/8, stated it this way:

For a long time now, I've taught my staff that the majority of
patient falls occur during the toileting process. Knowing, however, wasn't enough to hardwire actions to prevent patient falls.
TWI provides the hardwiring and rigor ... toileting is planned for
and built into my staff's work flow. It's really made a difference on
Level 8.

Handwashing Pilot Created "Pull"

Earlier in this chapter, we talked about the benchmark figure used to check
the percentage of times health care workers washed their hands before
interacting with patients. We noted that worldwide that number was as low
as 40% and even at Virginia Mason the figure was 83.5% the year before the
JI training was implemented. In the areas where the JI pilot was run, eight
nursing units totaling 467 RNs and nursing assistants, reliability of hand
hygiene went above 98%. For the rounding procedure, reliability was also
measured at over 98% and, where rounding was implemented, patient satisfaction scores were up 5–10%.

Besides these initial feedback statistics, the most immediate result of
the pilot was the flood of requests from other areas of the hospital to do
the hand hygiene training. This "pull" from other departments meant very

clearly that they all saw the value and need for the same training within their own areas. Departments that were scheduled to continue with the handwashing training included:

- Transporters
- Outpatient clinics
- Hospital nursing units not part of the initial trial (ED, RHU, CCU)
- Pharmacy
- Bailey–Boushay House (a nursing home run by Virginia Mason)
- Sterile processing
- GME (Graduate Medical Education) and Safety Curriculum Team
- MD section heads
- Surgery section

In this way, the trainers who did the pilot never stopped training, but continued rolling out the program into the pull from these other areas. All transporters throughout the hospital were immediately trained, and the JI trainers began going into the clinics directly thereafter.

Even as the handwashing pilot was still being conducted, many areas had already begun seeing the need for and planning the use of JI for other tasks. In anticipation of this surge in demand for Job Instruction technique, in September 2009, just as the pilot was winding down, the author and one other member of the Kaizen Promotion Office staff, Alenka Rudolph, took the JI train-the-trainer program to become facilitators of the JI 10-hour course. Once the pilot finished, they began teaching JI 10-hour sessions only admitting carefully selected individuals to take the training to be sure the program would continue growing in a strategic direction with continued momentum.

One good example of that growth was in the operating room where we had identified an immediate need for JI training: specimen labeling. Different from taking a blood or urine sample, where a test can easily be redone if in doubt, when a specimen is taken from a person's body in the operating room (OR), there is an "extreme chain of command" where the person carrying the specimen must not lose sight of it until it is properly labeled. In other words, it should never leave that person's hands. In spite of the protocol in place, though, we had experienced some near-misses where specimens were mislabeled and we wanted to eliminate the situation. Though these types of incidents were corrected without having to go back into the OR to extract another specimen, the near-misses pointed out the need for a better process.

Members of the OR team went into the JI class specifically with the intention of redesigning this process. While doing a breakdown for the job, in preparation for a practice demonstration of the JI method using an actual job from the trainee's worksite that each person attending the class must perform, they asked the question: "Why is it 17 steps?" Using the JI concept of Important Steps and Key Points, they were able to clear out the clutter and confusion in their current procedure and create a clear and effective teaching process that would ensure specimens were handled correctly each and every time they were labeled. We pointed out to them that when you design a process well, you do find the best way, just like the path that water takes when it flows downhill. But they first needed the JI model to show them that path.

Another example of how we saw the use of the JI method for problems we were trying to address was in the fire safety procedures at Bailey–Boushay House, a nursing home facility run by Virginia Mason. In fact, fires in nursing homes overall are a big problem and Bailey–Boushay had had three fires in three years, an unacceptable number, mainly due to a high population of smokers who did not always follow the rules around their habit. Bailey–Boushay followed national fire safety guidelines by teaching staff how to react to a fire using the acronym RACE: *remove* the patient from the area of risk, *activate* the fire alarm, *call* for help, *evacuate* if directed to do so. Even though people could remember the acronym, they didn't always remember what they were supposed to do.

The executive director of Bailey–Boushay, Brian Knowles, went to the JI class and used this fire procedure as his demonstration job in the training. He reframed the procedure into Important Steps and Key Points, the same steps as outlined by RACE, but without the acronym. After practicing teaching the procedure in the JI class, he went back to the nursing home and began training it to his staff. In subsequent fire drills, Bailey–Boushay staff not only remembered how to do the procedure, but were actually able to perform the actions prescribed proficiently and in a timely manner.

We knew that all of these priority jobs were problems that each area had already recognized and our staff knew what the right response needed to be in order to solve them. TWI didn't tell us what we had to do. In spite of this understanding of the need for good procedures and training, though, we didn't know how to frame the solution or how to "edit it correctly." TWI gave us a solid methodology we could follow in order to finish the job of developing true standard work that solved these pressing problems. In other words, just knowing you have to do a job doesn't get you to do it, but if you know how to do it, and why, then you'll follow the correct procedure every time.

Continued Application of Hand Hygiene Training

Since the introduction of this hand hygiene case at Virginia Mason Medical Center, countless other organizations, inside health care and out, have adopted the hand hygiene training method and used it with incredible success. In early 2016, Baptist Health Care, a not-for-profit integrated health care system with three hospitals, four medical parks, and a behavioral health network centered in Pensacola, Florida, was experiencing high infection rates related to central lines, with the Surgical Intensive Nursing Unit (SINU) showing the highest rate. Central lines are tubes placed in a major vein close to the heart for giving medications or fluids, or for collecting blood for medical tests, and can remain in place for weeks, even months. This makes them much more likely to be a cause for serious infection, especially when they are not kept clean. Looking for root causes to their high infection rate, Baptist specialists zeroed in on poor compliance with standard work related to taking care of central lines and turned to TWI Job Instruction for help.

Historically, from 2011 through mid-2016, Baptist was experiencing overall just under two infections per quarter while the SINU by itself had an average rate of 0.5 infections per quarter. As we pointed out near the end of Chapter 1, Central Line Associated Bloodstream Infections (CLABSI) are both lethal and expensive with up to one in four patients dying* and the cost to the nation totaling billions of dollars annually. Under the direction of the VP of Quality, the Baptist team held their initial TWI Job Instruction training for the SINU in April 2016 and kicked off a CLABSI pilot project in June consisting of three core jobs: Hand Hygiene with soap and water, Hand Hygiene with gel, and Scrub the Hub, the practice of cleaning the connectors between a patient's central line and any medication bags or equipment that are attached to the line. They used the exact same breakdown sheet for the hand hygiene instruction that was developed by Virginia Mason and presented here.

---

* Centers for Disease Control and Prevention (CDC): CDC Vitalsigns – Making Health Care Safer: Reducing Bloodstream Infections, March 2011, https://www.cdc.gov/vitalsigns/pdf/2011-03-vitalsigns.pdf.

Overcoming multiple obstacles, including initial front-line resistance to the training and challenges with sustainment, the newly established TWI Steering Committee developed 20 trainers who carried out one-on-one training in the SINU and three patient floors from June through August. The teamed joined up with the hospital hand hygiene campaign creating posters to encourage staff to tell patients, "Let me clean my hands…" and to make it OK to ask other team members, "Are your hands clean?" They established "TWI Touch Points" including Daily Management, New Hire Orientation, Nurse Residency Program, Annual Competencies, and Community Outreach. Most importantly, they celebrated their new trainers with strong support and high encouragement from management.

With promising initial results from the SINU pilot, they struck out to expand the effort to new areas delivering TWI JI training beginning in July of 2017 with a total of over 70 hand hygiene trainers and, by the end of 2017, a total of 2,000 people trained in hand hygiene. The results were that on February 6, 2018 (when the team presented at the annual TWI Summit in Savannah, Georgia), the SINU had gone 621 days CLABSI-free and the overall hospital had had only two infections since the initial pilot started in June 2016.

Conclusion

By following the time-tested method of good Job Instruction as developed by the TWI founders in the 1940s and used in companies like Toyota since the 1950s, the people at Virginia Mason Medical Center, as well as Baptist Health, were able to prove that this technique has a direct and powerful application in the health care field today. What is more, seeing the method in action gave us a vision of the true possibilities of what standard work could achieve when it is implemented correctly and fully. In Section II, we will look in detail at the contents of the Job Instruction method and how it can be applied to health care facilities. Then, in Section III, we will examine a leadership model that helps build motivation and cooperation in following the standard procedures people are instructed in. But first we need to examine the need for good instruction skills in health care and point out the various areas of health care practice that would be greatly influenced by people being properly trained. We will see how jobs in health care can be stabilized and improved in the same way that our manufacturing counterparts have so successfully done in the past.

Chapter 4

Need for Good Instruction Skill

Introduction

In any field of endeavor, the need for training our people well is a vital responsibility for all of us in charge of getting results from the organization. This is true for both our new employees who are learning their jobs for the first time and our veteran workers who need to stabilize and standardize their procedures to produce optimal performance. It goes without saying that in the health care industry, where our performance results are nothing less than the life and death of our patients, the quality of this training would be at the top of our list of priorities.

In the last chapter, we saw how the people at Virginia Mason Medical Center (Virginia Mason) introduced a single example of good training, a proper hand hygiene technique, and were able to move the organization toward safer and more consistent practice. Thanks to the careful and energetic way the team rolled out this initial use of the Training Within Industry (TWI) Job Instruction (JI) method, the entire hospital was able to witness the power of a strong method of training that positively affected the vital needs of the hospital. The entire workforce, then, from top executives and managers to the doctors, nurses, and staff, could understand what a good method for training could be and advocate its use.

The possibilities for the application of this good training technique are wide and varied. We already saw how the staff of Virginia Mason quickly embraced the JI technique for areas such as transporters, outpatient clinics,

DOI: 10.4324/9781003035305-4

sterile processing, and, in the operating room (OR), specimen labeling. After the initial TWI experience at Virginia Mason, TWI has since been introduced and applied in hospitals, clinics, and health care facilities across the country to a multitude of diverse tasks such as patient identification, central line dressing changes, GI scope cleaning, blood specimen collecting and processing, catheter care, and drawing up medications, just to name a few. It has also been used to great success in administrative work such as arriving and discharge of patients, Electronic Medical Records (EMRs), and outpatient scheduling. We must be careful not to jump to the conclusion that every job in a health care facility can or should be trained using this one-on-one training method (more on this topic in Chapter 7). But because so much of the work done in health care involves physical technique and defined processes, which are learned over time and based on experience and "tribal knowledge," the application of TWI-JI can benefit multiple facets of work in health care.

TWI Application in Health Care

What are some examples, then, of the areas that this TWI method of Job Instruction can be used in health care? One area in which the people at Virginia Mason felt they would get exceptional value out of a JI implementation was in telemetry, that area between critical care and routine patient care where staff are required to learn to use a variety of monitoring equipment as they care for patients in a high state of need. This was a bottle neck for Virginia Mason because of the unique expertise needed to care for very ill patients. There was also high staff turnover because they become very marketable once they are able to read the monitors and treat critical care patients. Nurses coming out of telemetry typically move up quickly to higher positions in clinical care, ICU, surgery, or even, in some cases, to becoming a flight nurse. Therefore, the need for good training here is constant and the department has become a "feeder line" for the entire hospital.

The telemetry unit at the hospital embraced the fact that they were going to be a training point for nurses and staff moving up their career paths and they embraced TWI as a steady means of providing this service to the organization. They ran with the initial hand hygiene pilot and, because of high morale in the department, received many questions when doing the training such as on the proper use of personal protective equipment (PPE). These questions were then passed on to the Department of Infection Prevention for further training development. Management thought that everyone knew these things and were surprised they didn't. In response, they took infection control procedures to new heights and used TWI to actualize these new standards even as they continued training the new nurses moving into the department.

Donna Smith, Virginia Mason's medical director at the time and a practicing clinical physician in pediatrics, participated in one of the first 10-hour JI sessions put on after the hand hygiene pilot was finished. While the plan was to have participants in the classes be practitioners who would actually train jobs, select administrators, such as Dr Smith, participated in order to elicit understanding and support from the top brass. As a practice job for the class, Dr Smith selected obtaining a throat culture where you reach into the back of the throat with a swab. When breaking down this job for training, she found a Key Point: "Don't touch tip until you reach tonsils," so that the patient, in particular a child, doesn't gag on the swab. The breakdown and instruction practice went extremely well and the medical director felt that, with this training, you could get a nurse's assistant to be able to do this job instead of relying on a doctor or a nurse. "There is no reason for me to do it," she proclaimed, "and no reason for a nurse to do it either." By aligning tasks with skills, and providing the appropriate training, we can enhance the work that is reflective of a person's level of ability and training. Most importantly, we can get whoever is doing these tasks doing them right, every time.

While Virginia Mason had been on the cutting edge of this reintroduction of the TWI methodologies into the health care industry, other hospitals and medical groups across the country also saw the application of this time-tested method in their organizations. Under the direction of newly hired chief improvement officer Skip Steward, Baptist Memorial Health Care began TWI training in January of 2014 based on a recommendation from Skip's boss, Dr Paul DePriest. Dr DePriest himself joined the Baptist team in 2012 as a chief medical officer after an extensive medical career at the University of Kentucky Medical Center where he learned about TWI from his close working relationship with the nearby Toyota plant in Georgetown, Kentucky. Headquartered in Memphis, Tennessee, Baptist Memorial Health Care consists of 22 hospitals and an extensive network of clinics throughout the tri-state area of Tennessee, Arkansas, and Mississippi. Under Skip's leadership, the TWI methods have been spread throughout all the Baptist hospitals and clinics and have been creating sustainable results.

An early win at Baptist, when the Job Instruction introduction was in its initial pilot rollout at NEA Baptist Hospital in the northeast Arkansas city of Jonesboro, was the teaching of GI scope cleaning. Because these scopes were used for colonoscopies, a common procedure which brought strong revenue to the hospital, proper cleaning was essential to prevent infection spread and it was thought, at the time, that only trained nurses could understand and perform the procedure. With the shortage of nurses and increases in the procedure, though, the hospital found itself incapable of keeping up and was calling in nurses for overtime hours just to clean scopes so they could be available for use in procedures. What is more, a "superbug" had recently appeared which was difficult to kill and that focused even more concern and attention on proper procedures for cleaning the scopes.

This dire situation posed a logical first application of the TWI instruction method. Because of the superbug, it turned out that representatives from Olympus, the scope manufacturer, would be coming to town to help NEA staff ensure proper cleaning techniques the very week after the initial TWI training was given. This presented the TWI team with a good opportunity to review the most up-to-date clinical practice guidelines we talked about in Chapter 2. The new TWI trainers prepared training documents based on the manufacturer's suggestions and used the instruction method to begin teaching staff, including non-nursing techs and assistants, how to properly clean the GI scopes. Within a few weeks, they were able to catch up with the backlog of uncleaned scopes eliminating the need for overtime and freeing up nurses to attend to the increased workload in colonoscopies.

Another big concern at NEA Baptist was the counting of instruments and supplies in the OR, both before and after surgeries. This was a safety precaution used to prevent retained foreign objects (RFO), oftentimes surgical sponges, from being left behind in the patient's body after surgery, wreaking havoc with the patient's body and creating extreme costs and liability for the hospital. The standard way for preventing RFOs, like sponges, is to do a sponge count both before and after surgery to ensure that all of the sponges in the OR are accounted for. However, there is a lot of history in health care for dismissing sponge counts. Errors also can occur when counts are done on bags of sponges instead of individual sponges. For example, if you have four bags containing 10 sponges in each bag, the assumption is that 40 sponges were used. However, one of the bags could mistakenly contain 9 or 11 sponges leading to an incorrect count. A study published in the *Journal of the American College of Surgeons* in 2009 reported that as many as 1 of every 1,500 operations may have a retained foreign object and that, of those, two thirds are sponges.[*]

---

[*] *Bulletin of the American College of Surgeons*, November 2009. Online at: http://www.facs.org/fello ws_info/bulletin/2009/brisson1109.pdf.

Because there was no consistent standard of how the counting was performed, immediate attention was paid to using the TWI training method to standardize and ensure the task was completed correctly each and every time without anything "falling between the cracks." OR nurses were part of the initial TWI training team and they enlisted the assistance of an experienced OR scrub tech to help with developing the training material who said afterwards, "I am confident now that we are counting correctly because everyone is doing it the exact same way." In their training breakdown, when counting sponges they were sure to include the Key Point of "break seal, separate and look for blue tag" to ensure the sponge packs were opened and sponges counted individually one by one (see Figure 4.1). This was a complicated training process because two people are always involved in the

V.1.1

JOB INSTRUCTION BREAKDOWN SHEET

Task/Operation: COUNTS
Supplies: CASE, CART PACK, PREFERENCE CARD, ADDITIONAL SUPPLIES, COUNT SHEET 0120.2014
Equipment: PEN

IMPORTANT STEPS	KEY POINTS	REASONS
AIDET-self and tech We are using this method to teach counting because it is a systematic method to count. It is less likely to result in an error or cause patient harm. (Item will not be left in body)	Can you tell me what you know about counting or the counting process? We will be teaching this process three times and then you will do the process 4 times to make you comfortable with the process.	
We are teaching 2 different roles the tech role and the RN role.	1. Scrub Tech does counting out loud. 2. RN confirms and records.	1. RN is responsible for room.
1. Arrange instruments flat on table.	1. Like pieces together. 2. Keep instruments on stringer.	1. Easier to count. 2. Easier to count.
2. Count Softs and Record.	1. Smallest first. 2. Break seal, separate and look for blue tag. 3. Each bundle individually. 4. Remove from room incorrect packs.	1. Easiest to lose. 2. Sponges stick together. 3. Easy to count. 4. Cause incorrect count.
3. Count Sharps and Record.	1. Don't touch sharp edges. 2. Don't recap needles.	1. Can contaminate and cut you. 2. Can contaminate and cut you.
4. Count Other Objects and Record.	1. Confirm w/count sheet. 2. If cut count each piece.	1. Confirm what is a countable item. 2. Correct count.
5. Count instruments and Record.	1. Use knife handle to separate. 2. RN calls out, count, confirm, record. 3. Get total for same instrument.	1. Don't miss anything. 2. Confirm correct count. 3. Confirm correct count.
6. Full count during cavity closure.	1. Same order smallest first. 2. Start at patient, mayo, back table. 3. RN counts from pocketed sponge bag. 4. Count instruments in order following count sheet.	1. Most critical first. 2. Most critical first. 3. Non-sterile & easy to visualize 4. Confirm correct count.
7. Count Softs and Sharps after each layer.	1. Same order smallest first. 2. Start at patient, mayo, back table. 3. RN counts from pocketed sponge bag.	1. Most critical first. 2. Most critical first. 3. Non-sterile & easy to visualize

We will follow up with you in a week to make sure you are doing the process correctly and we will place you with a preceptor that knows the process.

RN WORKFLOW 3/4/15

Figure 4.1   Job breakdown sheet for counting in the OR.

counting procedure: the scrub tech who counts the objects and the RN who records the totals. But the training was consistent and effective and today all new members going in to count in the OR are trained using TWI.

In almost every Baptist hospital where TWI was implemented, one of the first applications of Job Instruction was in the collection of blood cultures and the elimination of blood culture contamination due to inconsistent or improper technique. A key part of the instruction was to first collect blood in the anaerobic (without air) bottle which was marked with a blue cap and second from the aerobic bottle (with air) which was marked with a purple cap. It was critical to follow this order in drawing blood so the lab could properly test samples based on whether the blood was exposed to oxygen or not and if the order was reversed, the sample would be contaminated with air coming from the aerobic bottle. When they were told in the training the reason for this sequence, many nurses proclaimed that they never knew why they had to keep the order and had been performing the task "as best they could remember." One physician actually approached Skip after seeing a demonstration of the instruction asking, "Why *do* you have to use the blue bottle before the purple bottle?" He claimed he had been doing the procedure for years and didn't think it really mattered, so he just "went for it."

Another area of great potential for good training is in the Pharmacy where the compounding of medications is a critical function. In other words, while many medications are prepackaged and prepared for delivery, hospital pharmacy staff still mix ingredients to prepare medications in specific dosages for individual patients. Needless to say, this must be done carefully and with no mistakes. For example, in chemotherapy, drugs are compounded based on body height and weight and it is easy to transpose dosages when mixing the formula. If the correct dosage for a patient was 60 mg/m^2 of Adriamycin and 600 mg/m^2 of Cytoxan, an error of mixing 600 mg/m^2 of Adriamycin and 60 mg/m^2 of Cytoxan would create catastrophic results. To guard against these kinds of errors, a system of checks and balances has been set up to capture mistakes and herein lies a great deal of waste and redundancy. However, the safety aspect requires this redundancy. With more consistency in the work, using good training methodology, could hospitals create more stability in this critical area and reduce some of the redundancy?

The John D. Dingell VA Medical Center in Detroit MI had been implementing standard work procedures for several years under the guidance of Medical Center Director Dr Pamela J. Reeves. Seeing the need for consistent practice across all departments, both clinical and non-clinical, of the

Detroit VA, Dr Reeves and her team began TWI Job Instruction training in early 2020, continuing the training even through shutdowns caused by the pandemic because of the vital need for strong and active training skills among staff, including department managers. In the pharmacy, procedures were put in place to process all prescriptions that decreased inconsistencies between pharmacists and reduced out-of-stock medications ensuring veterans would get their medications on time. In addition, there were great financial benefits to be gained if they could teach veterans to make use of mail-order meds instead of picking up their medications at the hospital, an engrained practice of most patients at the VA. With TWI skills, they were able to increase patient satisfaction by dramatically lowering missing doses, which decreased from 107 to 83 in the first round of pilot training, and the wait time for veterans in getting medications.

A huge opportunity also exists in Sterile Processing where all instruments and equipment in the operating room must be cleaned, re-kitted, and sterilized for next use. This is the one area of a hospital that actually operates like a production line in a factory with, quite literally, a moving line, peak periods of output, and operators with well-defined tasks. Many hospitals have tried to apply manufacturing techniques in areas like this to improve their process, attempting to standardize work and create a better sequence of the flow of the processes. But, as is the case in manufacturing, when you don't have stability in the work processes and procedures, there is no visibility to find the vital areas that need attention and can be improved. At the Detroit VA, TWI trainers collaborated with both the OR nursing and the SPS (Sterile Processing Service) to create compatible standard work on both the delivery and receiving ends of dirty instruments moving from the OR to SPS. With the OR nursing team, they set up training for how to do the inspection and scope check before surgery as well as inspection and cleaning of scopes after surgery along with the proper method of sending them to SPS. With the SPS team, they trained on how to clean and sterilize scopes and prepare them for return to the OR when needed. With a unified and consistent process, they were able to reduce the number of missing and broken instruments which improved surgery scheduling which had been held up due to a lack of scopes.

When the coronavirus pandemic was unleashed, one of the first challenges the entire nation faced was getting people tested for COVID. Ginger Purvis, an experienced nurse manager and JI trainer who managed the Job Instruction practice at the Baptist hospital in Southaven, MS, described her experience when first volunteering to help in administering tests:

There was a great need for standardization from how to swab, what swab to use, completing the paperwork, where to place the paperwork and swab after collection, and what to tell the patient. Information was coming in so fast and changes were being made sometimes hour to hour. Once you had a process that worked, it may have been changed the very next day. Patients trust us to always use best practice and protect them. Swabbing the patient was a job that needed to be done correctly—every patient, every visit, every time!

Dr JoAnn Wood, chief medical officer for Baptist Memorial Health, along with the staff at the Southaven facility were made aware of this variation in how tests were being performed at the drive through line with the nasal test. Dr Wood called Skip Steward on the weekend to get his help. They quickly made a Job Instruction breakdown, road tested it making adjustments, and put it in place immediately so they could have consistent methods maintaining the quality of the tests being given.

These are just some examples of areas where the use of the TWI method of Job Instruction made a big impact in health care application. The possibilities are limitless. But when we have a sure and reliable method of training, we can better assure the consistent quality of the work and the safety of our patients and staff.

Implementation of New Equipment: Everyone Does It the Right Way

St. Joseph Health System (SJHS), which merged in July of 2016 with Providence Health and Services to become Providence St. Joseph Health, introduced TWI in 2010 through their Lean organization that deploys experts in activities like continuous improvement, waste reduction, and process flow, many of whom came with manufacturing backgrounds. While they began their Lean efforts three years prior to this introduction, they realized that they were missing a training technique that would allow them to enforce the standards they were trying to employ. For example, even though they would organize and carry out improvement events, they were continually frustrated in trying to actualize the benefits they were supposed to receive from these improvements. As Amber Gutman, a senior Lean facilitator at the SJHS system office in Orange, California, put it, "We wanted to make sure that our work on developing improvements had lasting impact." TWI helped them to implement those improvements.

In early 2011, just after the holidays, SJHS began the implementation of a new piece of equipment that it would place in each of its 14 hospitals that were, at the time, spread out in various locations in Northern and Southern California as well as West Texas/Eastern New Mexico. The new equipment used radio frequency (RF) identification technology to make sure no sponges were left behind inside patients' bodies after surgery, a problem we noted earlier. With its goal of "perfect care," it felt this was an investment that had to be made for every instance where a sponge might possibly be left behind. This included not only the main operating rooms but also areas where obstetrics (OB) surgery, such as C-sections, were being performed as well as labor and delivery rooms where sponges also were used. The machines were delivered to all 14 hospitals about the same time and there was to be a unified rollout for all personnel responsible for preventing retained foreign objects.

SJHS felt that this would be an excellent opportunity to use its new TWI skills to train a large group of people quickly. The new equipment was being purchased because SJHS knew it faced limits on where and how much its efforts at process improvements alone could be used to prevent errors from the system. With concerns like retained foreign objects, it was also too big a risk to rely solely on human vigilance. At the same time, though, SJHS was aware of the fact that when it tried to approach issues with technology, it didn't always get the results promised. In the end, the technology was only as good as the people using it. If SJHS didn't train people to use the machines properly, it would wind up spending a lot of money for suboptimal effect.

Machelle Theel, manager of patient safety and regulatory compliance, was charged with rolling out the RF project, which included everything from getting the equipment in place to setting a timeline for having the machines up and running. She also was charged with setting up a materials management system for handling the purchase and storage of specially made sponges that had chips embedded in them that worked with the RF machinery. She had seen a brief orientation given by the Lean operations team on the TWI Job Instruction methodology, which included an overview of the hand hygiene case study done at Virginia Mason Medical Center (see Chapter 3). She was encouraged by Mary Kingston, vice president over improvement performance and the St. Joseph Way (the SJHS system of Lean), to try integrating Lean methodologies like TWI into the clinical practice. Theel immediately saw the value of good training for new process implementation and was excited about the possibilities. She gave the directive to have all hospitals use the JI method to teach employees how to use the new equipment properly.

Theel began by reaching out to the respective leaders at all of the hospitals: directors of surgery, directors of labor and delivery, and directors of clinical education. She first needed to identify two or three people from each hospital who could act as trainers—those who could learn the TWI-JI method of training and then be responsible for teaching staff at the hospital how to use the new equipment. She had to coordinate each hospital's resources in terms of who they could provide to be trainers. Once these people were selected, they set up TWI classes—one in Northern California, one in Southern California, and one in Texas—to cover the regional areas. Fortunately, they had just recently, in October 2010, completed their first train-the-trainer session with the TWI Institute where four of their Lean leaders had been trained to deliver the JI 10-hour course: Mary Jordan from St. Joseph Hospital in Eureka, California; Jodi Judge and Bryn Risler from St. Mary Medical Center in Apple Valley, California; and Kendra Lange from Covenant Health System in Lubbock, Texas. Geographically, this gave them trainers in each of the three regions they needed to reach. And with two to three trainers from each of the 14 hospitals attending, they could set up the classes following the TWI format of 10 persons per class.

To begin the process of instructing how to use the machines, the training team first needed to learn for themselves how to use the equipment and then break it down in the JI format for instruction. Amber Gutman, a senior Lean facilitator who was coordinating the use of the TWI methods, set up a meeting with the equipment vendors and invited Theel, Judge, Risler, and one of the clinical educators to spend a full day at the organization's headquarters in Orange, California, to learn the system. In the morning, the vendors gave their typical presentation of PowerPoint® demonstrations, and hands-on trial runs. While observing all this, the JI trainers were busily taking notes, just like they did in the JI class, on what they thought were the Important Steps and Key Points in the processes. Following that, they listed all the training elements they felt needed to happen around the implementation of the equipment:

◾ What is the purpose? The importance of the new equipment and what they were trying to accomplish with it.

- What is the content? To understand the technical aspects of the new equipment.
- Logistical details: Where in the OR suite would the machines live? Would they always be turned on? What to do if they break down?
- Documentation requirements: Number of scans? Results of scans? What was needed for regulatory purposes? Equipment checks?
- How does this new equipment fit in with existing procedures? Standard sponge counts would still be performed even after the machines were up and running.
- Et cetera.

They took this big list, then, and determined what they wanted to accomplish using the JI method and what they would teach using traditional training methods like group classroom sessions. They decided to focus the JI portion on just those pieces where equipment users were in contact with the patients because that is where the quality issues could most likely happen. In fact, they narrowed down the jobs they would teach using JI to just two tasks—mat scanning and wand scanning.

> **MAT SCANNING**: This is a mat that is placed on top of the operating table, but under the patient, and validates sponge counts and locates missing sponges. Since OR staff already have skills at prepping tables and "layering" materials that go under the patient, there was nothing new or difficult here to learn about placing the mat. And since the mat itself would do the scanning, they simply had to teach how to run the scan.
>
> **WAND SCANNING**: The wand is a large circular tool that looks like a frying pan lid that is clear in the middle with a handle on the side. As with the mat scan, because the sponges all have RFID (radio frequency identification) chips embedded in them, scanning the wand carefully over the patient's body will detect and find any sponges that were not removed. The tricky part here is that the wand can inadvertently pick up things that are close to the patient, but not necessarily inside the body. Therefore, the user must be careful about, for example, something being in the pocket of a person standing next to the patient.

Working with the vendors, Gutman, Judge, and Risler made the original breakdowns that trainers would use to teach the two jobs. Interestingly, when the vendors questioned them on why they were including a certain Key Point into the training, the SJHS staff protested, "But you stressed that like 15 times in your demonstration!" By hashing out the procedure using the JI breakdown technique, the vendors themselves were able to pinpoint critical areas that needed to be stressed about their equipment. They were so impressed with the method, in fact, that they sat in on the 10-hour JI training sessions and began to reflect on their own method of training their customers. When it was all over, they claimed that they had never seen an implementation with this kind of energy and allocation of resources.

The people appointed to be trainers took their 10-hour JI training following the prescribed TWI program and did individual practice jobs that they broke down themselves to learn the proper use of the method. But, because the goal of the project was to create a standard work process for use of the RF equipment at all of the hospitals, the plan was to have all the trainers teach from the same breakdowns. So it was important for Gutman and her team to make sure that all of the trainers, at each of the hospitals, were teaching the same standard method. Because the hospitals had their own individual histories and, in most cases, differing systems of handling both administrative and clinical procedures, this would be a test case for implementing a standard procedure across all of the hospitals.

From there, the individual hospitals picked up the training and began teaching all personnel who were charged with handling the RF identification equipment. Approximately 50 or more people at each hospital were trained in the use of the new equipment, for a total of more than 700 people trained. In summary, four internal JI trainers conducted 10-hour classes in three locations where some 30 people were taught how to teach the new jobs using the JI four-step method. These trainers then went on to teach approximately 700 people how to use the new equipment. While they used the JI method to teach the actual handling of the machines with patients, the learners also were assured that they would get further training in other aspects of the equipment not covered in the JI training.

Following the training, Theel did a survey to get feedback on a variety of issues around the introduction of the new equipment. The positive comments assured her that they had taken the right course. One person noted, "We really liked the TWI concept; it just takes a little longer, but a much better method of training." Another person said, "The method was new to me, but I think will prove to be a valuable tool not only for this particular training but for others in the future as well." In addition to the hands-on JI training of the jobs, they also provided an online training component consisting of 10 PowerPoint slides to deepen their knowledge of the machinery. The overwhelming consensus at St. Joseph Health System was that this was the best rollout ever of any training on a new process or piece of equipment. The fact that they could start up a new system simultaneously at 14 different hospitals and get it up to speed quickly with safety and quality amazed even those who were initially skeptical about using a new method of instruction. The people who took the JI training, including members of clinical education who did this kind of work on a regular basis, had to change their ways of teaching. This was not easy, especially for those clinical educators who are accustomed to group training and not the one-on-one TWI style. But the results showed that they could do it better.

From Manufacturing to Health Care

As we mentioned before, many hospitals and health care organizations are today studying techniques developed in the manufacturing industry that have had dramatic results in improving quality, increasing output, and reducing costs. Many years ago, it was commonly thought that when buying products you could get high quality, low cost, and faster delivery, but not all three. If you wanted higher quality it would cost you more, or, if you wanted it faster, then you would have to sacrifice the quality. Companies like Toyota proved this adage wrong with a relentless effort to increase skills and improve processes by which they did their production. Over many decades they perfected techniques, such as just-in-time delivery, waste elimination, and process-flow mapping, which allowed companies to deliver high-quality products on time and at a reasonable cost, but these techniques were based on fundamentals Toyota learned as far back as the 1950s. One of these fundamentals was the TWI skills that were introduced into Japan after World War II.

TWI's Job Instruction component was the first module of the program to be developed and was, and still is, the most widely used. It is a method of teaching a person how to do a job correctly, safely, and conscientiously, and, when done properly and consistently, can help create the standardized processes that form the foundation of all the other improvement tools that came after it. For example, if we try to improve an unstable process where each person doing that particular job is doing it a different way, then the improved version of the job will be just one more way of many, many ways in which the job will be done. There will be no way to lock in the improvement and reap the benefits that were promised by the new method. Conversely, because improvement techniques always embody some kind of initial analysis of the current state in order to locate or discover where improvements can and should be made, an unstable process will not generate a reliable version of the current state, which, by definition, is in a state of flux. What we find from our analysis may, in fact, just be a random occurrence and certainly not an accurate picture of what is happening on a regular basis. First, then, we must stabilize the processes through a disciplined and thoughtful approach to how people should do their jobs on a consistent basis.

These fundamentals, which have worked so well in the manufacturing environment, are also what we need so desperately in the day-to-day work in health care. In the case of good instruction, whether we are talking about a manufacturing or a health care environment, when we train a person by having them observe and repeat the method used by an experienced person, we can only expect them to learn as much, or as little, as the person showing them knows about the job. It is not uncommon to hear people say, when they are struggling to do a job correctly, "Well, that's the way *my* instructor showed me how to do it." The implication here is that other people do it differently because they learned it from someone else. Thus, because everyone learned a different way to do it, then we can't hold that one person accountable for the problems they may create.

An example of this is when a person is taught how to properly use clean garments, say, sterile gloves. It is astounding to go into a health-care facility and hear all the different and contrasting ways people have been taught to don gloves. For example, many have been taught that it is acceptable to wear jewelry, such as rings, under their gloves because the gloves are so sturdy that they will not tear even if the ring has a stone or other jagged edges attached. Or was this just the opinion of that particular instructor who didn't like having to take off her rings when wearing gloves? And, because a new person is taught this way, when it is his or her turn (after becoming an experienced practitioner) to teach others, this same information is passed on in a cascading series of incorrect instructions that end up with no one really knowing what the truth is—the correct and "standard" way of wearing the gloves.

As in manufacturing, all of us in health care can and must improve all three of these factors at the same time: quality, cost, and delivery. One fundamental challenge we all face when attacking problems that prevent us from achieving our goals in these areas is the creation of a well-trained workforce that can perform their jobs correctly and consistently. For that, we need a standard method of training that can deliver on this promise each and every time it is used. What is more, we need a way of teaching this training method to our staff who are charged with the responsibility of training the workforce so that they can ensure that the methods being taught are consistent throughout the process.

Good Leadership Skill

How can we get the correct information for doing a job properly to each and every person who is responsible for doing that job? What is more, how can we motivate them to cooperate in following the set standards and continue to do the jobs in the prescribed ways? As we discussed in Chapter 1, we have to learn how to find best practices and put them into general use as quickly as possible. However, in order to achieve that, we must develop skill in communicating these best practices so that learners can understand them quickly and correctly, not only to *be able to do them*, but also to *want to do them* in the prescribed ways. Getting people to change their behavior (i.e., change the way in which they do their work) is nothing less than culture change, culture being defined as "the way most of the people behave most of the time." We know that culture change is by far the most difficult of all challenges to accomplish.

Our good leadership method must build on the confidence and trust people seek from the leaders of their organization in order to be successful in their jobs and careers. This skill must engage people on a personal level and build strong relationships so that people follow our instructions. Instead of just telling people what to do, we must motivate them to want to do their jobs in the prescribed fashion that we can call "best practice." Because people are all individuals with varying backgrounds and experiences, we must make an effort to understand each person as an individual and, while we continue to ensure work performance follows the standard procedures, make the necessary adjustments in how we treat each of these individuals. For that, finding ways to influence each individual learner requires skill in understanding how people behave, learn, and work. This is especially important when teaching experienced practitioners and trying to get them to follow a more standardized way of doing a job than what they are doing now and may have done that way for a long, long time. If we don't have real skill in motivating them, they will simply fall back to their old, more familiar methods.

Once we have built solid relationships of trust, our good training method must then deliver detailed knowledge and perhaps complicated techniques in a simple, easy-to-learn fashion. Without this kind of good skill, training events usually devolve into confusion on the part of the learners where they wind up, for the most part, experimenting on their own until they "figure it out." Of course, techniques are learned through practice and experience, but our method must ensure that learners can identify the difficult parts and quickly learn to do them the correct way. If we want to create standard work that is safe and ensures a quality outcome every time it is done, then we cannot leave it up to the discretion of the worker. Unskilled trainers will oftentimes say something like, "Just keep working on it and after a while you'll find your own way that works for you." Skilled trainers, on the other hand, will demonstrate the correct method and get the learner to perform it exactly that way the first time and every time thereafter because *they want to do it* that way.

Finally, we must have a mechanism to follow up on learners to ensure they have learned the jobs well and are performing them properly and consistently. It does take time to become proficient at a task, but, in the meantime, that does not mean we simply accept mistakes, accidents, and injuries as a "cost of doing business." Even though we may have done a good initial training of the worker, once we put them on their own and they begin doing the job, we have to follow up with them until they master the new technique. The work of training a person is not complete until the learner is fully functional to work on his or her own and trainers must be active during this period. Circumstances change and people come up with questions that need to be answered before they do something wrong. Making sure the new method is the only way the job is performed is the only sure way of achieving standard work.

In Section II, we will explain in detail the instruction method that meets all of these criteria. Then, in Section III, we will introduce a method of dealing with people that helps to solve, and most importantly prevent, problems in a way that builds strong relationships of trust and cooperation. Finally, in Section IV, we will present an improvement method that allows all employees, at all levels, to develop skill in questioning the current ways we do our work in order to find better methods that are safer, easier, and more productive. These methods come from the program called Training Within Industry, which was developed in the US during World War II when workers in factories and shipyards went to war and were replaced by inexperienced people, most of them women entering the manufacturing workforce for the first time. Because the US was to supply all the materiel to win the war, it was critical that these "Rosie the Riveters" were trained and motivated to work in, what was to them, a new and difficult environment. As it turned out, many doctors and nurses also went to the war and these methods were used extensively in health care settings as well. The TWI methods have been used throughout the world ever since, which shows how they are based on fundamental human principles of how people learn and prosper in a work setting. They continue to produce spectacular results today when implemented properly.

Now that we see the need for good leadership and instruction in the health care industry, let's take a look at these sure and reliable methods that get the job done and create stable working environments where quality patient care can be consistently delivered more effectively and efficiently.

JOB INSTRUCTION TRAINING

Chapter 5

Four Steps of Job Instruction

Introduction

We saw in the last chapter the vital need for good job instruction in hospitals and health care facilities. Training employees on job procedures, then, needs to be a regular task due to changing work demands, changes and improvements in procedures and standards, workforce turnover, the increasing need for cross-functional training, and the never-ending progress of medical practice and technology. At the very least, worker performance, regardless of whether people are new or experienced in their tasks, is not always where it needs to be. Moreover, we saw in Section I how proper training in standard methods, and ensuring that these standards are maintained on a consistent basis, created a baseline of standard work that is vital for continuous improvement to succeed. If health care facilities want to improve their performance and ensure the best possible patient care, they must start with a well-trained workforce.

Most organizations understand the need for good training and they provide a specified amount of time for this training, usually known as orientation. The orientation of a new worker in health care is often a shared responsibility involving the supervisor, a preceptor, and staff from a centralized education department. The supervisor has the final responsibility of evaluating the worker's performance and competency. The preceptor is a skilled and experienced co-worker who instructs from the work unit and shares patient care assignments with the new worker, gradually increasing the independence and assignment workload of the learner. Side by side, the

DOI: 10.4324/9781003035305-5

preceptor validates the new worker's ability to perform the tasks associated with the assigned job. The third party contributing to orientation is the centralized education team, often called the Department of Clinical Education, or something similar. This team provides training for jobs that are shared among work units regardless of the specialty, for example, medication administration. In this case, all nurses will need to know how to operate the equipment associated with this job: medication dispensing machines, computerized charting, and the safety procedures incorporated into the process. Medications specific to certain patient populations (such as sedating drugs used to treat intubated patients) would be covered by the unit-based preceptor. The clinical education team is most likely to train in a classroom or in a skills lab away from the clinical work unit where the worker is assigned.

So the issue is not usually in providing orientation or training. What is being questioned here is the method of instructing. Is it viable, effective, and complete? Let's look at two common, but insufficient, methods of instruction: Showing Alone and Telling Alone.

Showing Alone

It is a very common practice in health care facilities to instruct employees by *showing* them how to do a job. Showing a person how to do a job is a critical element of good instruction, but when used *alone*, can lead to very serious problems. Here's a true story of how one preceptor failed to train a person properly when she simply showed the person how to do it:

> The preceptor was teaching a new nurse how to attach an arterial line to connector tubing for the purpose of flushing the line. The job consisted of connecting the two tubes, one from the connector tubing and the other from the arterial line already attached to the patient's arm. The job had to been done fairly quickly and efficiently or else blood would leak out or air and contaminants could enter the line, so the supervisor showed the new nurse how to do it several times. What the new nurse failed to notice, however, was how tightly the connection had to be twisted on. When he was allowed to do it himself, the new nurse did not twist the connection on tightly enough into the locking position. The two tubes quickly snapped apart and blood from the patient's arm began draining the line, causing the patient to panic and the new nurse to scramble to correct the situation.

The failure to do the job correctly was not the new nurse's fault. No matter how simple it may seem, a job cannot be mastered by observation alone. Seeing a job does not always translate into being able to do it. Many motions are hard to copy, and most learners usually miss the tricky points. Even if they can do the job, it is usually no more than a copy of the motions and doesn't mean they understand the job. Yet, surprisingly, countless people today are simply being shown how to do their jobs with little more explanation than: "Do it like this." This type of poor instruction leads to many of the problems we face in health care facilities.

Telling Alone

Another very common practice when giving instruction is *telling* a person how to do the job. As with showing, telling someone what to do is a critical element of good instruction but, when used *alone*, can result in serious problems. To demonstrate how this style of training can result in failure, imagine you are a new worker in a health care facility and someone simply tells you the correct way of washing your hands, without showing you how and with no gestures or motions. The dialogue might go something like this:

Turn on the faucet and wet your hands with water so that they are completely wet. Get soap from the dispenser making sure that you have enough to cover all of the surfaces including the backs of your hands and the fingers. Rub the palms of your two hands together back and forth and in a circular motion. Then rub the palm of one hand on the back of the other hand backward and forward and in a circular motion. Repeat for the other hand. Interlace the fingers of both hands, palm to palm, and move your palms back and forth so that the insides of the fingers rub against each other. Curl the fingers of your right hand into a fist and rub the backs of those fingers backward and forward on the palm of your left hand. Repeat with the fingers of your left hand in the right palm. Take the tips of the fingers of your right hand and rotationally rub them backward and forward on the palm of your left hand. Repeat with the fingers of your left hand in the right palm. Take the thumb of your left hand and grasp it with the palm and fingers of your right hand rotationally rubbing the thumb in the palm of the hand. Repeat with the right thumb in the palm of your left hand. Rinse your hands thoroughly until all the soap is removed, being careful not to touch the faucet or the sink. Leave the water running. Dry hands thoroughly with a single-use towel and use the towel to turn off the faucet.

Would you be able to perform the task completely and exactly as specified just hearing this explanation? Things seem complicated when you are listening to words and most people don't "get it" simply by being told how to do something. Many movements, however simple, are difficult to describe in words and few of us can use the exact words or the right number of words to explain a procedure correctly and completely. When a person hears a long explanation, their minds do not piece it together in the same logical order in which it was described. The brain can only absorb so much information at one time, so details get mixed up and the person focuses on certain points while neglecting others.

Over time, with *enough* telling and *enough* showing, a capable person will be able to do the job. Through the process of trial and error, they may even learn all the nuances or tricks to doing the job. But this approach is not effective or efficient and contributes to mistakes, injuries, and delays while the job is being mastered. What is more, as each person "learns" the job at his or her own pace, the prescribed method will be "learned" differently by each person doing it. Depending on what troubles or difficulties they encounter, they will devise different means of accomplishing the task. The result is that we do not end up with standard performance that each person doing the job performs consistently each time they do it.

A Sure and Effective Method of Instruction

If we are to truly attain a standard method of doing our jobs, a better way of instruction is required. The Job Instruction (JI) four-step method fits this bill and, when used properly, can assure a successful training experience each time it is applied. This method works quickly and efficiently while ensuring that the learner remembers how to do a job *correctly, safely,* and *conscientiously.* The method is based on fundamental principles of human learning that are timeless and always true, a fact confirmed by supervisors who were formerly K-12 teachers and have noted that the JI method incorporates the fundamentals they were taught in their teacher education. Professional trainers as well have pointed out how the JI method covers all three styles of adult learning: auditory, visual, and kinesthetic.

Let's look at the JI method first by reviewing the dialogue an instructor has with a person learning a job. We'll assume this is a new employee without much experience working in a health care facility. One of the most important things he will need to do throughout each day of his work is to wash his hands properly so that he can protect both himself and patients by not contaminating them with harmful viruses or bacteria they might pick up from other sick patients with whom they come into contact. Of course, the employee being trained will both hear and see the instructor's words and actions, so refer to the diagrams and notes that accompany the dialogue and try to imagine the activity taking place.

Pay attention to both what the instructor says and does as well as the order in which these things are performed. After reviewing the dialogue, we will look in detail at each item the instructor did in order to teach the job of hand hygiene using the Job Instruction four-step method.

Teaching Hand Hygiene

Instructor: Hello, Bill. How are you?

Learner: Fine, thank you.

Instructor: My name is Sarah Jones and I'm the supervisor on this floor of the hospital. It's nice to meet you. This is your first week in orientation, isn't it?

Learner: Yes, as a matter of fact, this is my second day.

Instructor: Well, are you getting along OK?

Learner: I'm really glad to be here although there is a lot to know.

Instructor: It takes some time to get used to a new place. But, if you need anything at all, please let me know. Today I'd like to teach you how to wash your hands properly. Now, I'm sure you've washed your hands before.

Learner: Of course.

Instructor: But here in the hospital it's more than just washing your hands. You have to clean them thoroughly to be sure all the germs are killed. Have you ever had a shot and the nurse scrubbed your arm with alcohol where she was going to stick you? Why did she do that?

Learner: Well, if there are any germs on your skin, they'll get into your body.

Instructor: Right. Washing your hands properly is done for the same reason. Sick people coming to the hospital bring a lot of germs with them and they get on your hands while you're working. If you don't wash your hands thoroughly you could transfer those germs to yourself or to another patient and that patient could get sick with a disease they didn't even have before they came here. In fact, proper handwashing is the single most important thing you can do to keep patients and yourself safe.

Learner: I see.

Instructor: Okay, Bill, why don't you come around and stand behind me, to my left, and watch what I'm doing over my left shoulder. Can you see everything all right?

Learner: Yes.

Instructor: First, I'm going to do it while explaining the Important Steps of the job. Are you ready?

Learner: Yes.

Instructor: *(Instructor **performs the job** as she explains and points out the Important Steps: Figure 5.1.)*

- This job has six Important Steps
- The first Important Step is **wet hands**.
- The second Important Step is **apply soap**.
- The third Important Step is **rub hands**.
- The fourth Important Step is **rub fingers**.
- The fifth, and final, Important Step is **rinse and dry**.

Instructor: Did you get that all right?

Learner: Yes.

Instructor: Let me do it for you again. This time, I'll tell you the Key Points for each step. *(Instructor **performs the job again** as she explains and points out the Key Points.)*

- The first Important Step, **wet hands**, has one Key Point. That Key Point is **thoroughly without soap**.
- The second Important Step, **apply soap**, also has one Key Point. That Key Point is **enough to cover all surfaces**.
- The third Important Step, **rub hands**, has two Key Points. The first Key Point is **palm to palm**. The second Key Point is **palm to backs**.
- The fourth Important Step, **rub fingers**, has four Key Points. The first Key Point is **interlocking**. The second Key Point is **backs of fingers to palm** (Figure 5.2). The third Key Point is **tips to palm** (Figure 5.3). And, the fourth Key Point is **thumbs** (Figure 5.4).
- The fifth Important Step, **rinse and dry**, has just one Key Point. The Key Point is **use towel to turn water off**.

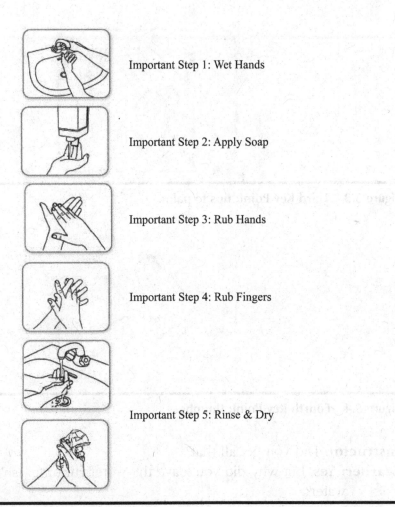

Important Step 1: Wet Hands

Important Step 2: Apply Soap

Important Step 3: Rub Hands

Important Step 4: Rub Fingers

Important Step 5: Rinse & Dry

Figure 5.1   Important Steps in hand hygiene.

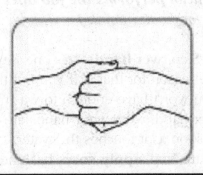

Figure 5.2   Second Key Point: backs of fingers to palm.

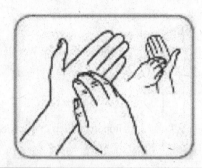

Figure 5.3   Third Key Point: tips to palm.

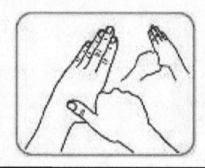

Figure 5.4   Fourth Key Point: thumbs.

Instructor*:* Did you get all that?

Learner: Yes, but why did you leave the water running. Isn't that wasting water?

Instructor: Good question. Let me do the job one more time telling you the reasons for all of the Key Points. Then that will answer your question. *(Instructor **performs the job once again** while explaining the reasons for the Key Points.)*

■ The first Important Step, **wet hands**, has one Key Point, **thoroughly without soap**. The reason for that is if you put the soap on first, it rinses away and you won't have enough to wash your hands completely. On the other hand, when your hands are already wet, the soap begins to lather as soon as it touches the water.

■ The second Important Step, **apply soap**, has one Key Point, **enough to cover all surfaces**. If you don't have enough soap to cover all the surfaces, you won't kill all the germs.

■ The third Important Step, **rub hands**, has two Key Points. The first Key Point is **palm to palm** and the reason is because it cleans the entire surface. The second Key Point is **palms to backs**. Here again, the reason is to clean the entire surface.

■ The fourth Important Step, **rub fingers**, has four Key Points. The first Key Point is **interlocking** and the reason is the sides of the fingers can be cleaned at one time. The second Key Point is **backs of fingers to palm** because it will ensure you clean the corners and creases of your cuticles and knuckles, areas where germs can hide. The third Key Point is **tips to palm** and we do this to be sure to clean the area underneath the fingernails. The fourth Key Point is **thumbs**. If we forget to wash our thumbs, the most active part of our hand, we certainly cannot say that our hands are completely clean.

■ The fifth Important Step, **rinse and dry**, has one Key Point, **use towel to turn water off**. We do this because we do not want to recontaminate our clean hands by touching the dirty faucet. We may use a little more water, but we keep our hands clean.

Instructor: Do you have any questions?

Learner: No. I think I get it.

Instructor: All right, then. Now let's have you try doing the job. Come around to the sink and just do it once for me without saying anything. *(Instructor has the learner come to her place and she goes and stands where he had been, behind him and to the left. Learner **does the job** and the instructor immediately jumps in and corrects any errors that the learner may make.)* That's very good. You're a quick learner. Do the job again for me, please. But this time, tell me each of the Important Steps of the job as you do them. How many Important Steps were there?

Learner: I think it was five; yes, five Important Steps.

Instructor: That's right. Tell me what the five Important Steps are as you do the job.

Learner: *(Learner **does the job again** while saying the Important Steps. Instructor helps him to remember any Important Steps he can't remember.)* The first Important Step is "wet hands." The second Important Step is "apply soap." The third Important Step is "rub hands." The fourth Important Step is "rub fingers." The fifth Important Step is "rinse and dry."

Instructor: Excellent! That's very good. Let me have you do the job again, Bill. This time tell me both the Important Steps and the Key Points for each of those steps.

Learner: *(Learner **does the job again** while saying the Key Points for each Important Step. Instructor helps him to remember any Key Points he can't remember.)* The first step, "wet hands," has a Key Point: "thoroughly without soap." Is that right?

Instructor: Yes, that's it.

Learner: Okay. The second Important Step is "apply soap." The Key Point here is "enough to cover all surfaces." That's the only Key Point for Step 2.

Instructor: That's right.

Learner: The third Important Step has two Key Points. The first Key Point is …

Instructor: What is the step again?

Learner: The step is to "rub hands."

Instructor: Right. And the two Key Points are?

Learner: The first Key Point is "palm to palm." The second Key Point is … I can't remember.

Instructor: What part of your hands do you need to rub besides the palms?

Learner: Oh, that's right, "palms to backs."

Instructor: That's right.

Learner: The fourth Important Step is to "rub fingers." There are four Key Points here. The first Key Point is "interlocking." The second Key Point is "backs of fingers to palm." The third Key Point is "tips to palm." And, the fourth Key Point is "thumbs."

Instructor: Very good!

Learner: The fifth Important Step is "rinse and dry" and it has one Key Point, "use towel to turn water off."

Instructor: You're really getting it. It sounds like you have a good understanding of the job. But, just to be sure, let me ask you to do it again and, this time, tell me the reasons for each of those Key Points.

Learner: All right. *(Learner **does the job again** while saying the reasons for each of the Key Points. Instructor helps him to remember any reasons he can't remember.)* The first Important Step, "wet hands," has a Key Point: "thoroughly without soap." And the reason is because if you put the soap on first, it rinses away when you splash it with water. *(Learner continues giving the reasons for all the Key Points until the job is completely finished.)*

Instructor: Well, it looks like you're ready to do it on your own. Please use this method every time you have to wash your hands. If you have any questions, just ask me. I'm usually on the floor, but if you don't see me, you can ask Jane, your preceptor. I've already told her that we would be covering this topic today and she is ready to help at any time. I'll come back and check on you a few times throughout the rest of the day, just to make sure you're getting on alright with the method. By that time you should be getting the hang of it and, after that, I'll just check on you once or twice for the rest of the week. But, never be afraid to ask a question if there is anything at all that is bothering you. I really believe that the best employees are the ones who ask lots of questions. If things are going well by the end of the week, I'll leave you on your own to make sure you are washing your hands properly at all times. Does that sound good?

Learner: Great. I think I should be fine.

Instructor: All right. Then I'll let you get back to work and I will be checking on you shortly.

This dialogue embodies the entire JI four-step method that is defined as *the way to get a person to quickly remember to do a job correctly, safely, and conscientiously.* The method is simple and straightforward, but it does follow some definite rules. These rules are captured on a pocket-sized card that can be carried by supervisors (instructors) at all times so that they can have the method at their fingertips whenever they need to train a job. Figure 5.5 shows the back side of the pocket card and the four steps of instruction (we will look at the front side of the card in the next two chapters).

Let's review each step along with all of the subheads for each step in order to understand how we can use the JI method in order to ensure correct instruction each time we teach a job. As we go through the details, refer back to the dialogue to see what the instructor said and did for each item. This dialogue will help you understand how to skillfully carry out all the facets of the method.

Step 1: Prepare the Worker

In the initial step, the instructor must do several things to put learners into the correct frame of mind. These may appear simplistic at first glance. But, because every person is unique, instructors must take into account attitude and demeanor at the time of training to ensure that the trainee is receptive to learning the job. Otherwise, you will have wasted your time or, even worse, created conditions that lead to problems.

4 STEPS FOR JOB INSTRUCTION

Step 1 – PREPARE THE WORKER
- Put the person at ease
- State the job
- Find out what the person already knows
- Get the person interested in learning the job
- Place the person in the correct position

Step 2 – PRESENT THE OPERATION
- Tell, show and illustrate one **Important Step** at a time
- Do it again stressing **Key Points**
- Do it again stating **reasons for Key Points**

Instruct clearly, completely and patiently, but don't give them more information than they can master at one time.

Step 3 – TRY-OUT PERFORMANCE
- Have the person do the job—correct errors
- Have the person explain each **Important Step** to you as they do the job again
- Have the person explain each **Key Point** to you as they do the job again
- Have the person explain **reasons for Key Points** to you as they do the job again

Make sure the person understands.
*Continue until **you** know **they** know.*

Step 4 – FOLLOW UP
- Put the person on their own
- Designate who the person goes to for help
- Check on the person frequently
- Encourage questions
- Taper off extra coaching and close follow-up

IF THE WORKER HASN'T LEARNED, THE INSTRUCTOR HASN'T TAUGHT

Figure 5.5   Job Instruction pocket card (back side).

Detail 1: Put the Person at Ease

People are, by nature, nervous and uncertain when they learn a new job. They may be afraid that they are not capable of doing the job or will have difficulty getting accustomed to the new work. They may have had a bad training experience in the past. Anxiety and uncertainty create "noise" in the minds of learners. They are a barrier to communication and cause learners to miss important points.

In the hand hygiene example, the instructor tried to put the new person at ease by asking him how long he had been with the hospital and by assuring him that she was there to help out if needed while he got accustomed to his new surroundings. You could begin as well by talking about local events or even the weather. Your task is to get a trainee to relax and focused on learning the job. While you don't want the training session to devolve into idle chatter, a little time spent putting them at ease helps to ensure training success.

Detail 2: State the Job

Amazingly, many trainers rush their employees into a training situation without informing them exactly what they are asking them to learn. Make sure learners fully understand, up front, the job they are being asked to do. Otherwise, they will be confused over where your instruction is going and will miss important points. It would be like trying to make a jigsaw puzzle without the picture on the box; you cannot connect the pieces if you don't know what it's supposed to look like.

For example, tell the learner the name of the job he or she is going to be learning and then show a completed sample, if appropriate, or explain the purpose of the work. This lets the learner see or know what the finished work should look like. Because you have removed the mystery of the work and the fear of the unknown, you have already made the learner less anxious.

Detail 3: Find Out What the Person Already Knows

The instructor should find out as soon as possible whether the learner has ever done the job, or something similar, or has a hobby requiring the same types of skills. A quick review of the process should provide this information. If the learner has never done this particular job before, finding out whether he or she has similar or related knowledge and skills can help the instructor evaluate and adjust the amount of instruction needed to teach the job properly. Accelerate or slow down instruction depending on the learner's background and experience.

By comparing the job at hand with something the learner already knows, even if only marginally related, you build confidence and reduce anxiety. In learning correct handwashing, for example, the instructor related it to swabbing an area of skin with alcohol before giving an injection, a process with which most people are familiar.

Detail 4: Get the Person Interested in Learning the Job

Job Instruction teaches people to learn to do their work *conscientiously.* That means that they have to take an interest in what they are doing and pay attention to details. The most effective way of getting people interested in learning a job is to make them realize the importance of doing the job right. For that, they need to know how their effort, no matter how small, fits into the bigger picture—the finished procedure or service. No one is ever enthusiastic about doing a mindless, meaningless task.

In the demonstration of proper hand hygiene, the instructor pointed out that, if done incorrectly, the person could pass on an illness to a person who did not have that illness when they initially came into the hospital. This explanation was not meant to scare the learner, but to show just how important the job is to their overall work. Moreover, the instructor pointed out how important it was to the learner himself in protecting against infection. Knowing the importance of the job honors the person doing it and motivates that person to learn to do it well.

Detail 5: Place the Person in the Correct Position

The final part of preparing learners is to make sure you place them in a position where they can best see and hear the instruction. This may seem obvious, but sometimes the obvious is the very thing instructors neglect to do. For instance, many an untrained instructor unwittingly trains an employee how to do a job backward—because the employee is facing the instructor.

The proper place for the learner to stand to watch the job demonstration is behind the instructor, looking over his or her left shoulder, the view the learner will have when performing the job. Because most people are right-handed, this gives them the clearest view of what the right hand is doing. If you are a lefthanded instructor, you may want to have the learner stand behind you looking over your right shoulder. However, be aware that the learner will do the job exactly as shown. Your procedure may be awkward for righthanded learners.

The best place to teach a job is at the actual spot where the work will be performed on a regular basis. If there is anything dangerous at the worksite, this is the time to be sure the learner is in a safe position. Be aware that it may be difficult for the learner to see or hear what you are doing or saying because of noise or inadequate space. Always ask if you can be heard and seen clearly. If not, you may decide to go to a training room or other suitable area, taking all the necessary tools and materials to teach the job with you.

Step 2: Present the Operation

In Step 2, Present the Operation, the instructor moves from the preparation phase to an actual presentation of the job. Here, the instructor gives a careful and detailed demonstration of the job to the learner. Again, it is imperative that you tell the learner what it is you are demonstrating.

In the hand hygiene example, the job was broken down into Important Steps and Key Points to facilitate the instruction. Preparing a job breakdown is the way to make sure that the learner understands all of the vital information in the right order and to avoid confusing the learner with information overload. Learning how to make job breakdowns using Important Steps and Key Points is a vital skill for supervisors proficient in JI. Chapter 6 provides a detailed discussion of the Job Instruction Breakdown Sheet, but for now, it is enough to know that an Important Step is a logical segment of the operation when something happens to *advance the work*. Key Points represent whatever is "key" to doing a step properly, such as things that *make or break* the job, anything that would *injure the worker* (i.e., safety), or things that make the work *easier to do*.

Detail 1: Tell, Show, and Illustrate One Important Step at a Time

Begin by *showing* the job one Important Step at a time, *telling* the learner what each step is as you do it. You can use sketches, diagrams, or pictures of the job or even lists to *illustrate* any fine points or details that may be difficult to conceptualize or remember. It is a good idea to start out by telling the learner how many steps there are in the entire job: "This job has *five* Important Steps; the first Important Step is …." By doing this, you give the worker a clear idea of what to expect, and you focus attention on the "five" important things to be learned.

Because Important Steps are the logical segments of the operation, do not make these steps hairsplitting, micromotion details of the job. They should be simple, common sense reminders of what is really important to "put across" the job to the learner. When demonstrating the job, be sure to:

- Speak clearly and deliberately.
- Make eye contact with the learners to ensure they are following you.
- As you move along, ask learners if they understand what you are demonstrating.

In Chapter 6, you will learn how to make a Job Instruction Breakdown Sheet, which lists Important Steps and Key Points, to ensure you explain the Important Steps in the right order without missing anything. This breakdown sheet is only for the instructor. Never show the breakdown sheet to learners because they must focus their full and undivided attention on the job you are teaching them to do.

Detail 2: Do It Again Stressing Key Points

Most people do not learn to do a job by seeing it demonstrated just once. With a second demonstration, people know what to expect the next time around, and this helps them understand what they saw the first time. Once people have an overall picture of what is going on from start to finish, they can begin to absorb the intricacies of the job. Here, you introduce them to the Key Points of the job, any relevant special trick or a knack that is not readily apparent, but which constitutes the real skill of the job learned over time.

Key Points are the skills and insights that make people "experienced." JI speeds up this maturing process and transfers this experience quickly and smoothly so that learners do not spend weeks, months, or even years trying to "figure things out."

As with the Important Steps, be sure to articulate each Key Point clearly as you demonstrate the job. The learner needs to see and hear your demonstration at the same time so synchronize what you are saying and doing to connect the words with the actions. Use your breakdown sheet to make sure you present all Key Points in their correct sequence.

Detail 3: Do It Again Stating Reasons for Key Points

Do the job one more time adding in the reasons for each of the Key Points. By knowing the reasons why each Key Point is important, learners will be able to remember to follow them each time they do the job. As thinking human beings, people need a reason to do what they do; if something is meaningless (i.e., no reason for it), they will not bother doing it or they may find a different way to do it. What is more, when they understand why they must do the job a certain way they will be able to recognize when conditions change or something is going wrong and will be able to take action to correct the problem.

Caution Point: Instruct Clearly, Completely, and Patiently, but Don't Give Them More Information than They Can Master at One Time

This line on the card is in *italics* to alert the instructor that this is a caution point that applies to all of the other items in this step. This method of instruction may seem cumbersome and repetitive, but what feels redundant to you is, for the learner, a natural part of the learning process. Each time you demonstrate the job, you give a little more information. In doing this, you avoid confusion and reinforce information presented before while adding depth of detail to the learner's understanding. In addition, you create a logical structure for the learner by drawing connections between each Key Point and its corresponding Important Step.

Learning is like eating—you can only chew and swallow small amounts at one time. In the same way, there is only so much information the brain can absorb and process at any one time. By clearly and patiently repeating the job several times, you have the opportunity to give an appropriate amount of information starting with the overall guideline and then drilling down into greater detail each time you go through the presentation. The more times the learner sees the demonstration, the more familiar he or she will become with the process. Gradually, the learner will become more capable of grasping and connecting information that is needed for doing a job. And, by covering all the Important Steps, Key Points, and reasons for the Key Points, you can be sure that your instruction is complete.

Step 3: Tryout Performance

In most cases, by the time you are satisfied that you have completed Step 2 successfully, the learner is already anxious to try doing the job. Do not feel that you have to rush into Step 3 until you are sure the learner has fully understood the job completely. Recognize, however, that if a learner is anxious to try the job out, it is likely that your efforts to motivate have succeeded.

Never assume the learner can do the job without verification. In health care, we like to call this the "teach back." In Step 3 you will confirm that the learner is able to do the job correctly and understands what he or she is doing.

Detail 1: Have the Person Do the Job, Correct Errors

First, have the learner perform the job silently, without having to say anything. This is the time for the learner to show you what he or she can do. At this point in the training, the learner merely needs to do the job and not worry about explaining how or why. (Exception: If the job entails a thinking process like judgment calls or inspections, the learner can confirm the call or state out loud what they are thinking.) When learners have to explain up front what they're doing, then this explanation becomes more important than doing the job itself and they will put more attention on the words than on the motions. This slows down the learning process.

Observe the work carefully and stop the learner immediately if he or she is doing anything incorrectly. Do not let the learner proceed because it is extremely difficult to unlearn something done incorrectly even once. This is the opposite of what is typically done when we let people "learn from their mistakes." The JI method is to do the job correctly the first time and every time thereafter. If a learner is unable to do any part of the job, show and tell again, as you did in Step 2, the correct way of doing that part or step. Then have the learner continue demonstrating the job using the correct procedure. In the worst case, you may have to go back and repeat Step 2 at a slower pace.

Many trainers get confused on this detail because they think they should not let the learner do the job silently, which is like "showing alone." While the *instructor* should never "show alone," it is essential for the *learner* to demonstrate his or her ability to do the job without having to speak or give an explanation. Good training always starts at the simplest level and moves toward complexity. Having the learner perform the job silently the first time is the simplest level. It allows the learner to focus on just doing the job.

On the other hand, you may occasionally get a person who has a habit of "thinking out loud" or "mumbling to themselves" when they do something new. If this is the most natural and relaxed mode of performance for them, then let them speak. If you didn't, it would make them more nervous and prone to make a mistake. However, this does not take away from the need to have them continue with Step 2 and explain the job completely following the breakdown. Their talk here is more a part of their physical activity and doesn't necessarily mean they understand what they are doing.

Detail 2: Have the Person Explain Each Important Step to You as They Do the Job Again

Now that you know the learner can do the job physically, you want to make sure that he or she understands the job mentally and is not just imitating the motions. Ask the learner to do the job again and tell you all the Important Steps. The learner does not necessarily need to repeat the Important Steps verbatim but listen carefully for accurate content. If the learner is having trouble remembering the steps, provide one or two keywords as a hint. This will usually stimulate a recall of the whole step. Use the same breakdown sheet used in Step 2 (in this case as a check sheet) to make sure the learner has stated all Important Steps in the correct order. Learning and maintaining the sequence of steps to complete the job *is* the standard for the work that ensures the job is done correctly each time it is performed.

If the learner cannot state any of the steps, stop the job and have the learner begin again. Interrupt when the learner gets to the end of an Important Step. Ask the learner to describe what he or she just did and sum up the learner's explanation by saying the Important Step. Continue this process with the next Important Step.

When the learner has completed doing the entire job, take a moment to examine the completed work carefully. Even if you are sure the job was done correctly, this careful review of the finished process shows the learner how much you care about the quality of the work. An encouraging "Well done!" after the inspection inspires confidence.

Detail 3: Have the Person Explain Each Key Point to You as They Do the Job Again

Have the learner do the job again, this time telling you the Key Points for each Important Step. This will confirm the learner understands the vital elements to do the job well. Use the breakdown sheet to make sure *all* Key Points were stated with the right step and in the correct order.

Because the job is still new, some learners may confuse Important Steps and Key Points. This is normal. Your job is to help the learner distinguish Important Steps from Key Points and one Important Step from another while mastering the Key Points for each of those steps. This may take some time and work, so have patience. This is the part of the process where they are really "learning" the job. There are always many details to any job that must be learned, probably too many for any person to learn at one time. However, if the learner can remember the Key Points "step by step" it will be easier and faster for them to remember them all. In other words, they are not having to remember nine total Key Points in the hand hygiene task but one Key Point for the first Important Step, one Key Point for the second Important Step, two Key Points for the third Important Step, four Key Points for the fourth Important Step, and one Key Point for the fifth Important Step. This breakdown, like peeling the layers of an onion one by one, makes learning and remembering all the details quick and easy.

Your breakdown sheet will show you how to do this. Asking questions reinforces the process: "What was the first Important Step again?" "How many Key Points were there in the first Important Step?" "So what is the first Key Point in this step?" And so on. Above all, make sure it is the *learner*, not you, who is restating the Important Steps and Key Points. Just like when helping young children with their homework, giving them the answers is not helping them learn. Giving them hints is better: "So how do you make sure there are no germs under your fingernails?" When they search and find the Key Points on their own, they commit them to memory.

Detail 4: Have the Person Explain Reasons for Key Points to You as They Do the Job Again

Have the learner do the job one more time, telling you the reasons for each of the Key Points. If the learner can explain why the job has to be done this set way, you will know that they have a true understanding of the job. By making sure they know the reasons for each Key Point, you can be better assured that they will remember to do the job the proper way each and every time.

Because the learner performs the job four times in this step, the instructor has the opportunity to have them repeat the Important Steps and Key Points several times. Learners usually struggle to remember these items the first time but, interestingly enough, begin to nail them down by the fourth repetition. This is why we should never "short cut" this step. It is tempting to let them go after one or two trials when they seem to be able to do the job. But it is not until they perform and explain the job four or more times that they truly make it their own and remember the procedure. In health care, we like to call this, "Hard wiring the procedure."

Caution Point: Make Sure the Person Understands

This caution point is *italicized* on the JI pocket card and applies to all of the other items in this step. In each part of the Tryout Performance step, the instructor's job is to make sure the learner physically and mentally understands the job while demonstrating it. The instructor's role is to be attentive to everything the learner says and does, jumping in whenever necessary. Never assume the person understands the job or you may run into problems down the road. If the learner is having trouble repeating the Important

Steps, Key Points, and reasons for Key Points, continue to review them until the problem is resolved.

Caution Point: Continue Until You Know They Know

This caution point is also *italicized* on the JI pocket card. There is no set number of times the learner should repeat the job while the instructor observes and gives instruction. *The correct number of times is the number of times it takes for the learner to fully learn and be able to perform the job.* Although the TWI card shows that you should repeat the Tryout Performance four times, you should continue this process until you are satisfied that all Important Steps and Key Points have been mastered. Do not leave the scene until *you* are confident that the *learner* knows how to do the job. Be patient. Reassure the learner that you are not going to bail out until the job is completely mastered. No matter how busy you are, you will avoid or minimize future problems if you take the time to instruct correctly and completely.

Many trainers feel self-conscious about this routine thinking they are "dumbing down" the learners or sounding "like a parrot." But while the trainer feels uncomfortable going through many repetitions of the job, have confidence that the learner is just fine. Learners routinely tell us after learning a job with this method of instruction that they "appreciate how patient" the instructor was because "they didn't leave until I got it." This is different from their previous learning experiences where the instructor may have shown it to them once and left them on their own to struggle trying to do the work.

Step 4: Follow-Up

The final step of the JI four-step method is follow-up. No matter how diligently you have performed the initial three steps—Prepare the Worker, Present the Operation, and Tryout Performance—you must never assume that you have achieved perfect instruction or covered every detail. And just because the learner has demonstrated the ability to do the job with full understanding does not mean they are experienced in doing the job—they are just getting started. Moreover, remember that people and processes can and do change. It is impossible to predict what effect changes will have on the work being done, which is why you must follow up on the instruction to make sure you are not blindsided by the unexpected.

Detail 1: Put the Person on Their Own

From the moment the instructor transfers the job, it is the worker's responsibility to do the job correctly each time, showing that he or she knows the job is important. The instructor needs to make it clear to learners that they have taken on this responsibility.

At this point, the instructor should advise the learner how much work is expected over a given time period (e.g., the next hour or the next full day) or how often the work is to be performed if it is not an ongoing task. Knowing how much work must be finished and by when will give the learner a sense of pacing, which is always a big concern when doing something for the first time. Without this knowledge, some learners might feel compelled to rush needlessly to prove themselves. This can lead to mistakes or accidents.

Detail 2: Designate Who the Person Goes to for Help

In the early stages of doing a new job, a learner will have questions or need help. Unless otherwise instructed, most learners have a tendency to ask people nearby. This can be disruptive and counterproductive, especially when the people nearby, regardless of their willingness to help, are not familiar with the job in question or do not know how to give correct instruction. The most appropriate person to get help from is you, the person who taught the job. Make this clear to the learner immediately. Obviously, you will not always be available, so you must designate someone else who can fill in (e.g., another leader in the area or an experienced worker). Be sure to let these individuals know that you have appointed them to help and that they have the appropriate knowledge to provide instruction.

Detail 3: Check on the Person Frequently

Most errors occur soon after the learner starts doing a job alone for the first time. During this critical period, check back frequently, even every few minutes if necessary. How often you check back depends on the nature of the job. In situations where accidents or serious failures can occur, checking frequently may even mean staying at the site and keeping an eye on the worker's performance for a period of time. In our example of hand hygiene, a worker has multiple opportunities to perform this job within an hour or two, so a good amount of time between putting them on their own and the first follow-up might be after one hour has gone by. Remember that it takes time to become experienced. Be available to help and give additional instruction when needed. As the worker becomes familiar with the job, check less frequently.

Detail 4: Encourage Questions

Most employees are hesitant to ask questions. Every worker wishes to be competent and to be seen as capable. Some fear that questions will show a lack of ability or experience and might jeopardize wages or promotions. They may even fear being fired. Even experienced workers hesitate to ask questions because they unrealistically, and mistakenly, believe they are supposed to know everything about the job. As a supervisor, you want all workers to be asking questions, especially if answers to those questions can help prevent problems. Encourage *all* questions and answer them.

The key to encouraging questions is to create a stable, secure, and open work environment where people are not afraid to ask questions. You must work hard at this by letting your people know that it is okay to ask questions and by taking the time to listen and respond. Furthermore, by creating strong and steady relations with your people you will create a mutual trust that will encourage people to ask any question without hesitation or fear of consequences. We will cover this aspect of building strong job relations in much more detail in the next section.

Detail 5: Taper Off Extra Coaching and Close Follow-Up

As the learner becomes more experienced, gradually taper off extra attention and bring the follow-up phase to a close. If you have used the JI method well, you can rest assured that the work will be carried out properly and with few problems.

If the Worker Hasn't Learned, the Instructor Hasn't Taught

The JI four-step method, when used properly, is a sure and reliable way of getting people to learn jobs. The key tenet to the JI method is: *If the worker hasn't learned, the instructor hasn't taught.* In other words, the supervisor has the responsibility of ensuring that employees perform their jobs well.

When things go wrong in a working environment, it is very easy and very common for supervisors to blame problems on the low skills or lack of proper attention on the part of the people who perform the work. The supervisor may even replace a person who cannot perform up to speed (and at times, this may indeed be the needed action). The truth of the matter is that most employees are actually capable of doing much more than what they are being asked to do. Moreover, most people go to work each day with the intention of doing a good job and are proud of the work they do. With proper training, most people not only do the jobs that are required of them, they also try to show their supervisors the full breadth of their ability and ambition.

Many supervisors feel it is an unfair burden for them to be held totally responsible for an employee's performance. After all, they protest, no matter how hard you try, some people simply refuse to listen or to follow good instructions. This is not an instruction problem, it is a leadership problem. Poor performers generally do not have a good relationship with their supervisor and resist the supervisor's guidance. In addition to good instruction skill, then, supervisors need leadership skill that helps them build and maintain strong relationships with the people they supervise and encourages their cooperation. This skill in leadership is the topic of Section III of this book.

In an environment that provides good leadership, employees depend on their supervisors to train them properly so they can succeed at their jobs. If supervisors are trained to instruct their employees, old and new, properly and continually, a good percentage of the problems we face on a daily basis in health care can be alleviated or eliminated, and changes can be addressed appropriately. The ability to train is, therefore, one of the most important qualities a supervisor must possess. Using the method described in this chapter will hone this training ability.

Chapter 6

Breaking Down a Job for Training

Introduction

In Chapter 5, we saw how an instructor taught a new employee at a hospital to properly wash his hands. Because the instruction method followed a specific pattern, you might think that this was enough to get the person to learn the job quickly and correctly. However, if not properly prepared before the training session begins, trainers may unwittingly give too much information and confuse the learner or fail to present the job as clearly as they should. They might also jump too soon from one point to another or have to backtrack because they missed a point earlier. In Step 2 of the method, Present the Operation, they might introduce new ideas in the wrong place or miss critical points because they have not clearly organized information about the job. In Step 3, the Tryout Performance, they might fail to confirm that the learner, in fact, has grasped all of the Important Steps and Key Points or confuse the learner by adding new information in Step 3 that was not presented in Step 2.

These training shortcomings are common throughout any industry. They show that instructors, although they may know how to do a particular job without even thinking, need to be fully prepared to deliver the training. Carefully considering the steps and critical points of a job before trying to teach it is the best way to begin. There is usually more to a job, even a simple job, than you realize, especially if it is something you do not do on a regular basis. For this reason, even if you fully understand the Job

DOI: 10.4324/9781003035305-6

Instruction (JI) four-step method, you need a solid foundation that will prepare you to teach it properly.

There are four important things that you need to do *before* you instruct a job. These four "Get Ready" points are printed on the front side of the JI pocket card introduced in the previous chapter. Titled "How to Get Ready to Instruct" (Figure 6.1), this side of the card lists things you need to do *before* you give instruction using the four steps listed on the other side. Let's examine these four Get Ready points.

1. *Make a Timetable for Training.* Do the training by plan, not by accident. You usually make plans for any part of your work, and training should be no different. When you make a timetable for training, you are planning *who* to train, on *which job*, and by *what date*.
2. *Break Down the Job.* List the *Important Steps* of the job and identify the *Key Points* for each of these steps; clearly organize the operation in your mind so that you can be sure you are correctly teaching the *one best way* of doing the job.
3. *Get Everything Ready.* Have all of *the proper equipment, materials*, and *supplies* needed to aid the instruction. If you use makeshift instruments or use the wrong equipment or forget something or don't have the necessary materials or supplies, you set a poor work standard for the person who has to do the job and undermine your authority as a supervisor or trainer.

JOB INSTRUCTION

HOW TO GET READY TO INSTRUCT

Before instructing people how to do a job:

1. MAKE A TIME TABLE FOR TRAINING
    Who to train…
      For which work…
        By what date…

2. BREAK DOWN THE JOB
    List Important Steps
    Select Key Points
    Safety factors are always Key Points

3. GET EVERYTHING READY
The proper supplies, equipment, materials, and whatever needed to aid instruction

4. ARRANGE THE WORKSITE
Neatly, as in actual working conditions

Figure 6.1 Job Instruction pocket card (front side).

4. *Arrange the Worksite.* Arrange things *neatly, just as you would in the actual working conditions.* A cluttered storage cabinet, a poorly arranged worktable, a cluttered desk, or any single thing that is out of place sets a poor example for employees.

Because the second Get Ready point, Break Down the Job, is the most important and the most difficult point to learn, it merits special attention. Thus, Chapter 6 will focus only on this subject, while Chapter 7 will cover Get Ready items 1, 3, and 4. Even though Break Down the Job is the most critical of the four preparatory items, the instructor must follow all four Get Ready points to ensure a successful training session.

Get Ready Point 2: Break Down the Job

If someone asked you to give a short speech at an event or to talk at a health care meeting about the progress of a project you were leading, you would probably make some notes beforehand, perhaps in outline form, so that you present your thoughts in an understandable, logical order. Doing this would help you to remember important information as well as keep you from digressing from the subject at hand. At the same time, you want your outline to be flexible so that you can adjust your comments in response to the audience reaction to what you are saying. In the same way, when preparing for JI, you also need to make notes regarding the jobs you want to teach to workers.

Specifically, you need to break down jobs into their *Important Steps* and then find the *Key Points* for each of those steps. You also will be finding the reasons for each of these Key Points, which you will use during instruction. When you break down a job, you document the *one best way* for doing that job and, thus, create a best practice standard for the work. However, the purpose of these job breakdowns is *not* to try to describe every conceivable step, motion, point, or precaution that may relate to the job. Nor are they instruction sheets that document in detail how to do the job. In fact, you don't even show the breakdown sheet to learners. The breakdown sheet is merely a tool for collecting notes "from yourself to yourself" to help you organize your thoughts and the job's procedures as you train the employee. Though we use the word "notes" here, we do not mean to imply random words jotted down on the back of an envelope. These "notes" will be carefully considered words and phrases that accurately capture the process of doing the task at hand.

JOB BREAKDOWN SHEET

Task: _____Hand Hygiene-Washing_____

Supplies: __Soap, Running Water, Disposable Towel_____

Instruments & Equipment: _____

IMPORTANT STEPS	KEY POINTS	REASONS
A logical segment of the operation when something happens to advance the work.	Anything in a step that might— 1. Make or break the job 2. Injure the worker 3. Make the work easier to do, i.e. "knack", "trick", special timing, bit of special information	Reasons for the key points
1. Wet hands	1. Thoroughly without soap	Rinses away with water; soap naturally lathers when put onto water
2. Apply soap	1. Enough to cover all surfaces	Fail to kill all germs
3. Rub hands	1. Palm to palm 2. Palm to backs	1. Clean the entire surface 2. Clean the entire surface
4. Rub fingers	1. Interlocking 2. Backs of fingers to palm 3. Tips to palm 4. Thumbs	1. Sides of fingers cleaned at one time 2. Corners and creases of cuticles and knuckles 3. Under fingernails 4. Most active part of hand
5. Rinse & Dry	1. Use towel to turn water off	Prevent recontamination of hands

Figure 6.2 Job breakdown of hand hygiene.

Figure 6.2 shows the breakdown of the hand hygiene example we used in the previous chapter. The breakdown sheet has three columns: one for Important Steps, one for Key Points, and one for the Reasons for the Key Points.

What Is an Important Step?

An Important Step is a logical segment of an operation when something happens to *advance the work*. Let's say you need to change the oxygen tubing for a patient and you keep the new tubing in a drawer. "Grasp the handle of the drawer" is not a step worth noting on the breakdown sheet because the worker will know to do this motion intuitively. What about:

"Pull open the drawer"? This is a step, but it is not an Important Step because simply opening the drawer does not advance the goal of changing the oxygen tubing. "Take out the proper tubing," however, is an Important Step and is the most important thing that happens to advance the work. For this step, it is not necessary to go into any greater detail. Keep in mind that during the instruction session, the learner will see the instructor taking out the tubing from the drawer and will know to grasp the handle and pull open the drawer without telling them.

It is important to keep in mind that these breakdowns are not hairsplitting, micromotion studies that people commonly use when documenting or analyzing a job procedure. They are simple, common sense reminders of what is essential when teaching a job. Remember that your purpose is to teach people to *quickly remember to do a job correctly, safely, and conscientiously*; so don't overload them with any more information than they absolutely need to have. For example, if you were to write down every detail of the procedure in the hand hygiene example, it would look like this:

1. Turn on the faucet and wet your hands with water so that they are completely wet.
2. Get soap from the dispenser making sure that you have enough to cover all of the surfaces including the backs of your hands and the fingers.
3. Rub the palms of your two hands together back and forth and in a circular motion.
4. Then rub the palm of one hand on the back of the other hand backward and forward and in a circular motion.
5. Repeat for the other hand.
6. Interlace the fingers of both hands, palm to palm, and move your palms back and forth so that the insides of the fingers rub against each other.
7. Curl the fingers of your right hand into a fist and rub the backs of those fingers backward and forward on the palm of your left hand.
8. Repeat with the fingers of your left hand in the right palm.
9. Take the tips of the fingers of your right hand and rotationally rub them backward and forward on the palm of your left hand.
10. Repeat with the fingers of your left hand in the right palm.
11. Take the thumb of your left hand and grasp it with the palm and fingers of your right hand rotationally rubbing the thumb in the palm of the hand.
12. Repeat with the right thumb in the palm of your left hand.

13. Rinse your hands thoroughly until all the soap is removed, being careful not to touch the faucet or the sink.
14. Leave the water running.
15. Dry hands thoroughly with a single-use towel and use the towel to turn off the faucet.

In this detailed description, there are 15 steps and 268 words, as compared with 5 steps and 41 words in the brief, but better, job breakdown of hand hygiene shown in Figure 6.2. Keep in mind that the instructor might need to use all 268 words in the course of explaining the job. However, for the purposes of organizing the procedure in your mind, 41 words are all you need.

Here is a simple procedure for choosing Important Steps. Using this checklist will help you create a concise but complete list of Important Steps for any task. The four steps of identifying Important Steps include:

1. Start doing the job, slowly and meticulously following the standard procedure.
2. Ask yourself at each stage: "Has the job advanced"?
3. If so, question what you have done.
4. If you think it can be an Important Step, write it down in the column for Important Steps on the breakdown sheet with a succinct phrase to convey the meaning.

Let's take a look at this process using the hand hygiene example (refer to Figure 6.2). You begin the job by turning on the water faucet so that you can wet your hands. Now ask yourself whether the job has *advanced* because of this action. While you certainly need to have the water running, just turning on the water does not get you closer to your goal of having your hands washed—your hands are just as they were before the water was turned on. The first logical step in the advancement is when your hands become wet, so the first Important Step would be **wet hands**. This action implies that you will need water, so there is no need to tell the learner to turn on the water. They will understand that when they see you demonstrate the job.

Continue washing your hands, applying soap. Ask yourself: Has the job advanced? This action definitely advances the job because you won't get your hands clean without soap. Therefore, the second Important Step is **apply soap**. Next, you begin moving your hands together in order to get the soap to lather without letting it spill down into the sink. So, **rub hands** would be the third Important Step because it moves the job forward. Here you might be tempted to think that this process of rubbing your hands together is the entire part of washing your hands, but you know that there are some special techniques you want to apply to getting the fingers and fingertips clean. Therefore, you separate that into a different step. That makes the fourth Important Step **rub fingers** because this part of the process requires special attention.

Now that your hands are completely clean, you continue doing the job, which is to rinse off the soap. Needless to say, this advances the job because we have to remove all of the soap from our hands and then dry them so they are not dripping wet. The fifth Important Step is **rinse and dry**. These five steps capture the essence of what it takes to understand this job quickly and completely. Because they are simple and direct, they are easy to remember and repeat. Notice that each step involves something that moves the job forward. It is not until you get to the Key Points for each step that you go into the details of the job.

The Important Steps in a breakdown should correlate with the learners' abilities. In other words, each step can be as precise or as general as needed. If the experience or skill of the learner is low, the steps can be shorter in content and more specific. If it is high, larger amounts of work can be captured in each step. This means that there can be different breakdowns for the same job.

You will notice in Figure 6.3 that there are two levels of detail depending on whether the learner is experienced or new. Example 1A is used for employees who have had experience with sterile processes and are already skilled at putting on sterile gloves. New people, however, have to learn each part of the process. Example 1B is the breakdown for just the third step: **don sterile gloves**. There can be breakdowns for any of the other operations; once the operator has learned them all, it will not be necessary to provide that level of detailed instruction. Your breakdowns can be as precise or as general as needed depending on a learner's skill level.

What Is a Key Point?

Five to ten percent of every job entails hard or tricky parts that take time to learn and that embody the real skill of doing the work. People gain these "know-how" skills through years of experience. Because these skills are developed over time, health care facilities value long-term, experienced employees. However, our objective with good instruction is to develop

Example 1A: Job Breakdown (Experienced Worker)	
TASK: Setting up Tray for Lumbar Puncture INSTRUMENT: LP Tray	
IMPORTANT STEPS	**KEY POINTS**
1. Open Tray	On flat surface
2. Unfold flaps	First flap away from you Only touch outside
3. Don sterile gloves	Maintain sterile field
4. Unfold Drape	Set aside on sterile field
5. Prepare Lidocaine	In 5cc syringe Attach orange needle
6. Prepare Specimen Vials	Open tops on all 4 tubes Stand in tray

Example 1B: Job Breakdown (New Worker)	
TASK: Don Sterile Gloves INSTRUMENT: Sterile Gloves	
IMPORTANT STEPS	**KEY POINTS**
1. Open package	Folding back creases Touching outer edges only Don't lean over open pack
2. Glove dominant hand	Pinching cuff Lift off paper Tuck thumb
3. Glove other hand	Sliding fingers in cuff Lift off paper
4. Adjust fit	Interlocking fingers Pinch & pull

Figure 6.3 Two levels of job breakdowns.

these new skills much more quickly. Training Within Industry (TWI) calls these know-how skills Key Points because they are the *key* to doing each step of the job properly. In fact, *knowing the Key Points of a job and how to pick them out quickly and easily is perhaps the most important thing in Job Instruction.*

A good instructor finds these Key Points and passes them on so learners can gain needed skills as quickly as possible. Knowing a job's Key Points helps to reduce the number of accidents and errors that occur while people are becoming "experienced." Supervisors can use breakdowns as well to capture the knowledge and skill of experienced employees and pass it down to a new generation of workers.

There are various kinds of Key Points, but these three conditions will help you recognize them in any given job:

1. *Make or Break the Job*: These are things that make for the success or failure in job performance.
2. *Injure the Worker*: Safety factors, no matter how small, are always Key Points.
3. *Easier to Do*: This includes any special knack or "trick of the trade," the special bits of information or feel or timing that make a job easier to do.

As with Important Steps, there is no need to identify everything that happens in a job, but if the activity meets one of these three conditions, you can consider it a Key Point. Some good examples of Key Points include:

■ When removing "dirty" gloves, the Key Point is to "peel off, inside out" so as not to spread germs.
■ When drawing up a medication, expel the excess air by inverting and tapping the syringe.
■ When using a suction machine, the sound will change if the tube gets plugged. Judging the sound will be the Key Point.
■ When cleaning used instruments, a Key Point is to avoid touching the part of the instruments that may carry infection.
■ When placing a peripheral IV, how far to advance the needle once you have entered the vein is the Key Point.
■ While performing CPR, when giving two breaths there are two Key Points: "tilt head/lift chin" and "pinch nose."
■ When connecting IV tubing to the hub of the catheter by "twisting the threads" to be sure you have a tight seal, how much power to put into the turn will be the Key Point.

After we have identified the Important Steps in the job we are teaching, we look for the Key Points step by step. Here is a procedure to use that will guide you through the process:

1. Do the Important Step.
2. While performing the step, recite the three conditions that define a Key Point: *make or break, injure the worker, easier to do*. This is what you are looking for.
3. If you find something you think might meet one of these conditions, ask yourself *why* you do it that way or *what if* you didn't do it that way.
4. Confirm that this is a Key Point by asking yourself which of the three conditions this would meet. For example, if you didn't do it that way and the job could not proceed, then this would *make or break* the job, and, thus, would be a Key Point.
5. If you conclude that it does meet one of the conditions, write the Key Point down on the breakdown sheet.
6. Repeat steps 2 through 5 for the same step until you cannot find any more Key Points in *this* Important Step.
7. Repeat the entire process for each remaining Important Step.

Now let's see how these seven steps were used to find the Key Points in the hand hygiene example. Note that all the bolded words are terms and phrases that went into the breakdown sheet.

Important Step 1: Wet Hands

1. Do the first Important Step: **wet hands**.
2. While performing the step, recite the three conditions for being a Key Point: *make or break, injure the worker, easier to do*.
3. Ask yourself if there is anything you are doing here that might meet one of these conditions. Yes, there is. Many people apply soap first before they wet their hands thinking that this is faster or easier. But you must first wet your hands **thoroughly without soap**. Ask yourself *why* you do it that way or *what if* you didn't do it that way. The answer is because if you put the soap on first it **rinses away with water** and, conversely, **soap naturally lathers when put onto water**. (*Note:* This is the Reason for the Key Point.)
4. To confirm that this is in fact a Key Point, ask which of the three conditions it meets. In this case, wetting your hands **thoroughly without soap** would *make or break* the job because if you rinse away the soap with water you will not have the proper amount of soap on your hands to wash them completely. Therefore, you can conclude that **thoroughly without soap** can be a Key Point.

5. Write the Key Point down on the breakdown sheet. All you need to write is "thoroughly without soap."
6. Repeat steps 2 through 5 for the *first* Important Step until you can't find any more Key Points in *this* step. (In this case, there are no other Key Points for the first Important Step.)

Important Step 2: Apply Soap

1. Do the second Important Step: **apply soap**.
2. While performing the step, recite the three conditions for being a Key Point: *make or break, injure the worker, easier to do*.
3. Ask yourself if there is anything you are doing here that might meet one of these conditions? Here, you have to make sure that you apply **enough to cover all surfaces** of both hands. Ask yourself *why* you do it that way or *what if* you didn't do it that way. If you don't, then you will **fail to kill all germs** that you may have on your hands. (*Note*: This is the Reason for the Key Point.)
4. To confirm that **enough to cover all surfaces** is a Key Point, ask which of the three conditions it meets. In this case, it clearly *makes or breaks* the job.
5. Write the Key Point on the breakdown sheet: "enough to cover all surfaces."
6. Repeat steps 2 through 5 for this step. (In this case, there are no other Key Points for the second Important Step.)

We continue using the same procedure for the remaining Important Steps. For the sake of brevity, we will just present the conclusions. However, the same procedure was used throughout to bring out these conclusions.

Important Step 3: Rub Hands

When you **rub hands**, continue reciting the three conditions for a Key Point—*make or break, injure the worker, easier to do*—so that you stay focused on what you are looking for. Key Points are usually hidden, almost invisible at first glance, so you have to be diligent about knowing what they are in order to flush them out. For example, when you **rub hands** it is important that you **clean the entire surface** of both palms without missing a spot and the way to ensure that this is done is to keep the palms flat and rub them together. This meets the condition *make or break*, and the Key Point **palm to palm** simply and effectively captures this.

Continue questioning the *same* step to see if there are any more Key Points. In this step, there is another Key Point. People very often neglect to clean the back of their hands thinking that this area is not used when working. However, the backs of our hands do come into contact with people, materials, and equipment and are excellent areas for carrying and passing on germs. Here again, the flat surface of your palms is the best thing to use to **clean the entire surface** because it ensures no spot will be missed. The Key Point then is **palms to backs** because it meets the condition *make or break*.

Important Step 4: Rub Fingers

We noted when determining the Important Steps for this job that there were several techniques needed to ensure that the fingers are cleaned thoroughly. When we wash our fingers, cleaning each finger separately would be cumbersome and time consuming. Here, by **interlocking** the fingers and moving the hands back and forth, the **sides of the fingers can all be cleaned at one time** and this meets the condition *easier to do*, so it can be a Key Point. The backs and tips of the fingers are areas where germs can hide, especially **under the fingernails** and in the **corners and creases of the cuticles and knuckles**. By rubbing the **backs of fingers to palm** and the **tips to palm**, two separate Key Points because they *make or break* the job, you can ensure to clean these critical areas.

Finally, you must not forget to clean the **thumbs** because this is the **most active part of our hand**. This meets the *make or break* condition for a Key Point. Notice that the Key Point does not specify the technique used which is to grasp the thumb and rotate it in the palm of the other hand. The learner will understand the motions by seeing the instructor perform the job and so no words are necessary. If the learner still has trouble performing this part during the Tryout Performance, the instructor can add additional explanation as needed.

Important Step 5: Rinse & Dry

In this Important Step, **rinse and dry**, you need to make sure you **prevent recontamination of hands** by not touching the faucet, which may have germs on it. While most people leave the water running while they wash their hands, they instinctively turn it off before they dry them. Because your hands were dirty when you turned the water on, there is a chance that germs were deposited on the faucet and you don't want to put them back onto your now clean hands. Because this would *make or break* the job, the Key Point is **use towel to turn water off** and, thus, **prevent recontamination of hands**.

When we find a Key Point, we check to see if it meets one of the three conditions—*make or break, injure the worker, easier to do*—by asking *why* we do it that way or *what if* we didn't do it that way. Based on the answer to that question, we can clearly see if it meets one of these conditions and, therefore, can be a Key Point. By following this procedure, we also find the reason for the Key Point because that is the answer to the question: "Why do we do it this way?" Writing this reason down on the breakdown sheet gives us this final piece of information we need to teach the job successfully using the JI four-step method. As noted in the previous chapter, if the learner knows why the Key Point is necessary, he or she will be more likely to remember and follow it.

Summary of Breakdown Procedure

As you have seen, the breakdown for Job Instruction consists of two major parts: Important Steps and Key Points. One easy way to remember the difference between these two items is that *Important Steps are the **what you do*** and *Key Points are the **how you do it***. Therefore, Important Steps usually consist of action phrases beginning with verbs: insert hypodermic needle, input data, swab injection area with alcohol, or turn up heat to 375 degrees. Key Points, on the other hand, usually consist of descriptive words using adjectives and adverbs: with shiny side up, feeding evenly and slowly, to two decimal places, or vigorously, with friction. When you put the two together, they make a complete and descriptive sentence as in: "Swab injection area with alcohol vigorously, with friction," where "swab injection area with alcohol" is the Important Step and "vigorously, with friction" is the Key Point. When you add the reasons for the Key Points, it makes for a complete description of the process.

These breakdowns may seem complex, but you can do them quickly and easily after a little practice. Because they are notes to yourself, *few and simple* words are required, and the fewer the words the better. If you make your breakdowns too precise or use technical jargon, you will only confuse the learners and important parts of the instruction will be left unclear or misunderstood. With a good breakdown in hand, when you demonstrate the job in Step 2 of the JI four-step method, you will be able to explain each of the Important Steps precisely and emphasize all of the Key Points to each step in the correct order without missing any. In Step 3, the trial phase, you can use this breakdown as a check sheet for making sure the learner has understood all of the Important Steps, the Key Points, as well as the reasons for each Key Point, with nothing omitted.

Experienced trainers may know a job so well that they seldom think about how to put it across to others, so when they teach it, they carelessly miss important parts. They assume that because they are able to perform the job quite easily, then anyone can do it. Consequently, they fail to gauge just what learners need to know in order to do the job. On the other hand, sometimes trainers incorrectly think they fully understand a job that they really don't and only notice their ignorance when they try to teach it to someone else. We may be able to do a job even though we don't understand all of its details, but, when we have to teach it to someone, we will be forced to explain these details. Even when we know a job well, with the best of intentions the tendency is to give too much information by saying everything we know about the job and this only serves to confuse the learners. Oftentimes, the more we try to explain something, the more confused the learner becomes.

These are all common faults and the reason why so much faulty instruction is being given throughout the health care industry. That is the reason why we need to think through jobs and make a breakdown sheet for each job before instructing it. When we analyze a job by doing a breakdown for instruction, we can plan out beforehand how we will explain the job clearly and judge the proper amount of information the learner must remember. We should never assume that we can come up with a clear explanation right there on the spot.

The following four sample breakdowns are from four different areas of the health care industry (see Figures 6.4–6.7).

Below is a summary of how to make a breakdown.

1. Do the job on your own. You may want to refer to any available written materials such as work standard forms or "instruction sheets," and you should talk with experienced workers to be sure you have determined the "one best way" of doing the job.
2. Write up the Important Steps of the job, making sure that each step is a logical segment of the operation that advances the job.

JOB INSTRUCTION BREAKDOWN SHEET

Task: Install IV Catheter and inject contrast material for CT Examination
Supplies: Needle, syringe, IV connecting tube
Instruments & Equipment: Rubber gloves, tape, tourniquet, alcohol, cotton pad, clear band aid,
                                      sodium chloride, contrast material.

JI No._____   Date: October 9, 2004

IMPORTANT STEPS	KEY POINTS	REASONS
A logical segment of the operation when something happens to advance the work	Anything in a step that might— 1. Make or break the job 2. Injure the worker 3. Make the work easier to do, i.e., "knack," "trick," special timing, bit of special information	Reasons for the key points
1. Apply tourniquet	Adequate pressure to increase the size of veins	To make the best vein available stand out from the rest
2. Select vein	Straight and large enough to accommodate a standard size catheter	So contrast can enter vein at the rate desired. Otherwise a smaller catheter must be used
3. Cleanse area with alcohol pad	Letting the alcohol air dry	Arm sting when a needle is put in the skin when wet with alcohol
4. Insert needle into vein	1. At the same angle the vein is running 2. Pushing the needle in to the length of the catheter	1. To prevent going through the vein 2. To assure stability while in the vein
5. Attach syringe to the catheter	Drawing back on syringe until you see blood flow	Needle is not properly in vein if blood does not flow
6. Inject 2cc of sodium chloride	Use the full amount	Clear blood from catheter
7. Secure catheter to arm	Applying clear band aid at the site of entry	1. To prevent catheter from coming loose when attaching IV line 2. Ability to see entry site
8. Attach IV line	Firm connection	So line will not come off when contrast is going into vein
9. Inject contrast	Feeling vein as contrast is entering vein	To make sure contrast is going into the vein
10. Remove catheter after the injection, apply gauze and tape to arm	Firmly over the point of entry	To prevent continued bleeding

Figure 6.4   Job breakdown: Example 1. (From P. Graupp and R. J. Wrona. 2006.
The TWI Workbook: Essential Skills for Supervisors. **Boca Raton, FL: Taylor & Francis**
Group. With permission.)

3. Do the job again, step by step, and find the Key Points for each Important Step. When finding the Key Points, keep in mind the three conditions for being a Key Point: What makes or breaks the job? What might injure the worker? What makes the work easier to do? As you find the Key Points, record the reasons for each Key Point and this will make the explanation complete.

4. Number or label your breakdown sheet. Doing this will make it easy to find in your files, and you will be able to use it again and again whenever you have to teach that particular job.

No. _____

JOB INSTRUCTION BREAKDOWN SHEET

Operation: ___Label Blood Culture Specimen_____

Parts: ___Specimen, Label_____

Tools & Materials: ___Pen_____

IMPORTANT STEPS	KEY POINTS	REASONS
A logical segment of the operation when something happens to advance the work.	Anything in a step that might – 1. Make or break the job 2. Injure the worker 3. Make the work easier to do, i.e. "knack", "trick', special timing, bit of special information	Reasons for key points
1. Select label	1. Correct test 2. Rectangular	1. Patient safety 2. Several same labels
2. Position tube in hand	1. Label on tube up 2. Open space on back	1. Easier to place 2. To inspect the blood in tube
3. Place label	1. Length wise 2. Covering old label 3. Straight	1. Not to jam in machine 2. Correct scanning 3. Correct scanning

#010
20160105

Figure 6.5 Job breakdown: Example 2.

Structure of a Good Breakdown: Simple Words and Few

We said that breakdowns for Job Instruction do *not* include every single thing that can be said about a job. So, selecting what should be included in the Key Points and what should be left out is a matter of good judgment and training experience. If we include too much information, we confuse the learners and they miss or overlook the critical items that they really do need to have in order to learn the job well; in other words, these critical items get lost in the deluge of information. If, on the other hand, we trim down that information to only the vital things the person needs to hear and retain in order to understand and perform the work, we can be sure they will be able to do exactly what is needed. That means that the Key Points can differ depending on the learner. For example, for new people even small details can be Key Points because they are not as familiar with the intricacies of the jobs as more experienced people. Or, for unskilled, unmotivated, or careless workers, we may have to change the Key Points to suit their demeanors.

No. 1_

JOB INSTRUCTION BREAKDOWN SHEET - HEALTHCARE

Task: <u>Central Line and PICC Dressing Change</u>

Supplies: <u>Clean gloves, dressing kit, CHG dressing, sterile saline syringes</u>

Equipment & Materials: <u>Trash can, bedside table</u>
- AIDET/HAND HYGIENE (HH)

IMPORTANT STEPS	KEY POINTS	REASONS
A logical segment of the operation when something happens to advance the work.	Anything in a step that might – 1. Make or break the job 2. Injure the worker 3. Make the work easier to do, i.e. "knack", "trick', special timing, bit of special information	Reasons for key points
1. Prepare room & patient	1. Prepare table and patient 2. In bed on back 3. Elevate bed 4. Masks 5. HH before gloves	1. Safety and decrease risk of infection 2. More stability, avoid line displacement 3. Good body mechanics 4. & 5. Decrease risk of infection
2. Remove and inspect site	1. Slowly toward insertion site 2. Squirt saline on CHG gel-don't touch 3. Assess for infection 4. Look & feel	1. Avoid line displacement 2. Loosens gel to come off more easily, skin integrity 3. Decrease risk of infection 4. Identify and treat infection
3. Clean with alcohol	1. HH/don sterile gloves 2. No alcohol on the PICC catheter. 3. From insertion site outwards 4. 3 sticks to 3 inches 5. Air dry	1. Decrease risk of infection 2. Prevent breakdown of PICC catheter. 3. Clean contaminants away from insertion site 4. Removes biofilm 5. Dry time is kill time
4. Disinfect w/CHG	1. If prevantics-flat side to skin/both sides If chloraprep-squeeze wings 2. Back & forth to 3" from site 3. Air Dry 30 sec	1. Correct Chg. Distribution, decrease risk of infection 2. Clean both sides of the epithelial cells 3. Dry time is kill time
4. Apply new dressing	1. Holding by handles 2. Gel pad over site 3. Notch over tubing 4. Smooth surface to edges 5. Change hep-locks with green caps	1. Prevents contamination of dressing 2. Provides continuous antimicrobial action 3. Seals dressing 4. Avoid air bubbles or wrinkles 5. Decrease infection risk
6. Label dressing	1. Remove PPE/HH 2. Date/time dressing 3. Lower bed 4. Document in EMR	1. & 2. Decrease risk of infection 2. Communicates with Care team 3. Patient Safety 4. Communicates with Care team

#010

Figure 6.6   Job breakdown: Example 3.

JOB INSTRUCTION BREAKDOWN SHEET

Task: Discharge to SNF
Supplies: Kardex, Census Board, Chart Copies, Transfer Envelope

IMPORTANT STEPS	KEY POINTS	REASONS
WHAT *I am doing* *A logical segment of the operation when something happens to advance the work*	**HOW** *I must do the work* *1. Things that make or break the job* *2. Things that injure the worker* *3. Things that make the work easier to do; a "knack" or a "trick"*	**WHY** *I must do it this way* *Reasons for the Key Points*
1. Transcribe discharge order	Write on kardex and census board	Staff awareness
2. Confirm discharge order with RN and CM	1. Page RN 2. Verbally tell CM	To prevent delays in discharge
3. Update census board	1. Write D/C next to patient's name 2. Write time next to D/C	Staff awareness
4. Place copies of chart in transfer envelope	Copy required data from chart (see list on transfer order sheet)	Information for the receiving facility
5. Give completed packet to RN/driver		
6. Log D/C at station	Write name, time, and destination	For future reference
7. Input into system	Discharge under patient activity	To complete discharge (notifies Beds and EVS of D/C)

Figure 6.7   Job breakdown: Example 4. (From St. Joseph Health System, Orange, CA. With permission.)

(See again Figure 6.3 where we had two levels of breakdowns, one for more experienced people and one for new workers.)

As an example, if the Important Step in a job is to "connect IV to central line," we could consider it as a Key Point to turn the fastener "clockwise" when making the connection. However, because most connectors used in medical equipment (though not all) follow the pattern of tightening by turning clockwise and loosening by turning counterclockwise, an experienced practitioner would know this without telling him or her. This would not be a Key Point worth mentioning, though it is certainly an important part of doing the job successfully. If the learner, though, were a person new to health care who had very little experience in the working world, they might get hung up on this point and not be able to complete the step correctly. We would have to tell this person which way to twist the connectors in order to connect the lines.

When making breakdowns for instruction, then, we must be careful not to think that there is one and only one correct way to break down a job, as if it were a mathematical formula with only one correct answer. In fact, we can say that there is no right or wrong breakdown. A good breakdown is one that succeeds in teaching the job well. This means, though, that we must develop the skill of finding and selecting the Key Points for each job so that learners can learn jobs quickly while getting all the necessary information. As with any skill, the best way to do this is through practice.

When we break down a job and then train someone using that breakdown, we will get immediate feedback on how well the breakdown is working. If they struggle to accomplish a certain aspect of the job, that means we have missed a Key Point and should try to identify what it is and add it into the breakdown so that the next time we teach it we avoid that trouble. If we find when training a job that the same question keeps coming up, we can include that information up front as a Key Point. When training hand hygiene, for example, we regularly were asked whether it made a difference using hot or cold water. Because it makes no difference to the outcome of washing your hands properly, this was not originally a Key Point, but we can mention it because so many learners had the question. If, on the other hand, learners find the job fairly easy to do, but are having difficulty remembering all the details, then perhaps we have included too many Key Points and can eliminate those that learners pick up on their own without being told.

In addition to deciding which Key Points to include or not to include in a breakdown, another difficult skill to learn is finding the right words to express them. Our inclination is to write these breakdowns as if we were writing a report and to explain each point in long, detailed sentences that read like a book. Keep in mind, though, that these breakdowns are like "notes" to cue trainers on what they need to cover while training so that everything is delivered in the right order without missing anything. The trick is to find just the right word, or (few) words, that succinctly, but accurately, grasp the concept of what we need to express. Again, if we try to be too detailed, we only wind up confusing the learners. Therefore, instead of writing, "Twisting the connector tightly onto the hub until it snaps into place," you could write as the Key Point: "Tightly, until it snaps." Keep in mind that during the instruction the learner will see the instructor performing this Key Point as it is explained, so the action of "twisting connector onto the hub" will be learned visually without the need for a verbal prompt.

In Chapter 3, we saw how the instructors at Virginia Mason Medical Center initially broke down the hand hygiene job by making a breakdown that looked more like a full-blown standard operating procedure document rather than "notes" for training (see Figure 3.1). This is very typical when we first begin using the Job Instruction method because we are trained to express ourselves completely and in great detail when writing. After studying the method in more depth, they were able to cut this down to just the essential bits of information that they would then go on to use successfully in training the job (see Figure 3.3).

Following are some words and expressions that can be used as examples of good Key Points:

- Firmly, tightly, neatly, loosely
- Taut
- Carefully, thoroughly, accurately, completely
- Until you see ...
- All over the surface
- Uniformly, evenly, equally
- Slowly, gradually, softly
- At an even speed
- All together, with ...
- Alternately
- According to ...
- Adjusting ...
- Making ... even
- Before it cools, after it cools
- As soon as ..., before ...
- Counterclockwise/clockwise
- Without force
- Forcefully
- Until dry
- By twisting, by stretching, by pulling
- At the same time as ...
- After checking ... By paying attention to ...
- By watching ...
- A little bigger than ..., a little longer than ..., a little thicker than ...
- A little above midline
- Circular from the inside out
- Just like squeezing the air out of it
- Until you can slip it in
- Until you feel a slight resistance

- When you hear a "click"
- When you feel it snap in
- Sliding in at an angle
- With a quick flick of your wrist

Teaching "Feel"

Many jobs, especially in health care, require some kind of a feel or knack. Some supervisors tend to think that these skills are somehow mysterious or difficult to teach because they are generally the result of years of experience. But, if you teach the learner *what* and *where* the feel or knack is, they will be able to pick it up much faster. Also, if you teach the correct "feel" for the job right from the start, the learner will master it with little difficulty and few problems.

Key Points that express feel and knack are sometimes impossible to describe in words, so you have to think of creative ways to teach them. Using expressions like "with finger power," "with wrist power," "with arm power," or "with body power" when showing the degree of force that needs to be applied may help, but demonstrating "feel" by letting them try it out for themselves in connection with these verbal cues is better. Have the learner do it and keep checking their performance until it "feels just right."

For example, when applying a tourniquet to a patient's arm in order to draw blood, how tight we wind it around the arm is a matter of feel. If we don't apply enough pressure, we will not get the blood vessels in the lower arm to enlarge so that we can find a good vein and insert the needle easily. If we make it too tight, we might cut off circulation and cause them undue discomfort. To get across the proper feel:

1. The instructor first applies the tourniquet properly.
2. The instructor then has the learner feel the tightness of the tourniquet and remarks, "This is the correct tightness. Remember this tightness."
3. The instructor then allows the learner to apply the tourniquet himself or herself recalling the "feel" of the tightness.
4. The instructor checks the tightness and praises the learner if it is done correctly or, if not, asks him or her to try again until the proper tightness is achieved.

By applying the tourniquet in this manner a few times, the learner quickly learns the "feel." Usually, in Step 2 of the Job Instruction method, Present the Operation, the learner does not touch the job and simply observes the instructor's demonstration of the correct method. However, teaching "feel" is an exception. When the instructor teaches this kind of Key Point in the Present the Operation phase, the learner can actually try it out to properly understand the "feel" that is the Key Point.

When Key Points are impossible to express in words, then you will have to find other means of communicating them. For example:

- How tight: Let them feel it
- How to hook your finger: Show it
- How to grasp something: Demonstrate it
- How wet: Let them touch it
- How to adjust a needle: Show a drawing
- How it sounds: Let them hear it
- How it smells: Let them smell it

Common Key Points

In many jobs, there are Key Points that apply to all of the steps in a given job, and it is cumbersome and confusing to repeat the same Key Point for every Important Step. Often these are Key Points concerning safety (e.g., "wearing gloves," or "putting on protective eyewear"). Some Key Points refer to the way an instrument is used or held or how a part is used throughout the entire process (e.g., "cutting away from you" or "with large opening facing up" or "pushing plunger all the way"). You should teach Common Key Points as an integral part of the job procedure, listing them on the breakdown sheet as the "Zero Step" or "0. Common Key Points" (Figure 6.8). In this way, it will not be confused with the actual number of Important Steps in the job.

When teaching a job that contains Common Key Points, in Step 2, Present the Operation, you can demonstrate the job the first time just giving the Important Steps starting with the first Important Step. Then, when you do it again stressing the Key Points, start out by saying the job contains some Common Key Points that apply to the whole job and present them. Continue by going through the Important Steps of the job one by one explaining the Key Points for each Important Step. In Step 3, follow the same pattern making sure that the learner can repeat the Common Key Points each time they demonstrate the Key Points of the job.

IMPORTANT STEPS	KEY POINTS	REASONS
A logical segment of the operation when something happens to advance the work	Anything in a step that might— 1. Make or break the job 2. Injure the worker 3. Make the work easier to do, i.e., "knack," "trick," special timing, bit of special information	Reasons for the key points
0. Common Key Point	1. Wearing sterile gloves 2. Pushing plunger all the way	1. To prevent contamination 2. Apply correct amount of medication to wound

Figure 6.8   Common Key Points: The "zero step" on the breakdown sheet.

How Big Should a Breakdown Be?

Trainers oftentimes ask, "How many Important Steps and Key Points should a good breakdown have?" This depends on the job, but there is a limit to how much a person can understand and retain at one time. The important thing to keep in mind here is our method of teaching the job in stages: first demonstrating the job giving only the Important Steps; then demonstrating the job again reviewing the Important Steps, but adding in the Key Points, step by step; finally, demonstrating the job a third time reviewing the Important Steps, the Key Points, and then adding in the reasons for the Key Points. Keep in mind the caution point of Step 2, "Don't give them more information than they can master at one time." We give a little more information each time we do it until we get to the core details of the job. That means that at each stage we can learn and remember another level of information.

In the initial stage, when giving the Important Steps, generally speaking a person can remember four or five or six things with a bit of effort. If you give them seven or eight or nine things to remember, you are starting to push the limits of what they can retain at one time. If you give them 10 or more things to learn, they probably won't be able to remember them all. In the same way, there is a limit to how many Key Points the learner will be able to remember for each Important Step. Two or three Key Points are just about right. Four or five Key Points and you're starting to push too hard. If there are six or seven Key Points in a step you should start considering breaking the step into two separate Important Steps, splitting up the Key Points appropriately between them.

When we find an Important Step that has too many Key Points, break it into two or more Important Steps so that each step has about the same amount of content and complexity. Even if this revised step does not nec-essarily "advance the job," the rule of thumb for what makes an Important Step, the better balance between all of the Important Steps to the job will improve the breakdown and make the job easier to teach. When we go up a staircase, it's a good thing that each stair is the same height, as that makes it easier for us to anticipate each step we make without tripping and falling. In the same way, when each Important Step is about the same volume, it makes it easier for the learner to pick up the steps one by one and remem-ber them all. It also helps create a kind of rhythm or cadence to the job that, again, makes the job easier to learn and remember.

The secret to the Job Instruction method and the reason it is so effective in getting learners to quickly remember to do jobs correctly, safely, and con-scientiously is the skillful way in which we break down the job into just the right amount of content between the Important Steps and Key Points. For example, if we focus the training on just the details of the job being learned, the learner will be overwhelmed by too much information. However, in our Job Instruction method, because we are learning the Key Points *step by step*, we have the learners remember the details two or three or four at a time for each Important Step. Here, it is important that the learners first remem-ber all the Important Steps so they can relate and connect the Key Points to each Important Step. In this way, they can retain a relatively large amount of detail in a short amount of time.

Nevertheless, big jobs or procedures may contain more content than a person can learn and retain in one sitting. Some jobs may actually take several hours or even days to perform. In these cases, we should break them up into smaller sections, or "teachable elements/units," and teach one segment at a time within the learner's ability to understand. For example, in a long procedure the instructor (or another experienced worker) should do most of the operation while having the learner try just the easiest part at first. After having mastered that segment, then the instructor can teach the second easiest unit and have the learner do that together with the first one. Continue in the same way until they can perform the complete operation. (More on this point in the next chapter.)

Observing and Involving Experienced Workers in the Breakdown Process

If supervisors know a job well, they can make breakdowns on their own. However, with the help of an experienced person, you will be able to build better breakdowns that everyone can follow. Getting experienced people involved in the breakdown process will provide invaluable information on how to do a job, as well as many insights into the best way of doing it. These people have spent incalculable amounts of time gaining wisdom and experience creating what we sometimes call "tribal knowledge." We should never fail to respect and value this "know-how" and indeed that is what we capture in JI when we find the "key points" to doing a job. You can perpetuate the real value of your organization's work by passing on these important skills to future generations of employees.

For example, when teaching a Job Instruction class with the St. Joseph Health System, we had one participant who was from the physical therapy department and he did his class demonstration on how to assist a patient to stand up. In breaking down this job, Paul, the person teaching the job, pointed out how the trick was to squat down in front of patients in wheelchairs as you speak to them so that you could look at them directly in the eyes at their level. "This gives the person confidence in you, looking you in the eye, so they can trust you when they try to stand up knowing you won't let them fall," Paul explained, giving the reason for this excellent Key Point. As he demonstrated how to help patients stand, having them place their hands on Paul's shoulders and going up together "on the count of three," the class noticed another Key Point that he had failed to mention. They pointed out how it looked as though Paul was assisting patients in standing up.

"No," Paul protested, "I want them to stand up completely on their own power."
"Then why did you place your hands on his hips?" they asked.
"Oh," Paul said, "I didn't realize I was doing that."

Paul went on to explain that it was not his intention to lift or even guide patients as they stood up, but simply to give them confidence that they could do it by themselves. By placing his hands gently on the patient's hips, he explained how this "touch" gave the patients confidence that nothing bad was going to happen because the therapist was "right there" if assistance was needed. The thing to notice here is how these tricks are done unconsciously by experienced workers who do them without thinking. The job of the good instructor, then, is to find these Key Points by observing and quizzing our experienced people.

When working with a team of JI trainers at Baptist Memorial Hospital in Memphis, we assembled 10 nurse trainers to break down together the job of Central Line Dressing Change in an effort to reduce CLABSIs (Central

Line-Associated Blood Stream Infection). In addition to these nurses who taught the job to all hospital staff, we also had in the room with us Dr JoAnn Wood who was leading Baptist's efforts to reduce hospital-acquired infections as well as various other subject matter experts whose specialty was infection control. In short, we had the hospital's leading experts and practitioners of this job. We spent over six hours breaking down the job together because, as it turned out, each of the 10 trainers taught the job differently and vigorously defended their own varying methods. For example, there were differing opinions as to whether *both* alcohol and CHG (chlorhexidine gluconate, a powerful cleaning product) were needed to clean the insertion site since both products kill germs. The decision of the experts was that both were needed in order to completely kill all germs, so we modified the breakdown to include two Important Steps—*Clean w/ alcohol* and *Disinfect w/ CHG*—to clearly distinguish both actions. This was different from our original breakdown which used only one Important Step here—*Clean the site* (see Figure 6.6).

The next day, one of the trainers said she had spoken that morning with an experienced nurse on her floor about the work we were doing. The veteran nurse told her the story of how "many years ago" when she had been trained with other new nurses on cleaning central line sites, they were told by their preceptor, "Alcohol is really good to get the goop off." What the new nurses took this to mean was that if the site was "goopy" then they were to use alcohol; if not, then no need for the alcohol. This kind of unclear training had a big effect that stayed with them for years to come. And by working with experienced practitioners on the breakdown work, we could glean many insights both for what to do and what not to do in a task.

It is not unusual for some employees to resist sharing their special techniques or tricks with others. They may do this for job security or simply because they put in the time it took to become experienced and believe others should do the same. This attitude may be especially true in the medical field where having unique, one-of-a-kind abilities can give a person the aura of a superhero or "rescuer." But, for organizations that want to improve, it is imperative to create a culture where employees act as team members and not like Lone Rangers riding in at the last minute to save the day, and the patient. If you honor the experience of your veteran employees, you can make them mentors for others. If this occurs in a way that does not threaten their job security or their status as expert practitioners, they will become useful partners in creating and improving organization standards while passing on their know-how to a new generation.

As we discussed in Section I of this book, good training gives us the opportunity to influence culture and change it from being one where employees must go through a "rite of passage" to become accepted members of the health care community to one of welcome, inclusion, and collaboration. For the expert workers contributing to the breakdown, this is a chance to honor their expertise allowing them to leave a legacy. It also honors the new workers by elevating their practice to that of a "seasoned" worker as quickly as possible. When we share our knowledge instead of hoarding it or rationing it, we focus on returning to our core mission of helping patients by enabling everyone to perform at the highest known level of practice.

Breakdown Sheets and Standardized Work

Learning to make breakdowns of jobs and putting this skill into use is a big step toward the greater goal of work standardization in health care, which we discussed in Section I. These Job Instruction breakdowns, however, should not be confused with Work Standards. Strictly speaking, Job Instruction breakdown sheets are well-considered notes for the trainer to use during the instruction process. They are a tool of the trainer. "Instruction sheets" or standard work forms, when available, can be used as references as you create your breakdown sheets for training. Usually, these forms are very detailed and describe "everything" about a job. Breakdown sheets for Job Instruction, on the other hand, give only the amount of information needed to "put across the job to the learner."

Even if you have instruction sheets or standard work forms, you should still *perform the jobs* when making breakdown sheets because doing so ensures that you are capturing just the right descriptive and simple words for the tasks. There is absolutely no substitute for actually going to the worksite and doing the job yourself to make sure you have the procedure down correctly. What is more, standard work forms usually miss many Key Points because they were written to describe the "what to do" and have overlooked the "how to do it" in a job or task. Therefore, we cannot depend solely on the written standards to guide us in making our breakdown sheets for instruction.

Once organizations learn JI training, they quickly realize that their "instruction sheets" for employees are too complicated. These documents typically have the steps, details, and reasons intermixed in long narrative descriptions. In most cases, to our dismay, they are not used or even read by the employees. We do not mean to imply that these documents are not useful—they certainly are. But they are not particularly useful *for training*. In good instruction, as embodied by the JI four-step method, both what is seen and what is heard make up the full extent of the training. Therefore, these breakdown sheets are designed with this specific purpose in mind. They are not a comprehensive written record of the job and you should not use them as such.

Keep in mind as well that just because we have two separate documents describing a job does not mean that we have two "standards" for doing the work. This is a common misunderstanding. It would be like looking at two drawings of the same house. One may be an isometric 3D rendering of what the home looks like from the outside, an image of what the house looks like in real life, whereas the other may be a schematic drawing of the inside details from three different angles—front, side, and top—that shows floor dimensions, room layouts, window and door locations, etc. Both drawings still represent the same house. In the same way, having another written description of the job does not mean we have another, different standard. Both documents describe the same standard process of doing the work, but from different points of view.

We cannot emphasize enough that the Job Instruction breakdown sheets do *not* replace detailed instruction documents, which are the proper references for both operators and supervisors to use to confirm details of the work (more on these tools in Chapter 12). They also may be used, for example, when regulators or auditors, or even vendors, come into a facility and need to confirm how certain tasks and procedures are being performed. Just because the names of the tools are similar doesn't mean they perform the same function. We need *both* types of documents and they should be used appropriately for the purposes they were designed to perform.

Training Soft Skills: Hourly Rounding to Prevent Patient Falls

Now that we have noted the many subtleties of making the Job Instruction breakdown sheet, let's take a look at an actual case study of how this breakdown skill was applied to a health care problem. This is a case where so-called "soft skills," that is, non-technical and interpersonal skills related to *how* one works and interacts with others like communication and empathy, were used and how the training method achieved outstanding results. Trainers mistakenly assume that we can only use the Job Instruction method for procedural-type jobs where something is physically done to a person or object. For example, they may think that this method *can* be used when we teach someone how to set up an IV or give an injection, but that it *cannot* be used when we, for example, teach someone to interview a patient to assess their needs. These "soft skills," which are not physical hands-on work, may seem, on the surface, to be too ambiguous or variable to be set down into a defined procedure, so we let people use their own wits and intuition to figure out how to get them done. The result is that there is never a standard method of doing them and we, therefore, can never seem to improve them when we run into problems. The following example shows how just one such "soft skill" problem was broken down for training to capture the real skill of doing the work.

One of the most persistent and costly hospital problems, in terms of actual dollars spent and amount of patient discomfort, is inpatient falls and all hospitals are trying to figure out ways to solve this problem. Costs involved with injuries incurred while in the hospital due to falls can be phenomenal and the safety of patients would be greatly enhanced if a way could be found to reduce them. What is more, an injury due to a fall in the hospital can be a major setback to the health and mobility, not to mention mortality, of an already frail or otherwise ill patient.

While traditional approaches have been to look at the patients' physical and mental state in relation to the falls—weakened bodily conditions, light headedness, tied to medical equipment, etc.—and to try and mitigate these conditions in order to prevent falls, the people at Virginia Mason looked at the problem from a different root cause. For the entire year of 2008, we took data on where the falls occurred and what the patients were doing when they fell. The largest situation, 32% of total falls, occurred when patients were trying to get to the bathroom. Of the 87 people who fell while toileting, 57% of these occurred as they ambulated to and from the bathroom and 43% of these patients fell off the toilet.

Nurses and hospital staff are always ready to assist patients in going to the bathroom. However, patients are reluctant to ask for help or overestimate their ability to self-ambulate. After getting their initial TWI training in the spring of 2009, the Job Instruction trainers at Virginia Mason felt we could tackle this problem by training staff to better approach the patients in a way that would make it easier for them to acknowledge this need and get help before a fall took place. But this kind of skill was different from the more routine jobs, like washing your hands or collecting a specimen, where there are actual hand motions and physical techniques. We questioned if the Job Instruction method could even be used here.

The group felt that these falls could be reduced by having staff make hourly rounds of the patients where we would ask them if they had to go to the bathroom and offer help if needed. Here, we felt we would have to appeal to the nurses' sense of being caregivers—to their "inner nurse" and the real reasons they came to this profession in the first place. However, we faced many obstacles from patients as well as nurses and assistant nurses. Patients typically were embarrassed to ask for help, even when offered, for this most private of needs. What is more, patients reported that they "did not want to bother the nursing staff who are already so busy."

Getting Patients to Ask for Help

First, we looked at how nurses approached patients and what we could say in offering help that would get an honest response. We felt that asking "How are you?" was such a colloquial question that the answer would almost always be a simple "I'm fine," no matter how poorly the patient might actually be feeling. We wanted a more therapeutic, clinical opening phrase and many in the group felt the key word should be "pain" as that would indicate something specific, and clinical, about the patient's condition: "Are you in any pain?" But not all patients hospitalized experience pain and most people might not consider having to go to the bathroom a kind of "pain." At that, someone threw out the word "comfort" as a way of greeting the patient, an "opening line" that conveyed concern for their well-being: "Are you comfortable?"

We weren't sure if "comfort" was the right word for the task, so, in order to come to a stronger conclusion, we had the group quiz a whole unit of about 25 patients what they thought about the word "comfort" and to write down what they heard. To our big surprise, we got an avalanche of responses and requests ranging from needing to go to the bathroom to how to order lunch to one person who said, "The social worker told me she would be back, but that was yesterday and I'm getting nervous about going home." The word "comfort" brought out so much more about what was really going on with the patients that we became convinced this was the approach we were looking for. The second Important Step to the breakdown, then, after the first step of knocking and announcing your entry, became, "Ask about comfort" (Figure 6.9).

JOB BREAKDOWN SHEET — HEALTH CARE

Task: Hourly Rounding

Supplies: (Patient Room)

Instruments & Equipment: Bed

Instructions before job demonstration:

1. HH before and after this job
2. How this differs from being in room often
3. 3 script choices for toileting

IMPORTANT STEPS	KEY POINTS	REASONS
A logical segment of the operation when something happens to advance the work	Anything in a step that might— 1. Make or break the job 2. Injure the worker 3. Make the work easier to do, i.e., "knack," "trick," special timing, bit of special information	Reasons for the key points
1. Enter	1. Knock 2. Announce	1. Courtesy 2. Prevent embarrassment
2. Ask about comfort		
3. Offer toileting	1. Assess mobility status 2. Select approach 3. Document elimination	1. Get help/assistant 2. Correct script 3. Care management
4. Items within reach	1. Call light 2. Table	1. In case of emergency 2. Easy access
5. Check bed setting	1. Low/locked 2. Alarm 3. Surface power—heel zone	Reduce skin breakdown and falls
6. Leave	1. Ask if anything else 2. Tell planned return 3. Initial grid	Help patient judge better when to call for help

Figure 6.9 Breakdown sheet for hourly rounding. (From P. Graupp and R. J. Wrona. 2011. *Implementing TWI: Creating and Managing a Skills-Based Culture*. Boca Raton, FL: Taylor & Francis Group/CRC Press. With permission.)

Next, when it came to actually offering patients assistance to the toilet, we felt that this had to be done tactfully so as to respect the person and maintain their dignity. In this way, we could mitigate the embarrassment around needing help to go to the bathroom. So, the group looked at why patients were hesitant to ask for help and we found we could categorize the level of functioning into three groups:

1. **Independent People**, who find themselves unexpectedly in the hospital with limited mobility and find it mortifying to need and ask for someone's help to go to the bathroom.
2. **Chronically Ill People**, such as people with cancer, who consider it a setback in their recovery to find themselves, again, in the hospital and, thus, deny the fact that they need help getting around in an attempt to prove that they are getting better.

3. **People with Loss of Faculties**, such as those with dementia, or those who are not in control of their bodily functions and, thus, not even aware of their need to go.

We felt that we would need specific and different strategies to address each of these groups and, thus, the Key Point here was to "Select approach" and take the right tact. We came up with phrases that we could use in each case and practiced giving these lines during the training sessions; they would be taught before the person was given instruction in the rounding. For the first group of independent people who felt shame in needing help to the bathroom, we would ask, "I want to measure your intake and output, so let me know when you go." For the second group of chronically ill patients who needed help, but were reluctant to ask, we would say, "It's been a few hours since you last went. Would you like to go now? I have time." And, for the final group of people who didn't know when they needed to go, we would say, "It's been two hours since you last used the bathroom, so let's go now." In this way, by determining which of the three approaches to use, we were able to maximize the effect of the rounding service.

One more line we found to be quite effective, after asking if the person needed help, was, "I can help you, I have time." Most patients tend to be very cognizant of the busy nature of the nurses' jobs and are afraid that their own personal needs are interrupting that routine. By letting the patients know that it is a good time to be asking for help, this further helped to eliminate the barriers to seeking out and getting that help. It also let them know that the staff was happy to assist and that there was no shame in needing this help.

Once the toileting is completed and documented, the next two steps in the Hourly Rounding process are to check "Items within reach," especially the call light so they can call for help if needed, and "Check bed setting" so that the bed is in the proper position to minimize the effects of a fall if they do try to get up. These two steps provide some backup against falls during the time between the rounding visits. While making this breakdown, we also kept in mind Lean concepts, such as flow in the work. Initially, the breakdown had checking the bed settings, which are located at the bottom of the bed, before tidying up the bedside table. However, as they walked through the job, we found that the flow of the work through the room would be shorter with no back tracking if we did the bed settings last, on the way to the door and out of the room. We were able, in this way, to teach the job in the most efficient way without any waste of time or walking and, by creating a natural flow of the work, the staff could feel the job was being done with simplicity and ease.

Finally, the Key Point to the sixth and final Important Step, "Leave," after asking if there is anything else they need, is to tell the patient when you plan to return: in 15 minutes with the next medication, in half an hour with a meal, etc. This innovation proved extremely effective because patients can judge whether they should put on the call light if they need to go or just wait until the nurse returns. As it turns out, patients agonize over whether they should call a busy nurse, even if they are in great pain. If they know when the nurse is going to be back, they can make a better choice of whether to wait or not hesitate to push the call button.

As you can see, the Key Points that the group garnered in this job were both subtle and difficult to describe. We had to think long and hard about just what technique would allow us to get the job done and make sure patients travel to and from the bathroom without falling and injuring themselves. While these Key Points did not deal with "feel" from the aspect of actually touching something, like the tightness of a fitting, they certainly did have everything to do with how people "feel" about embarrassing things like asking for help to the toilet. We had to teach nurses and staff just the right "touch" when it came to dealing with people around these delicate subjects. And, by finding the right Key Points, this could be accomplished.

We experienced the effect of having a good breakdown for training when we were following up on one nurse who wanted to show her skills at rounding. She was the charge nurse and we visited a man who was not her regular patient, so they did not know each other. The young nurse, polite and patient, asked him, "Are you comfortable?" to which the older gentleman just growled at her. "It's been a while since you've gone to the bathroom," she continued, "I have time to help you." He reluctantly went along with her and, after they returned, the nurse made sure everything was in reach and tidy on the bedside table and then checked the bed settings. "So, is there anything else you need?" she asked. He scowled. "I'll be back in an hour with your lunch," she told him. At this point the man, who had been grouchy and rude the entire time, turned to her and said in a low voice, "Well, it'll be nice to see you again." We found out what his real problem was, he was lonely. And that was information we could all act on.

"We're Too Busy to Do This"

When the JI team began teaching the Hourly Rounding routine to the staff, the first reaction we got was, "We're too busy to do this!" The staff certainly was busy with their already hectic work schedules. But we saw that they were *in* the patient rooms at least every hour already, so we wanted to work it into their routine versus adding it as a special trip. Thus, this job instruction needed a great deal of tact and skill to teach effectively. Having experienced the teaching of the rounding job while fine-tuning the breakdown and getting the procedure working the way we wanted it to, the team also perfected the way we would train it in order to overcome this resistance.

Instead of simply telling them when to perform the rounding work, we devised a process of "self-discovery" where we would let the skeptical nurses and nursing assistants find out for themselves when they could insert the routine into their work. We would ask them, "What are you doing already, like taking vital signs, delivering food, giving medications, and so on? How would you fit this into that routine?" For example, if you were already coming in to take the patient's vital signs, what would the sequence look like? Then we would let them actually practice it, walking through the routines in the empty room we were using for training to see what it would actually look like to perform the rounding steps as they did the work they were already doing. They would practice the job under different scenarios thinking it through thoroughly and that is when the light bulbs started going off.

For example, if a trainee was attempting to do a certain task while rounding, like checking vital signs, they might say, "I can put it between Steps 4 and 5."

"Try it out," their trainer would say to them.
"Well, it doesn't work real well there, does it?"
"What else could you do?"
"How about putting it between Steps 2 and 3?"

They would try that out and find that, in fact, they could perform the rounding tasks without adding significant time to the work they were already doing. But they had to discover that for themselves to be convinced that the procedure could be performed in an effective and efficient way. This experimentation was done during the training of the job at the end of Step 3 of the JI four-step method, the Tryout Performance. Once the person learned the standard method, then the trainer would ask them to do it one or two more times, integrating jobs they already did on a regular basis. The "amended" breakdown would look something like this:

1. Enter
   a. Knock
   b. Announce

2. Ask about comfort
3. OBTAIN VITAL SIGNS (the job already being performed)
4. Offer toileting
   a. Assess mobility
   b. Select approach
   c. Document
5. Items within reach
   a. Bedside table
   b. Call light
6. Check bed setting
   a. Locked/low
   b. Alarm
   c. Surface power/heel zone
7. Leave
   a. Ask if anything else
   b. Tell planned return
   c. Initial grid

Another adjustment we made, which was key to gaining their acceptance, was answering the question, "What if you are coming in to answer a call light?" The answer was to add this between Steps 1 and 2: "I see you have your light on, may I help you?" Once these immediate needs were met, they could then proceed through the remainder of the sequence as appropriate.

Right from the start of the training, the follow-ups the team performed began showing that we were getting strong reliability. In other words, the procedure was being performed regularly. One morning the team came in and heard that there had been a fall the night before on a unit they had trained. We were very concerned and went to investigate right away. Because the last step of the rounding process includes initialing the grid to show that the event has taken place, we went to the log to see if the rounding had been completed and, sure enough, there were two hours in the middle of the night where the patient had not been visited. That is precisely when the fall occurred. The team then began work on how we would arrange our work so that Hourly Rounding would be done reliably, every single hour. We rearranged the sequence of our work and inserted signaling so that we could achieve a higher degree of reliability.

In addition to preventing falls by helping people get to the toilet, this method, perfected through many trial runs and modifications, was able as well to provide the staff with much-needed and useful information from the patients. What is more, it improved the customer service and the overall image of the hospital to its patients. And this "soft skill," it turns out, could most certainly be taught and practiced using the JI method. The following list of "Top Soft Skills Employers Value"* shows, in italics, the many soft skills we were able to "engineer" into the job through good training.

Communication

Listening
Negotiating
Non-verbal communication
Persuasion
Public-speaking
Reading body language
Verbal communication
Writing skills
Story-telling

Teamwork

Collaboration
Empathy
Emotional intelligence
Networking
Team building
Influencing
Intercultural competence
Social skills
Self-awareness

Leadership

Conflict management
Decision-making
Facilitation
Inspiring people

---

* "Top Soft Skills Employers Value with Examples," www.httm/thebalancecareers.com, accessed Feb. 2, 2021.

Giving clear feedback
Mentoring
Dispute resolution
Deal-making
Delegation
Project management
Successful coaching

Positive Attitude

Confidence
Cooperation
Courtesy
Energy
Patience
Humor
Respectfulness
Friendliness
Honesty

Critical Thinking

Problem-solving
Flexibility
Adaptability
Resourcefulness
Tolerance of change and uncertainty
Troubleshooting

Work Ethic

Attentiveness
Dependability
Motivation
Persistence
Reliability
Resilience
Staying on the mark
Punctuality

Results-oriented
Following directions
Time management

Patient Falls Were Reduced

Before TWI was introduced to Virginia Mason, the effort to reduce falls using our Lean tools was put into practice and good results were obtained. This became an organization-wide initiative in 2007. The average number of patient falls per 1,000 patient days was 3.33 in 2006 and we were able to reduce this total to 3.04 and 3.10 in 2007 and 2008, respectively. More significant than the total number of falls, however, is the number of Falls with Injury—the ones that really count. This figure, as well, was reduced from 1.04 in 2006 to 0.77 in 2007 and 0.99 in 2008.

As we described in Chapter 3, the initial TWI training of 10 JI trainers was done in May 2009, but the pilot training of the Hourly Rounding job was not put into full production until July 2009 when 467 RNs and assistant nurses were trained over a nine-week period ending in the middle of September. Looking at Figure 6.10, we can see the number of patient falls

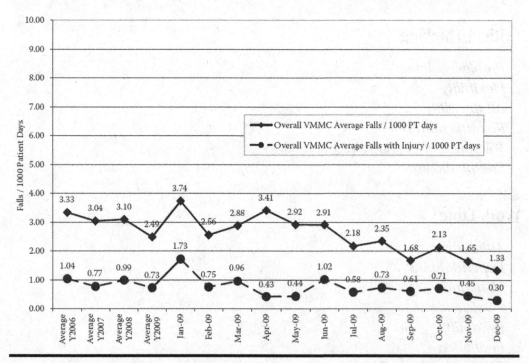

Figure 6.10 Falls and falls with injuries/1,000 patient days overall. (From Graupp and Wrona, 2011. With permission.)

on a month-by-month basis drop off dramatically beginning in July and hold steady, if not continue to fall lower. Even with just half a year of training results, the average for the entire year of 2009 went down to 2.49 patient falls per 1,000 patient days and 0.73 patient falls with injuries. For just the six-month period since July, the totals would be 1.89 and 0.56, respectively.

Patient falls were always considered inevitable at the hospital, one of those things that, in spite of our best efforts at prevention, would always be one of the "costs of doing business." However, inspired by these dramatic results from the pilot training using TWI Job Instruction, the people at Virginia Mason found a renewed commitment to get this number down to zero, something most had thought would "never happen in my lifetime," and this created a big shift in morale.

Chapter 7

How to Organize and Plan Training

Introduction

Chapter 6 covered the most difficult part of the "How to Get Ready to Instruct" items, *Break Down the Job*. This chapter examines the other three "Get Ready" points listed on the Job Instruction (JI) pocket card: *Make a Timetable for Training*, *Get Everything Ready*, and *Arrange the Worksite* (see Figure 6.1). These areas complete the preparation phase for training and it is here that we take the time to make sure we are training the right people on the right jobs and that we set a high standard for the work they will be learning. Supervisors often ignore or forget to apply these three points. Don't. Although they are easier to learn than *Break Down the Job*, they are just as important. Their proper use can mean the success or failure of your training effort.

As we saw in Section I, the need for good training in health care is great and supervisors encounter a multitude of problems when they fail to train their people and to train them well. There is always a lot of pressure to keep up with patient needs and there is never a shortage of important work that needs to be done every day. Under these conditions, many busy supervisors tend to see training as a problem or as something that someone else will do for them. When these attitudes are expressed in words, you hear:

We don't have the resources to provide good training.
New staff should be fully trained when they arrive.
Let them learn by watching others. That's the only way.

DOI: 10.4324/9781003035305-7

Such attitudes and statements are counterproductive. Good hospitals and health care facilities know that it is well worth the trouble and effort, in the long run, to arrange schedules to accommodate training in the same way they make plans for any other part of the business. That begins with making a Training Timetable so that training is well planned and executed.

Get Ready Point 1: Make a Timetable for Training

When you *Get Ready to Instruct*, the very first thing to do is to plan your training. *Make a Timetable for Training* means that you will do the training according to a plan and not by accident. More specifically, it means that you need to determine:

- *Who* should be trained?
- For *which job*?
- By *what date*?

Making plans on a regular basis helps to ensure that work proceeds smoothly, meeting demands and important deadlines. The same concept applies to training. It is very common to be caught unprepared thinking that we have enough trained personnel to cover for a person, say, who called in sick only to find ourselves scrambling to find someone to work overtime, someone who can rearrange their schedule, or some poor staff member who can deal with the situation trying to do the best she can with some hurried notes she took before the change of the shift. The purpose of planning is to avoid this kind of "firefighting." Many hospitals use a simple tool called the *Skills Map* as a loose planning guide. The Skills Map, however, is a static document that shows only who can do which job, whereas the *Training Timetable* is a dynamic document that guides and organizes your training effort. It is easy to make.

Figure 7.1 presents a partially finished Training Timetable. In the left-hand column of the grid is a list of jobs done in a department, in this case, an OR (operating room) team of neurology scrub nurses. The jobs, listed one by one, are *Gown and glove, Table setup, Draping patient, Sponge scan* (this is the new piece of equipment described in Chapter 4), *Case cart to Sterile Processing Department (SPD)*, and *Scrub craniotomy cases*. Similar lists can be created for other working environments or departments. In some cases, where everyone on a team is performing the same work, you can modify

Name: Sarah Jones Dept.: OR (Neuro Scrub RNs) Date: 1/05/xx	Breakdown No.	Smith	Lark	Morse	Taylor	Massy	Peters	Baker				Changes In Schedule
Gown & glove		✓	✓	✓	✓	✓	✓	✓				
Table setup		✓	✓	✓	✓	✓	✓					
Draping patient		✓	✓	✓	★	✓	✓	✓				
Sponge scan		✓	✓	✓	✓	✓						
Case cart to SPD		✓	✓	✓		✓	✓					
Scrub craniotomy cases		✓		✓								
Turnover Work Performance												

Figure 7.1   Job Instruction Training Timetable (partial).

your headings by listing classification, position, level of skill, type of equipment, or any other logical way of differentiating the skills required of the people doing the work. The critical question to ask is: *What makes one person's work different from the work of others?* In a billing office, for example, even though all of the people may be processing insurance forms, some may work exclusively on large company accounts while others may specialize in overdue accounts.

After listing the jobs, put all of the workers' names across the top of the grid in each column. The names can be listed alphabetically or organized to reflect workers' experience or seniority. Depending on the number of people in an area and the number of jobs, or whether you want the timetable to be laid out in landscape or portrait orientation, you can switch the axes and put the people's names down the left side and the job names across the top. Then check off all the jobs each worker can do, as shown in Figure 7.1. You will notice that all of the checkmarks are the same except for the star mark for Taylor's draping the patient. Jones, the supervisor making this timetable, used this mark to show that Taylor, although already trained on the draping job, was a bit slow and not working at the optimal skill level.

Not everyone in a working area necessarily needs to know how to do every job. You may, for example, consolidate the expertise in a few individuals because a skill is complex or infrequently used. The Training Timetable can show you how many people are able to perform the skill when it is needed. Knowing that you always need, say, two nurses who can scrub craniotomy cases, a difficult and irregular job, will allow you to be sure you have that area well covered while not training too many people who will ultimately lose the skill because it is not used regularly. You can note the ideal number of people, if appropriate, on the timetable.

The completed Training Timetable (Figure 7.2) illustrates that Jones then reviewed the timetable to see if there were any urgent training needs in her department. First, she looked for possible *turnover* due to retirement, promotions, transfers, etc. She knew that Morse was scheduled to retire at the end of February and made a note, "*Scheduled to retire on 2/28*," at the bottom of the timetable in the column under Morse's name. She then reviewed the list of names from the perspective of *poor performance* (e.g., errors, injuries, damage to equipment, etc.). As the timetable shows, Jones felt that the performance of all her people was satisfactory except for Taylor's patient draping skill. At the bottom of the grid, under Taylor's name, she wrote, "*Needs more training.*"

Finally, Jones reviewed the job headings from the perspective of *changes in schedule*, considering how she was meeting the current operating

Name: Sarah Jones Dept.: OR (Neuro Scrub RNs) Date: 1/05/xx	Breakdown No.	Smith	Lark	Morse	Taylor	Massy	Peters	Baker				Changes In Schedule
Gown & glove		✓	✓	✓	✓	✓	✓	✓				
Table setup		✓	✓	✓	✓	✓	✓	2/21				Need one more worker at beginning of March
Draping patient		✓	✓	✓	★ 1/28	✓	✓	✓				
Sponge scan		✓	✓	✓	✓	✓						
Case cart to SPD		✓	✓	✓		✓	✓					
Scrub craniotomy cases		✓	2/7	✓		2/14						Need one more worker at beginning of March
Turnover **Work Performance**				Scheduled to retire on 2/28	Needs more training							

Figure 7.2 Job Instruction Training Timetable (complete).

schedule in all of the jobs and whether there might be any upcoming increases in the operating schedule. Then she learned that a rotation of new surgeons was coming at the beginning of March that would require an additional nurse to scrub craniotomy cases. In that case, she thought, one more worker would be required to do table setup so that a more experienced person could be available to scrub craniotomy cases. Jones noted, *"Need 1 more worker at beginning of March,"* in both timetable rows for table setup and scrub craniotomy cases. The notations highlighted for Jones the three issues that would require urgent training: Morse's retirement, Taylor's patient draping, and the anticipated need for additional people to do table setup and scrub craniotomy cases.

Jones was now ready to make plans to meet these training needs. Specifically, she needed to consider *who* was to be trained on *which job* and by *what date*. With Morse's retirement, she would be short one person to scrub craniotomy cases. She decided that Lark was the most suitable person to scrub craniotomy cases and she will be trained by *February 7*, as shown in Figure 7.2. Lark's training was to be completed on or around this date. Because this was a specialized procedure and one that was not performed regularly, that would give Lark plenty of time to practice and ask questions before Morse left the hospital. Then the department would be prepared when Morse retired at the end of February.

Next, Jones addressed the problem of the time it takes Taylor to drape patients. Because Taylor was already skilled enough to do the job partially, Jones determined that she would need only a few days to prepare for the training—to make a breakdown for the job and schedule time with Taylor. She scheduled Taylor's training for *January 28*.

Finally, to prepare for the rotation of new surgeons, Jones selected Baker as the most suitable person to do table setup. Because Baker was the newest person on her team, she thought this would help him expand his skills in the OR at a time when it was needed, at the beginning of March. Jones did not want to do the training too early, knowing that people trained too soon will forget what they have learned before they have a chance to perform the work. On the other hand, she did not want to wait until the last minute, in case Baker needed more time to learn the job. After weighing these issues, she set *February 21* as the date to complete the training.

Then, with this help, Jones felt that Massey could learn to scrub craniotomy cases. She was the next most experienced person of all those remaining in the group and would be capable of learning this job. Jones would have Massey trained by *February 14*, after completing the same training with Lark. As with Lark, this would give Massey time to practice and ask questions and she will have been trained before the new surgeons arrive, so the rotation will go smoothly.

Using this kind of Training Timetable grid may seem simplistic, but it is amazing how simple practices like this can create real order and discipline in a department. It also can help you flush out hidden problems and avoid them down the line. At this point, the timetable is basically complete. All that remains is to put in the breakdown number for each breakdown. For this number, you must first break down a job that requires training, number that breakdown sheet, and then put that number into the column headed *Breakdown No.* The first thing to do is break down the job of draping patients because it requires training by January 28. Once the breakdown number is entered on the grid the breakdown sheet can easily be retrieved when it is time to train Taylor on that job. The next step is to break down the job of scrubbing craniotomy cases, as that training schedule is coming up soon. The same is true for the table setup process.

The model presented above is invaluable and can be replicated for any department. The procedure for making a Training Timetable includes:

1. Fill in the supervisor's name, department, and date
2. Put in the job headings down the left side column
3. Put in the staff names across the top (axes may be switched for Steps 2 and 3)
4. Check off the jobs that can be done by each person
5. Look for urgent training needs
   a. By worker: Turnover, Poor performance
   b. By job heading: Meeting present schedules and quotas, Contemplated schedule increases
6. Plan to meet these needs
   a. Who to train
   b. On which job
   c. By what date

The Training Timetable is an invaluable way to bring the needed skillsets of the department into visual management and shows, at a glance, what skills are available at any given time according to who is on the job and what each of them can do. Using this tool, any shift supervisor can manage the skills of his or her work team ensuring that proper training is given and there are no "gaps" in needed capabilities at any time. It is also a great way to engage teams in the critical skillsets needed to efficiently manage their departments. Seeing gaps on the Training Timetable posted on the department's huddle board is a great way for leaders to identify needs in advance and to get support for needed training to take place.

Many companies and organizations that have implemented TWI Job Instruction have improved on the usage and application of the Training Timetable. Instead of using just a checkmark in the grid for each job a person is able to do, for example, companies like Toyota use different symbols to represent the different levels of knowledge and experience a person has in a particular job. The simplest level, represented by a circle that has only one quarter of its center filled in, means that the person is currently in training while half of the circle filled in means they can just perform the job. Three quarters filled in means they are proficient in the job, while the highest level, a completely filled-in black circle, means that the person not only has great skill and experience in the job but also has enough ability to teach that job to others.

Application of Training Timetables

At its most basic level, the Training Timetable is a simple "skills matrix" showing who can do what, but it can be so much more when used as a planning tool for making sure we always have capable people ready to handle the jobs that need to be done. A nursing department manager was overheard saying, "I'm worried because I don't have any heart nurses for this weekend." "What are you going to do if you need one?" we asked. She didn't have an answer but continued looking worried. In a different situation, a patient came into the ED with a bad pacemaker and none of the nurses on shift that day knew how to deal with it because it was a rare problem they had never seen before. The ED manager, who herself had not done the procedure in over 10 years, was forced to deal with it because no one else was available. What comes into play here happens far too often in health care.

Developing the working skills of our people is the vital role of Job Instruction and is effectively managed using the Training Timetable. Here we can quickly and effectively find our urgent training needs and then apply good job instruction to fill those gaps by determining who we need to train, for which job, and by what date. In Chapter 1 we spoke about the alignment of frontline work to prevent CLABSIs and CAUTIs (catheter-associated urinary tract infections), in-hospital infections caused through poor care of central lines and catheters. We saw how success in training would directly lead to reaching hospital-wide goals of reducing infection rates. Once we have determined that training can standardize procedures like Central Line Dressing Change and Catheter Care, which will reduce the variation in these procedures that can allow infections to set in, we set up the Training Timetable to plan and direct the successful training delivery. Figure 7.3 shows the Training Timetable for an ICU unit training these jobs along with a few other jobs directly connected to infection control.

A critical aspect of good Job Instruction is the follow-up process that ensures operators and staff are performing jobs to the standard taught in the training. We saw in Chapter 3, the Hand Hygiene Training Case Study, how trainers at Virginia Mason would conduct follow-ups after the initial training where they could view the job being done in the actual flow of work to ensure the new method was being adhered to (see Figure 3.6). Even though learners have shown, in the JI instruction, that they can perform a specific task following the standard and know the reasons why they have to do it that way, it is human nature to fall back on old habits. Embedded in the JI method is a series of repetitions of doing the work, performed by the learner during the Job Instruction process, to help create the new habit, but

JOB INSTRUCTION TRAINING TIMETABLE

Name: Debbie Jones Dept.: ICU Date: March 23, 2018	Breakdown No.	Donna G.	Mary K.	Billy B.	Sarah L.	Janie S.	Joe T.	Bobbie K.				Changes In Schedule
Hand hygiene – soap & water	001	✓	✓	✓	✓	✓	★	✓				
Hand hygiene – gel	002	✓	✓	✓	✓	✓	★	✓				
Scrub the hub	003	✓	✓	✓	✓	✓	✓					
Central line dressing change	004	✓	✓	✓	3/28	3/28	3/30	4/3				Updated procedure
Replace stat-lock	005	✓	✓	✓	★	✓	✓					
Catheter care	006	✓	4/5	4/10	✓	4/5	4/10	4/12				Updated procedure
Changing connectors	007	✓	✓									Testing new procedure
Turnover **Work Performance**					Struggles with stat-lock change		Needs refresher H.H. training	New staff member				

Figure 7.3 **Training Timetable for ICU Jobs Around Infection Control. (From P. Graupp, S. Steward, and B. Parsons. 2020.** *Creating an Effective Management System: Integrating Policy Deployment, TWI, and Kata.* **New York, NY: Taylor & Francis Group. With permission.)**

inevitably it takes time after the person begins to perform the job on their own for the pattern to be fully ingrained, to be "hard wired."

Many organizations have modified their Training Timetables to assist in this follow-up process by using them like a control sheet for job audits and process confirmation. The timetable will show not only the date that the training takes place but also the dates, and perhaps results, of the follow-up checks to determine when the person is "signed-off" on being fully capable of doing the job. Figure 7.4 shows an example of a Training Timetable for just one job, Foley Insertion, the most common type of urinary catheter, and you can see that after the initial training for each nurse was completed, a *verification* was made in the next week to a month to ensure the trained nurse was correctly and consistently using the method. Then, the trainer performed quarterly *validations* to make sure the nurses had not fallen back on their old ways or changed the standard.

Another common issue that comes up with training is when jobs are only rarely, if ever, performed. This was the case we saw above when the ED manager had to deal with a failing pacemaker, not a regular occurrence but something that can happen. For rare diseases, like Ebola, while we probably will never see a case, we must nevertheless be prepared for it, especially if your hospital is picked as the designated treatment site in your city. In a hospital or office, there are rare times when machinery breaks down (e.g., paper jams in the copy machine) and we would be better served fixing it ourselves rather than waiting for the maintenance crew to show up. Or there may be special procedures or special requests in health care that are both rare and small in number but must still be attended to.

A good use of the Training Timetable would be to keep track of when employees have had the opportunity to perform these rare or infrequent procedures so that we can then provide timely training using the Job Instruction method of repetition and practice. For example, if we think a person should perform a certain task at least once in a three-month period to retain proficiency, then we would give them refresher training if they have gone for three months without doing it. Our Training Timetable can keep a track of that work activity. And because the Job Instruction method includes the learner performing the job several times, we can use the training method as a means of getting "hands-on" practice for a task that, by definition, only rarely comes around.

Good hospitals have "training lab" facilities equipped with expensive training equipment like mannequins that talk, breathe, and bleed. But are these facilities being utilized optimally for training other than basic skills?

TWI Training Schedule

JIB:	Foley Insertion
Unit:	ICU
Trainer:	Joyce Bing (JB)

Skill Level

Level 1 - NOVICE: Beginning Level of Skill
Level 2 - ADVANCED BEGINNER: Moderate Level of Skill Development
Level 3 - COMPETENT: High Level of Skill Development
Level 4 - PROFICIENT: Meets Level 3 and can train others

				Verification		Validation Quarter 1		Validation Quarter 2	Q1 Level	Q2 Level	Validation Quarter 3	Q3 Level
Date of Training	Staff Name	Initial Train Time	Trainer	Level								
4/18/2017	Judy Nurse	45 min	JB	2		7/1/2017 JB	2	9/26/17 JB	3	1/5/18 JB	3
4/21/2017	Samuel Parker	32 min	Jackie Parton	3		7/2/2017 JB	2	9/26/17 JB	2	1/6/18 JB	3
4/24/2017	Dianne Jackson	43 min	JB	1		7/6/2017 JB	2	10/1/17 JB	2	1/10/18 JB	3
4/28/2017	Sarah Brown	38 min	JB	2		7/24/2017 Jackie P	3	10/6/17 Jackie P	3	1/18/18 JB	2
4/30/2017	Jodie Crown	48 min	JB	1		7/25/2018 JB	2	10/9/17 JB	2	1/19/18 JB	2
5/2/2017	Laura Sanders	41 min	JB	1		7/25/2018 JB	1	10/21/18 JB	2	1/25/18 JB	2
5/3/2017	Theresa Needles	37 min	Jackie Parton	3		8/1/2017 JB	3	11/1/17 JB	3	1/31/18 Jackie P	3

Figure 7.4 Training Timetable with Quarterly Validation and Skill Level Grading. (From Graupp et al. 2020. With permission.)

We recommend using these facilities much more frequently and on a regular basis for training experienced workers on jobs that are done rarely so that their skills are fresh when they are called upon to do them.

Get Ready Points 3 and 4: Get Everything Ready and Arrange the Worksite

The final two points on the *How to Get Ready to Instruct* side of the card are *Get Everything Ready* and *Arrange the Worksite*. Because these two points are self-explanatory, supervisors often overlook them. You may feel that you cannot take the time to attend to these points of the JI process, but not doing so can jeopardize successful training with the JI four-step method. Once you understand their importance, you will always remember to do them and do them well.

Getting everything ready to instruct means that you assemble all the proper things that aid the instruction and have them on hand. At the top of the Breakdown Sheet is a space to list all of the supplies, instruments, and equipment needed to complete the job. Use this as your guide to make sure you have not forgotten anything before you instruct. You don't want to end up halfway through teaching a job and then realize that you do not have the proper clamp to complete the job correctly. Telling the learner, "Oh, just pretend this paper clip is the clamp and I'll bring you the correct one later," shows poor preparedness and sets a poor standard. The learner will not see the actual work being done with the proper equipment and will be left with the impression that you don't think the job is important enough to take the time to prepare properly for the training. Furthermore, the learner may feel that if it was not important enough for the trainer to bring the right instrument, then it must not be that important to use that exact instrument in any exact way.

Arranging the worksite means arranging the work area neatly, just as you would expect to find it during actual working conditions. First impressions last, and a positive first impression of the workplace will set a good example for the worker to maintain. Neatness will promote a high standard of work as well because there will be no extraneous materials that might distract from or interrupt the work. It does not take long for a supply cabinet to become cluttered and disorganized or for a desk to become piled with papers. Set a high standard right from the start by arranging the worksite and cleaning up this clutter *before* the new person comes to learn the job.

Supervisors should never be too busy to set a good example for people in their departments. Setting a good example is what supervisors and instructors should be doing as a regular part of their daily responsibilities. As members of the organization's management, you are models of the hospital's standards, ideals, and culture. Teaching a person a new job is the ideal time to begin setting that good example.

Training Large Jobs: Divide Them into Teaching Units

One of the concerns we hear with Job Instruction is that it is just fine for simple jobs that take only a few minutes or less to complete, but is not suitable for many jobs that are more complex and take a long time to finish. These kinds of jobs contain so many items that they simply cannot be taught all at once or even in one sitting. However, the truth is that these are just the kinds of situations where correct instruction is *most* important because both learners and instructors tend to get confused and "lost" when a job has an overwhelming amount of detail. The answer is to break up the long job into smaller units and, using the JI four-step method, teach it one segment at a time within the limits of the learner's ability to understand and remember at one time.

One of our caution points in the four-step method is *Don't give a person more information than they can master at one time*. This also applies to the total amount of work you can teach at one time. Consider the example of giving an injection, which is an important procedure that takes skill and attention. Many things go into doing this job. Here we can divide them into four units:

Unit 1: Preparation of materials and supplies
Unit 2: Prepping patient for injection
Unit 3: Administering injection
Unit 4: Difficult situations (e.g., small veins)

Here, we would only have to do Step 1, *Prepare the Worker*, and Step 4, *Follow-up*, once each, as these steps will cover the same ground for all of the four units. However, what is different is that we will do Steps 2 and 3, *Present the Operation* and *Tryout Performance*, independently for each of the units. That means that there will be a different breakdown sheet for each unit and the learner will not proceed to the next unit until he or she masters the unit before. When we master one skill at a time, instead of everything at once, we learn more quickly and avoid mistakes and accidents.

For a long operation that cannot be stopped in the middle, the instructor can still break it up into smaller units but will have to do most of the operation himself or herself, or get another experienced person to help out, while the learner is instructed in each unit. It is a good idea to teach learners the easiest parts of the job first, so they can pick it up quickly. Then teach the more difficult units, one by one, while you (or another person) continue to complete the other untaught units until the learner can do the entire job without assistance. This may seem to take a lot of time, but how much *more* time would it take the same person to learn the entire job all at once, and how many problems would occur while they struggled learning it?

Many complex jobs share common elements, such as putting on protective equipment or setting up a sterile field. By learning each of these jobs first, you learn *the building blocks* to the complex job and these more difficult jobs become easier to learn because the common elements are already known and well rehearsed. For example, some common building blocks to many procedures would include:

■ Hand hygiene
■ Donning sterile gloves
■ Setting up a sterile field
■ Patient ID validation
■ Labeling a specimen
■ Site (skin) preparation
■ Labeling medication
■ Labeling samples

If we were teaching thoracentesis, paracentesis, knee arthrocentesis, or lumbar puncture (all procedures that remove fluid from the body, each from a unique site), each of these procedures would require knowledge of all of the aforementioned jobs. When students come into the learning lab already knowing all of these, the instructor can concentrate on the remaining, differentiating elements of each procedure and focus on the actual removal of the fluid.

By listing all of the required basic skills, we can then begin planning our training to be sure that all the needed skills are properly taught in the right sequence. Figure 7.5 shows a timetable version of a Safety Curriculum Skills Map for a variety of different positions in a hospital. Notice that these

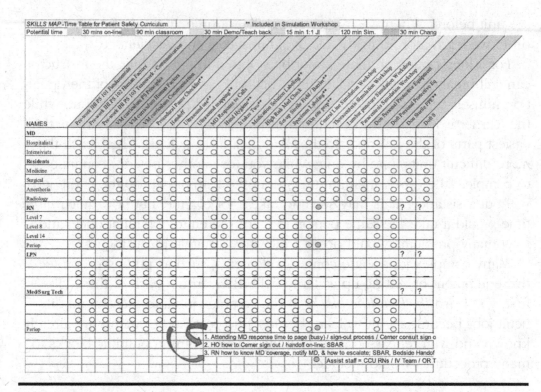

Figure 7.5 Timetable for Patient Safety Curriculum. (2011 Virginia Mason Medical Center. All rights reserved.)

skills are taught using different techniques, Job Instruction being one of them. Depending on the content of the training, we select the best way of learning it.

When, and When Not, to Use Job Instruction

As we saw displayed in Figure 7.5, not all jobs can or should be taught using the JI four-step method of instruction. To begin with, some problems can be solved better by simply improving, or automating, the method for how the job is performed, thus eliminating the need to teach someone how to perform an inherently difficult procedure. In other instances, we can create a "mistake proof" procedure so that it can be done correctly and safely without the need for detailed instruction. More than that, though, we need to remember that the JI method is just one of many styles and types of training and it should be used appropriately. Specifically, the JI method is *one-on-one skills training* where the learner is being asked to perform a defined task that takes practice to learn.

In many tasks and procedures, there is a great deal of knowledge that has to be obtained before we can begin actually doing the work. For example, before you can learn how to give injections or set up IVs, you need to know some basic things about the circulatory system and how medication is delivered intravenously. These things can best be learned in a classroom setting with many people present or by reading books or perhaps in an online class, and learners can even be given a test at the end to see if they have retained the content. You would not, however, want to be learning these things "on the job" while actually sticking someone with a needle. We need to separate, then, the learning of *knowledge* and the learning of *skills*. While knowledge can be learned in a classroom, skills must be learned through practice and repetition and the JI method of instruction is set up to teach just these kinds of skills.

The question oftentimes comes up whether we can teach groups of people using the JI method. Our definition of good job instruction is "The way to get *a* person to quickly remember to do *a* job." This means that we are teaching *one* job to *one* person at a time. While it may seem, at first glance, to be more "efficient" to train people together in a group when they are all learning the same job, the reality is that, in total, it takes longer. When we attempt to group train skills, we cannot adjust the training to fit each person's unique background and experience and we cannot confirm that each individual in the group can actually remember how to do the job correctly, safely, and conscientiously. When members of the group go on and fail at the job, the time it takes to retrain them and correct the problems caused by their mistakes will inevitably be greater than the time "saved" by group training. That is why the JI method must be practiced one on one.

The Job Instruction method is designed to be used "on the job," which means that learners are actually performing real work even as they go through the steps of learning the job. However, in many cases, especially when the job is performed on a patient's body, we would not want to practice and perfect our skill on a live person. So, we will simulate the work using, for example, a special mannequin or even a piece of fruit instead of real muscle tissue when learning to give an injection. This kind of "offline" training has the advantage of being able to make mistakes without incurring disastrous consequences. Remember that in the JI method we said that we should "correct errors" and never allow the learner to do it incorrectly as this creates bad habits. When you are working on real patients, this is certainly true. However, learning from our mistakes *can be* a good method

Authors: Deborah Kelly, MN, RN & Martha Purrier MN, RN AOCN

Steps	Tools	IDENTIFYING TRAINING NEEDS AND METHODS Outcome
1. Understand the process	• Ask "Why?" five times • Paredo the issues • Fishbone diagram • Observation • Quality data/metrics	May require multiple corrective strategies beyond training → SS, Mistake Proof, Set up Reduction, SW/SP, Training
2. Understand the gap	Separate Out Tool "Can't Do" vs. "Won't Do" vs. "Too Difficult to Do"	Training Issue → USE TWI JOB INSTRUCTION Leadership Culture HR Issue → USE TWI JOB RELATIONS Improvement Issue → USE TWI JOB METHODS
3. Identify Training Issue	Determine reliability of knowledge/skill **Low (Passive):** HLC, Article, Share/Inform, Data **Medium:** Case study, Exemplar **High (Active):** Return Demonstration	High need for reliability/skills with active learning methods = *Instructor required • Job Instruction • Lab/simulation • Role play • Validation/verification of performance *Need for Clinical Education expertise, use of adult learning principles

4. Determine Return Demonstration set up	1. How many people? (Person, Unit, Multiple Units, Organization)
	2. Cycle time of training and follow up?
	  a. Short < 20 min.
	  b. Long > 20 min
	3. What equipment/set up is needed?
	  a. Lab vs. Nearly anywhere
	(Use SWS, Time table, LTO, TAKT time calculation)
		→ Determines size of training team
		→ Determines off-line vs. on-line
		→ Determines location (lab vs. on-line in work area)

5. Evaluate results (Did you solve the problem?)	Refer to Step 1 data and review/re-measure/re-observe	Report results

Figure 7.6 Identifying training needs and methods. (2011 Virginia Mason Medical Center. All rights reserved.)

of instruction when it is done, as with simulations and role plays, in a safe environment where no one will get hurt.

The key, here, is to determine which method of training—JI one-on-one training, classroom training, simulations, role playing, etc.—is most appropriate for what you want to teach. Figure 7.6 shows a model that was developed to help determine which training methods would fit with which training needs. It begins by analyzing and understanding the process to determine, first of all, if training and creating standard work is what is needed to correct the problem. A common "rookie error" is to think that we need standard work and, thus, a Job Instruction breakdown for every single job. When we need reliability, when there is a need to do the job the same way, every time, for every patient, when there is a quality or safety outcome, then, yes, we need standard work and training. But, we also may find from our analysis that there are other strategies of correcting the problem beyond training, such as improving the process.

Once it is determined that it is a training issue, the next step is to decide whether the problem may be, in fact, a personal problem where what the person needs is good leadership and guidance to create motivation for doing the work. In other words, if the person is not motivated to do the job, all the good training in the world may not get him or her to do it correctly. So, this issue must be addressed before you move on to the training. The Job Relations component of TWI is an effective method that helps get people to cooperate in the work and is critical for success in creating and sustaining standard work. (Section III takes up the JR method.)

Now that we are ready to move on to the training, the next thing is to prioritize the issue so that we don't throw large quantities of resources at minor issues. If the reliability we need to have around a certain task is low, in other words, it is a *passive* knowledge or skill that is not engaged on a regular basis, we could simply have people read articles or share the information with them at regular meetings. We could ramp up this information exchange to include case studies and other examples if there was more need for it. If, though, we needed to have high reliability around certain *active* skills that must be performed correctly and safely on a regular basis, then we should devote time and effort to more interactive training methods. In particular, having learners demonstrate that they can perform the duties is critical to ensuring a successful training process. The final step, then, is to plan the training determining which type of training to use, how long the training will take, how many trainers will be needed to cover all the learners, whether it should be done online or offline, and what equipment or workplace setups will be needed.

JOB RELATIONS TRAINING

Chapter 8

Four Steps of Job Relations

Introduction

In Section II we reviewed in detail TWI's Job Instruction method of getting people to quickly remember to do jobs correctly, safely, and conscientiously. In carrying out this powerful method of instruction, we said that we must believe, "If the worker hasn't learned, the instructor hasn't taught." It is not unusual, however, for supervisors and others who are in charge of directing the work of others to protest, somewhat forcefully, "No, you can't put that on me. You don't know the people I have to supervise!" After a little discussion they will oftentimes admit, "Even if I had a good instruction method, they still wouldn't listen to me." That may be true. But this is not a failure of instruction; it is a failure of leadership.

Whereas TWI addressed the need for skill in instructing with the Job Instruction method, there is another module which addresses the need for skill in leading called Job Relations. In Job Relations, TWI clarifies that a leader is a person with followers. If people are not following your instructions, then we cannot say you are a leader. So it goes without saying that we need leadership skill if we want to successfully train people—they have to *follow* our instructions. In order to have good supervision of standard work we need to develop leadership skill.

DOI: 10.4324/9781003035305-8

What Is "Good Supervision?"

There are many models, programs, and "how to" books that define good supervision. However, when dealing with people, there is never an easy fix or secret formula to success. The Job Relations method, like all of the TWI programs, goes back to basic principles learned and passed down to us by countless generations of good supervisors. It is in their experience and knowledge that the real wisdom of working with people lies. To appreciate the value of this, you need to remember just one thing: Social norms and technology change; human nature does not.

The TWI founders developed the following paradigm of good supervision: *Good supervision means that the supervisor gets the people in the department to do **what** the supervisor needs done, **when** it should be done, and the way the supervisor needs it done, because **they** what to do it.* In other words, as a member of the organization's management team, the supervisor knows the demands being placed on the organization—what procedures are due and by when— and must divide and delegate the work in order to meet these demands. Moreover, the supervisor must see to it that the work is done according to standards that ensure the work is done in a way that meets patient expectations in terms of performance, quality, safety, accuracy, etc. By far the most difficult task for a supervisor is motivating people to do that work in a way that makes them want to accomplish the *what*, *when*, and *how* of the work.

How do we get people to work "because they want to do it"? The essence of leadership is to get people to take charge or ownership of the requirements of their work so that it becomes a source of pride in their own doing. A leader is a person who has followers, not simply a "boss" who issues orders. By definition, the act of following implies a certain amount of free will and people who work under this boss-style are not being led, they are simply being told what to do. And they instinctively dislike "the boss" who treats them this way. Being the "boss" does not invite dedication or cooperation so true leaders get their people to understand the importance of their work and motivate them to do the work by making it their own and something "they want to do."

To meet all of their responsibilities successfully, not the least of which is developing and maintaining standard work practices, a supervisor must have a relationship of some kind with each of his or her people. When you look carefully at this relationship, it is by no means a one-way street. It is a two-way relationship that affects the kinds of results you will get when striving to meet your responsibilities. Good relationships will give you good results. Poor relationships will give you poor results. When you experience difficulties with people or when trust is strained, relationships will be adversely affected, a signal that you need to deal with a situation. When trust is high, people give you the benefit of the doubt because they feel you have their best interests in mind and they believe you will do right by them—that you will *lead* them to a better place. When that trust is missing, however, you will find yourself "drowning in a puddle," struggling over the most minor details and unable to move forward on even simple issues. The goal, then, is to keep job relations with our people as straight, strong, and correct as possible.

What Is a Problem and How Do You Solve It?

A problem is *anything the supervisor has to take action on* when not doing so will have a negative impact or influence on the overall results of the organization. Keeping job relations straight, strong, and correct is critical here because it is often "people problems" that get in the way of the supervisor's efforts to produce good results. Often it is hard to define just what the problem is. Because people are at the center, it may not be easy to understand or to fix.

When asked what problems they have had with people in their departments, supervisors never find it difficult to compile a long list. The list provided here is typical:

- An employee loses interest in the job
- A person continually fails to come to work on time
- A person wants to change jobs all the time
- Hospital safety regulations are not followed
- A drop off in an individual's output
- Friction between shifts
- Arguments between individuals
- New workers do not get along with long-term employees
- A person who is lazy and goofs off on the job
- Prospective change in hours is apt to cause trouble
- A person doesn't follow orders
- A couple who has broken up but still work together don't get along
- A person's poor personal hygiene angers co-workers

These are real issues that surface on a regular basis. To resolve any of these problems and to continue meeting his or her responsibilities, a supervisor needs to understand individuals, size up situations, and work with people to resolve them. All supervisors need to have or develop the skill to do this and this is at the core of effective leadership skill.

Handling a Problem

There are good ways and bad ways to handle people problems. The example below provides some useful insights.

The Joe Smith Problem

A hospital was building a new wing and created a project team of staff members from each department to help design it. One of the team members was Joe Smith, a nurse who was in charge of oncology. Joe loved the job and was a highly motivated worker.

Some time ago, Joe began to frequently skip the weekly Tuesday meetings of the project team and his absence from the meetings had a bad effect on the team's atmosphere. The team leader had spoken to Joe about it several times but Joe said, "I'm doing what I'm assigned to do. Isn't that enough?" The team leader tried to appeal to Joe's loyalty but saw that he did not get anywhere.

Then the project started getting into the oncology areas that were Joe's specialty and Joe began attending all the meetings. The team leader thought that since Joe was in charge of those areas, and was quite outspoken about the accomplishments and needs of his department, that's why he came to the meetings regularly. Joe kept up the good record for several weeks.

Then, just when the oncology work was coming to an end, Joe was absent from the next meeting. The team leader decided that Joe's absence was because the work he was in charge of had fallen off. He decided that he no longer wanted Joe on the team. When Joe showed up at the next meeting, the team leader called out, "Hey Joe, we don't need you in our meetings anymore. I talked to my boss and we took you off the team. You should know why it's important to be at all the meetings."

This team leader certainly had a problem. How do you think he handled it? What was the team leader trying to accomplish? What did he want out of Joe? It's pretty clear he wanted Joe to come to the meetings regularly. Instead, he kicked him off the team!

The team leader made no attempt to find out why Joe didn't come to the meeting that particular day. He jumped to the conclusion that Joe, in spite of the special skills he brought to the team, was after all just an irresponsible person who thought only about the needs of his own department and nothing for the whole team. He thought that Joe only cared about the things he could boast about. Another important factor the team leader did not take into consideration is the effect his disciplinary action had on the other team members. What do you think their reaction was to Joe's supervisor's action? ("Wow, can you believe what happened to Joe?!")

Here's what happened next:

The Joe Smith Problem (contd.)

The team leader kicked Joe off the project team. A few days later, at lunch, another supervisor came up to him and said he'd heard he had been pretty hard on Joe Smith. Joe's father had been hurt in an accident the previous Monday night. Joe had left word with the receptionist that he would be out the next day, but the receptionist forgot to tell the team leader. When Joe came to the next meeting, he didn't know that the team leader hadn't heard about what had happened.

Do these additional facts throw more light on the situation? Joe had a good record for a while, but the team leader had decided that the drop off in oncology work was the reason for his not coming to the meeting. But Joe's failure to come to the meeting had been for a good reason. And he thought the team leader had been notified. Let's consider the consequences of the team leader's actions from three angles.

1. *How does Joe feel toward the team leader?* Without a doubt, Joe is bitter about being punished for behavior that is valued by all of society, taking care of a parent. How do you think this will affect Joe's attitude toward development of the new hospital wing?
2. *How do the other people on the team feel about the way Joe was treated?* Word spreads fast in an organization, especially when something happens that affects the people that work there. Other people on the team must feel uneasy, perhaps even angry, about the action taken against Joe. They may worry about what might happen to them if they have to

miss a meeting suddenly due to an emergency in the family. The team leader misunderstood what was happening with Joe. Could the same thing happen to them?

3. *What did the team leader's action do for patient care?* If the work of the project team was upset by Joe missing one meeting, it would certainly be disrupted that much more by his being kicked off the team. Did the team leader's action help patient care or hurt it? Will this have an effect on the hospital?

The team leader was wrong on all three counts. Because his relationship with Joe and the team members is strained, the supervisor now finds himself working with people who do not trust his judgment and will probably not be very cooperative. Moreover, he has created an atmosphere of fear and anxiety instead of trust and respect. Below are four steps that might have made the supervisor handle this situation differently. Every supervisor should follow these steps when trying to handle a people problem:

- **Step 1: Get the Facts.** Be sure you have the whole story. These facts will form the basis of what you do to resolve the problem.
- **Step 2: Weigh and Decide.** Weigh the facts carefully and then decide what to do. Resist the temptation to jump to conclusions.
- **Step 3: Take Action.** Carry out your decision. Don't pass the buck to others. Do not make the Human Resources Department or higher-level management responsible for the situation. You are responsible.
- **Step 4: Check Results.** Follow up to see if your decision and action worked out. Did it help patient care?

By following the above Job Relations four-step method, there is an excellent chance that you will take the correct action that best solves the problem and avoid the kind of trouble Joe's supervisor created. The Job Relations method, just like the Job Instruction method we saw in Section II, uses a four-step method as shown on the JR pocket card (see Figure 8.1). This handy tool contains everything you need to follow when applying the JR method and you should keep it with you at all times.

Get the Objective

To solve a problem well you need to have a clear idea of where you want to end up so that you can take the appropriate steps to get there.

HOW TO HANDLE A PROBLEM

DETERMINE OBJECTIVE

STEP 1 – GET THE FACTS
Review the record
Find out what rules and customs apply
Talk with individuals concerned
Get opinions and feelings
Be sure you have the whole story

STEP 2 – WEIGH AND DECIDE
Fit the facts together
Consider their bearings on each other
What possible actions are there?
Check practices and policies
Consider objective and effect on individual, group, and
patient care
Don't jump to conclusions

STEP 3 – TAKE ACTION
Are you going to handle this yourself?
Do you need help in handling?
Should you refer this to your supervisor?
Watch the timing of your action
Don't pass the buck

STEP 4 – CHECK RESULTS
How soon will you follow up?
How often will you need to check?
Watch for changes in output, attitudes, and relationships
Did your action help patient care?

DID YOU ACCOMPLISH YOUR OBJECTIVE?

Figure 8.1   JR four-step method pocket card: back side.

In other words, before beginning the JR four-step method, you need
to determine the objective that you want to achieve and create a thesis
statement that defines your objective. The objective is something to shoot
at and, hence, may be difficult to determine. Moreover, it may have to
be changed in the course of handling the problem. But be sure it is not
shortsighted or too narrow in scope. Asking these kinds of questions can
help:

■ What makes this a problem?
■ Just what are you trying to accomplish? What do you want to have hap-
   pen here?
■ What effect is this having on patient care?
■ Are any other people in the department involved or concerned?
■ What results do you want to get out of this?

In this problem, the supervisor wanted to have Joe attend the meetings regularly but more than just that, because this was an interdepartmental project, he needed to lead each team member to think about how their participation contributed, not just to their own department's benefit and interest, but to the hospital overall and ultimately to patient care. His objective should have been, "Have Joe attend all meetings and create strong teamwork leading to optimal patient care in the new wing." Note that in most problems the objective tends to take on two parts, the immediate objective with the target of the problem, having Joe attend all the meetings, and the larger objective that is being affected by the problem, creating teamwork and optimal patient care.

Step 1: Get the Facts

Joe's supervisor did not have the facts, and this led to a bad decision and poor action. Collecting facts effectively is the basis of any successful resolution to a problem, but this means having *all* relevant facts. Supervisors often make the mistake of thinking that "the facts" include only data and details from physical evidence. But because *we are dealing with people*, you also need to include what people think and how people feel about the situation.

Item 1: Review the Record

To understand a current problem, the supervisor needs to review the employee's previous record on job performance, career, achievement, attendance, problems, disciplinary actions, etc. Organizations typically keep such records on file in the form of attendance sheets, performance appraisals, disciplinary reports, and so on. Not all records are paper records. A review of the record includes looking at what the supervisor knows. Joe's supervisor recalled vividly Joe's previous poor record, when he had regularly missed meetings, but he overlooked or ignored Joe's more recent good record. Also keep in mind that a review of the record means looking at all behavior, not just unacceptable or inappropriate behavior.

Item 2: Find Out What Rules and Customs Apply

When supervisors deal with any problem, they invariably run into something covered by the organization's rules and customs. These guidelines help maintain fairness and equality in the workforce. Rules are written standards in the organization's policy manual or handbook that everyone needs to follow. An organization's customs, on the other hand, are not necessarily in a policy manual; they are precedents set by many accumulated cases that were handled in a fixed way. At Joe's hospital, for example, it was apparently a custom for people to call in and let someone know if you were not coming to a meeting. Such unwritten customs are just as important, and sometimes even more important, than written rules.

Item 3: Talk with Individuals Concerned

If supervisors don't talk with the people involved, they may never discover the critical elements that caused the problem in the first place. Joe's supervisor did not take the time to do this. He took action without even asking Joe why he had not come to the meeting the week before. To a certain degree, this is understandable. Dealing with people problems usually entails uncomfortable situations for supervisors, and there is a strong temptation to avoid confronting people directly about difficult issues. Some supervisors feel it is more appropriate or easier to have someone more senior or more experienced handle these problems, someone from Human Resources, for example. However, if you are to build strong relationships with your people and strengthen job relations, you must embrace this communication role, no matter how unpleasant, and take responsibility for getting the facts from the people involved. By doing this, you build trust and respect.

Item 4: Get Opinions and Feelings

When you talk with the key individuals concerned, you should be looking for their opinions and feelings. Joe's supervisor didn't think at all about how Joe felt. He focused only on his own preconceived notions about Joe and on his own feelings. Many supervisors, in fact, disregard feelings because they are not based on "fact." A key point in JR is that *what a person thinks or feels, whether right or wrong, is indeed a fact to that person and we must consider it as such.*

For example, some people feel their supervisors do not like them. This may or may not be true. Nevertheless, if a person *feels* disliked, this feeling is a fact to that person. It is an important piece of information. You cannot understand the real gist of what is happening in a situation without knowing the personal emotions involved.

Caution Point: Be sure you have the whole story

This is a caution point for the whole of Step 1. The more facts you gather, the better the judgment you will make. The better the judgment you make, the more likely the action you take will be correct and successful. We pointed out that Joe's supervisor did not have the whole story.

Whenever you deal with a problem concerning people, it is easy to think you understand everything based on your own experiences and then incorrectly assume everyone has had similar experiences. But each person's situation is unique, and it is up to you to get this "unique" story before taking any action on a problem.

Step 2: Weigh and Decide

This step consists of two activities, analyzing the facts and determining what you will do to resolve the problem. These two processes are interwoven, and you must do them at the same time. TWI uses the word "weigh" because, with people problems, the issues are not always black and white or easy to understand. So you want to "weigh" the facts and try to determine meaning from what you know, even if you have contradictory facts or are missing pieces to the overall picture. Only after this thorough analysis and review do you decide on the best course of action.

Item 1: Fit the Facts Together

Once you list all the facts concerning a problem, you fit these facts together in a logical pattern (by content, by time sequence, by subject, etc.) and begin looking for gaps or contradictions. For example, in Joe's case, "Joe's father was hurt" was an important gap in the facts. If the supervisor had known about this, he might have taken a different course of action.

Many times when we fit the facts together, we also find that certain facts contradict each other. Joe's failure to come to the meeting that day contradicted his recent behavior of coming to meetings regularly for several weeks. Contradictions can tell you a lot about the real nature of a problem. For example, a person sees another employee's aggressive actions as coercive and threatening while that employee sees their own attitude as positive and "getting the job done." This underscores the fact that different people see things in different ways. Your job is to see the contradictions and consider the reasons behind them.

Item 2: Consider Their Bearings on Each Other

Once you begin fitting the facts together, you can consider what bearing they have on each other. A good way to understand this process is to examine the difference in meaning between "facts" and "information." "Facts" are just the raw data. By themselves, they don't really mean anything. You obtain "information" when you take these facts and give meaning to them. By taking the facts gathered in Step 1 and looking at what bearing they have on each other, you turn them into useful information that you can act on.

Putting facts side by side may reveal cause-and-effect relationships you may not have realized up front. For instance, if today is the first day of hunting season and half of your team has called in sick, you can put those two facts together, consider their bearings on each other, and deduce that team members are not really sick but out hunting. (Some companies deal with just this situation by making the first day of deer season a paid holiday.) Joe's supervisor looked at the work drop off in oncology and Joe's previous bad record. He decided that these two facts accounted for Joe's absence and came to the conclusion that all Joe cared for was what he could boast about. If he had looked at Joe's recent good record, he might have understood the situation in a different light.

Item 3: What Possible Actions Are There?

Joe's supervisor thought that there was only one option for his situation. This is a common perception among supervisors facing people problems. Because supervisors depend so heavily on their own experiences, they often fall back on what has worked for them in the past and believe that this is the "one and only one way" to fix a person. One of the most important lessons to learn from JR is that *when you carefully weigh all of the facts in a case, there is usually **more than one** possible action to resolve the problem.*

Take a person who is not performing up to standard. You might simply warn that person to "get up to speed." But a careful look at the reasons for this problem might suggest other possible actions. If, for example, the person is having trouble doing the work, you can provide additional training. If a health problem is involved, you can suggest medical attention or some time off to rest. If marital problems are involved, you can suggest some form of counseling. You might even discover that the problem may be somewhere else further up the line and that the person's performance might improve if that problem is fixed.

Some supervisors strongly resist the idea of looking for more than one possible action sticking to the notion that there is one clear penalty for any given infraction. These supervisors have learned from the "school of hard knocks" that if they don't rigorously apply a well-defined set of rules and consequences, they will not be able to handle the people doing the work (e.g., if you don't call in when you're out, you're suspended—no exceptions). There may be many reasons for holding to this "draw-the-line" and "one-size-fits-all" mentality, but it is counterproductive to handling people well. Because people are individuals and each one is different, and their motives for what they do and how they behave are unique to their own background and situation, good leaders must consider a variety of options, or possible actions, to get them successfully to their objectives.

The Job Relations method *does* take into account an organization's practices, policies, and customs to make sure that every possible action complies. It advocates, in all cases, a fair application of all organization rules to all employees. But it also advocates that supervisors consider the complexity of people and make a concerted effort to understand each individual and their unique situation. It follows that the corrective action should reflect the particular set of circumstances and people involved. People must be treated as individuals. Listing several possible actions presents the opportunity of weighing the merits of each and picking the one that is best suited to solving a particular problem with a particular person.

What about the case when the employee has broken a "no tolerance policy"? When it comes to issues such as critical safety violations, violence in the workplace, or sexual harassment, it is important and appropriate for organizations to enforce strict rules regardless of the individual circumstances. In these situations, there may be only one course of action. However, it is still a failure of leadership because these problems did not start when the employees broke the no tolerance rules. They began as smaller issues which, through supervisor neglect, were allowed to escalate until an unfortunate action was taken. When problems are small, before any egregious acts have taken place, many avenues will be available to prevent them from growing and getting out of hand. In the next chapter, we will see how supervisors can recognize and get into problems early when there are still many possible actions that can be taken to solve them.

Item 4: Check Practices and Policies

Your possible actions must comply with the organization's practices and policies or else they are, quite simply, not "possible." A supervisor has to know the ground rules by which the organization operates and know whether a possible action falls within those rules. Like long-established customs, practices built and developed over a long period constitute the way things are done in an organization, even if they are not written down or formalized in an organization's policy manual. If an organization has established a practice that there is no excuse for not calling in when you fail to come to work, then that practice has to apply to everyone in the hospital. You may also have to follow standards that society sets, many of which are dictated and controlled by state and federal laws. In Joe's case, it would seem unreasonable to most people for the organization to penalize him for his actions. Moreover, even though he failed to contact his supervisor, it would seem fair to take into consideration that he made a positive effort to do so.

Item 5: Consider Objective and Effect on Individual, Group, and Patient Care

This item is the evaluation part of Step 2, in which you look at each of the possible actions and consider whether they are viable. In JR, you make that decision by checking whether a possible action will meet the objective. Then you consider what effect that possible action will have on the following factors:

1. The individual who is the target of the action
2. The group that will be indirectly influenced by whatever action is taken
3. The patient care of the department and the facility overall.

What Joe's supervisor really wanted was for Joe to come to meetings regularly. This was the supervisor's objective in resolving the problem. When he decided to kick Joe off the team, he did not consider whether that action would meet *any* of these criteria.

In TWI classes, one of the possible actions that invariably comes up during a review of actual problems is "Fire the worker." Sometimes, this is indeed the best thing to do. However, the objective we started out with in solving the problem is usually some variation on "Make Joe (or Mary) a good worker." If you check to see if "Fire the worker" meets this objective, the answer is an emphatic "No." Good supervisors who use the JR method know you should always consider if there is anything else you can do to help make an employee a better worker before taking this final option.

If the possible action will help meet the *objective* and have a positive effect on the *person*, the *group*, and *patient care*, then it is probably worth pursuing. Occasionally, the possible action may be a mixed bag that cannot have a positive effect on all three of these. Say you changed a person's job and the department approved of the action because that person's poor performance was causing everyone to struggle. However, the job change, if perceived as a demotion or a lack of confidence in the employee's work, might demoralize the individual and lead to new problems. In situations like this, someone (or something) benefits and someone (or something) does not, and you have to "weigh" such options very carefully and decide if the pluses outweigh the minuses.

Caution Point: Don't jump to conclusions

It is pretty clear that Joe's supervisor jumped to a conclusion when he assumed pride was the only reason for Joe's absence. He jumped to the conclusion that he was not going to be able to count on Joe—that Joe was just an irresponsible person. It is very easy to fall into this mode and, because of human nature, very difficult to resist doing so. Because JR emphasizes knowing *all* the facts before drawing conclusions, this caution point is extremely important.

Step 3: Take Action

Sometimes taking action means making someone unhappy or causing emotional upset, so it is understandable to want someone else to do the task. This is a mistake. It is imperative that you directly and personally handle this very important responsibility, no matter how uncomfortable or difficult, and handle it well. If not, you will lose the respect of your people.

Item 1: Are You Going to Handle This Yourself?

The first question to ask when taking action is whether you are *responsible* for handling this problem. This has to be decided by the supervisor. Joe's supervisor, in spite of his other flaws, understood that dealing with Joe's failure to come to the meeting was his responsibility. If you determine that you are the right person to take action on a problem, then it is your responsibility to take the appropriate measures to deal with the problem. In some cases, the problem may be outside a supervisor's area of responsibility—for example, a problem with an outside vendor—and has to be referred to another authority.

Item 2: Do You Need Help in Handling?

This item addresses your *ability* to handle the problem well. This does not mean you pass off the problem to someone else. It simply means that you take action with the help of someone who may be a specialist or someone from a department that specifically handles certain aspects of personnel issues. For example, you may not have the knowledge, experience, or expertise to deal with legal, medical/psychological, or financial aspects of a particular problem and you need assistance from these specialists.

You can also turn to many other people for help in providing solutions to problems, not the least of which may be the person who is the target of that action. This approach may have a better chance of addressing the real cause of a problem. Other people in the department may also be good sources of assistance because they are indirectly affected by any action you take. In either case, when people involved in a problem take a part in its solution, there is a better chance that the action will have good results. Additionally, you may get good assistance from other supervisors who have faced or are facing similar situations.

Item 3: Should You Refer This to Your Supervisor?

Many supervisors like to take action and then inform their boss so that he or she is aware of the situation should it come up again. But if your action is beyond your own *authority*, then you will need approval before you act. Before acting, you need to determine whether your action is within your own *authority* or if you need your superior's approval. For many day-to-day situations, you may not need to bother your own boss; for other issues, you may want approval or may want to make sure the boss knows what is happening. (Recall that Joe's supervisor informed his boss and got approval to kick Joe off the team.)

Some supervisors claim, with some frustration, that they have no authority to act when it comes to dealing with people. Keep in mind, though, that **recommending action** *is an action in itself and an important responsibility of supervisors*. The better you get at sizing up situations and recommending good actions, the more confidence your own superiors will have in you and the more authority you will earn going forward.

Item 4: Watch the Timing of Your Action

Joe's supervisor didn't waste any time in removing Joe from the team after he failed to show up for the meeting, but was this the time for him to act? As with most things in life, the timing of actions aimed at resolving people problems is critical and influences the effectiveness of the action taken. Even a good action can be spoiled if the timing is missed. Someone who is upset, for example, will have difficulty seeing past emotions. No matter how rational your action is, this person is not likely to understand or agree at this time. On the other hand, if people are aware of a problem and you wait too long to act, they may get discouraged. This is especially critical when morale, safety, or even legal issues are involved. If you do not act quickly, these issues will only fester and grow. As a rule, the most effective way to handle people problems is to deal with them early, when they are still manageable, or to anticipate them and prevent them. Timely actions are one way of maintaining good relations with your people.

Caution Point: Don't pass the buck

This caution item does not need much of an explanation as everyone knows it is bad form to push a "dirty job" on someone else. Joe's supervisor, to his credit, did not do this. However, it is not uncommon to hear supervisors say, when enforcing unpopular policies or rules, "Don't blame me, it wasn't my idea!" This is a form of passing the buck and not taking responsibility for their role as leaders and members of management. We lose the respect of our people when we do this.

Step 4: Check Results

When you take action on a people problem, it is always necessary to see if you succeeded in resolving that problem. An action that was successfully used with one person in the past will not necessarily work on another person, even if the problem is similar. Joe's supervisor never even considered checking the results. It was only when another supervisor made him aware of what had actually happened that he discovered that his action was incorrect. Even when supervisors follow the first three steps of JR, they often fail to *follow up* on the results of their actions. This step lets you see if the action worked and will also help you learn to make even better decisions in the future.

Item 1: How Soon Will You Follow Up?

When it comes to implementing solutions to people problems, you need to make your first check as soon as you can reasonably expect results. This sometimes calls for a waiting period, especially when people's feelings are involved. You may need to give them some time to let their emotions run their course. On the other hand, if urgent issues, such as quality or safety, are involved, you may need to check right away to prevent errors or accidents.

Item 2: How Often Will You Need to Check?

You can settle some problems quickly and decisively, but with most people-related issues, you may need to keep an eye on the situation for quite some time to be sure that it doesn't recur. Moreover, you should be aware that an action you have taken can cause other problems. Although this is generally not intentional, it does occur, and it is something you need to watch out for. Solutions to people problems are almost never slam dunk. Most supervisors, in fact, find that they have to continue checking on many of their actions indefinitely because of the possibility that the problem will resurface.

Item 3: Watch for Changes in Output, Attitudes, and Relationships

When you go to check on the results of your action, just what is it that you will be looking for? First, you look to see if your actions have improved or adversely affected the *output* (the work of the person involved). This is a quantitative issue. Your role as a supervisor is to help the organization continue providing effective patient care. If your efforts are not succeeding here, then we cannot say we have solved the problem.

When dealing with people and people problems, however, you cannot check results by looking only at objective figures, such as infection rates or patient feedback scores. You have to observe people's behavior, and this will be a strong indication of the success of your action. Checking the *attitude* of the person involved will let you see whether that person has accepted your actions. Even if a person does not like the action you took, experience shows that most people will accept an action so long as they feel they were treated fairly. If you have built strong relations with each of your people, they are more likely to accept the action because they trust you and believe you are trying to represent the best interests of everyone concerned.

The third thing to look for is the effect your action had on the overall group. Even when other people in the department are not directly involved in the problem, their ideas and opinions are important because the outcome will most likely affect them or their jobs. When you examine the *relationships* among people in the department—are they getting along, how are they treating the person who was the subject of the action, do you detect any resentment between them—you will know if your actions are working by how they are behaving.

Caution Point: Did your action help patient care?

In spite of the best intentions, supervisors often take actions that have a negative impact on patient care. Because Joe's supervisor didn't get the facts, he chose an action that gave him poor results. Kicking Joe off the team hurt the patient care of the entire hospital. Regardless of what your organization does in the health care industry, you need to be sure that what you do as a supervisor contributes in a positive way to that overall effort.

Did You Accomplish Your Objective?

You begin the JR four-step method by determining what the objective of our problem-solving effort will be and you end it by questioning whether you achieved that objective or not. If you have a clear vision of the end results you want, you can determine how successful you were in handling the problem. There will be times when you will not achieve your objective, but your efforts will give you invaluable experience analyzing where you went wrong and how to avoid these failures in the future.

There is no recipe for handling people nor is there ever only one way to respond to a people problem, but the JR four-step method will serve as a steady guide for leading your efforts in the right direction. Combining the method with your own *common sense and judgment*, which you develop through experience, you are certain to achieve good results.

Applying the JR Four-Step Method to the Barbara Problem

Let's take a look at another people problem as the best way to understand the four-step method is to see how to apply each item of each step to an actual problem in a workplace. This is a real problem that occurred in a large city hospital in the mid-South and illustrates the vital need for good job relations skills if we are to obtain the cooperation and dedication of the workforce in following the best practice standards we set for health care.

The Barbara Problem

A unit manager received a disciplinary report on Barbara, a new Patient Care Assistant (PCA) who was still within her 90-day probation period. The report came from Sally, the Registered Nurse (RN) who had been supervising Barbara's work the day before, and stated that Barbara, the PCA, had repeatedly failed to answer her Voalte phone,* refused assignments, and was disrespectful in front of patients. These were serious allegations that could easily lead to disciplinary actions.

Sally was an RN who had 14 months' experience on this unit. She was hardworking, ambitious, and had stated that she wanted to become a charge nurse because she had many ideas on how to improve the unit's function, including how to make assignments. Her working philosophy was that she was "in charge of her patient's care" and she delegated as she saw fit to meet the patient's needs. Sally primarily delegated to the PCA assigned to her patients but was willing to go to the nurse's desk or even other hallways to find someone else to fulfill the work if needed. Sally was direct and could be slightly abrupt in her communication style, but this was not viewed as disrespectful by the other staff. Most believed her approach and attitude was because she was from Boston now living in a southern culture.

Barbara, the PCA, had been on this unit for less than three months; this was her first PCA role in a hospital. She had worked before as a sitter/companion for homebound patients prior to this position so she could have the self-scheduling flexibility she needed to care for her children while they were pre-school and elementary school aged. She had good evaluations from her preceptor, an experienced co-worker assigned to give personal instruction and guidance to new workers, and had received no complaints against her. In fact, she had been recognized once or twice during patient rounding as someone special.

On the day in question, Sally and Barbara were assigned patients in rooms 6 to 14. While Sally was in the middle of administering the 9 AM medications to the patient in room 7, the patient requested to sit in the chair

---

* Clinical communication device.

after using the bathroom. Sally said she would get help and instructed him to wait in the bed. She stepped outside the room and called Barbara on her Voalte phone, but it went to voice mail. She started preparing the meds for room 9 and called again with the same outcome. When she went into room 9, she saw Barbara bathing the patient there. Sally told Barbara to go next door right away to assist the patient in room 7 up to the bathroom and then get him in the chair. Then she could come back and finish the bathing after Sally was done giving meds. Barbara replied that she was almost done, and suggested Sally wait a few minutes on giving the meds and help the patient in room 7 on her own. Sally cut her off saying she was the RN and asked her to step outside to the hallway.

As soon as Barbara emerged from the room Sally, who was waiting, shouted:

> Barbara, you were wrong to tell me what to do in front of the patient. The RN is in charge and I am the RN and you are the PCA. I delegate to you and you should respect that. I find your pushiness out of line and offensive. I tried to call you twice, but you refused to answer the phone. I am in the middle of administering medications and I should not stop and be distracted by doing *your* work.

Barbara responded:

> I *didn't* refuse to answer. I was almost finished giving a bath which was very important to the patient before her family arrived and I wasn't trying to be pushy, I was trying to find a solution to …

Sally cut her off saying:

> This isn't the first time I have seen this behavior from you. You have not answered my calls before. So, you think that my plan is wrong. Well, let me tell you that is not your role. I am the RN—I worked hard to get my degree. Maybe you should go back to school and get your RN if you want to be in charge.

As Barbara turned to walk away, Sally added:

> I'm not going to let this slide; I think your behavior could be insubordination.

Later that day, Barbara asked the charge nurse if she could have a differ-ent assignment but was told that wasn't feasible. The charge nurse reported the situation to the unit manager and said that Barbara kept a low profile the rest of the day, always making sure she answered calls on the first ring. The charge nurse also noted that Barbara would seek out Sally every few hours to see if she needed anything and that Sally responded in short, curt answers.

The following morning, the unit manager called Barbara into her office and encouraged her to explain what had happened and how she felt she was treated. She did remind Barbara that the role of the hospital PCA was a big transition from her previous work with homebound patients and Barbara agreed saying she liked her new work even though she was accustomed to working on her own. Barbara explained how it was the patient's first day after surgery and she had asked Barbara to help her bathe before her family arrived to visit. Barbara had just refreshed the warm water and the grateful patient had asked Barbara not to stop to answer the phone so it wouldn't cool off. "The patient asked me for a little extra soaking—so I was delayed a bit," Barbara said.

At this point, you can begin to apply the JR four-step method to the Barbara problem. Refer to the JR pocket card, Figure 8.1, "How to Handle a Problem," so you can see how the unit manager, Sally's and Barbara's super-visor, used the four steps. In a typical business scenario, the report given by Sally on Barbara's refusal to follow orders, the so-called "insubordination," may have been enough cause to dismiss her, especially considering she was still within her 90-day probation period when it is still relatively easy to get rid of a "bad apple." While most large organizations have some type of progressive disciplinary system where an employee must first get a series of warnings, verbal and written, before he or she can be fired, insubordination is typically one of those "no tolerance" violations, which made Sally's final threat to Barbara all the more biting. Nevertheless, there is always much more we need to know about and address in a situation before we "jump to conclusions" and that is where the Job Relations method helps us avoid hasty and poor decisions that lead to poor outcomes.

Determine Objective on the Barbara Problem

The first thing the supervisor did, before applying the steps, was to get the objective. The question here is, *just what was this supervisor trying to accom-plish?* What did she want from Sally and Barbara, the two people under her charge? She wanted to have Barbara, the PCA, willingly follow instructions from her supervising RN without disrupting patient care. But, at the same time, she wanted Sally, the RN, to manage the assisting workforce in a motivating way that created good teamwork across the floor. Putting these together, she determined that her objective was *to have Barbara willingly follow RN instructions without disrupting patient care and have Sally manage the workforce in a motivating way that created good teamwork.*

Notice that the objective is a simple, clear, and direct description of the desired outcome of the problem. It gives Barbara and Sally's supervisor something to shoot for as she goes through the problem-solving process using the JR four-step method. It also addresses the immediate concern of Barbara's work with patients as well as the bigger picture of creating good teamwork in the workforce. Now, let's look at how the supervisor used each of the four steps and the items under each step to get all the facts and find a good solution to this problem.

Step 1: Get the Facts on the Barbara Problem

The unit manager reviewed the facts she had and listed them after talking to the two women and looking closely at the situation:

- Sally—14 months' RN experience on unit
  - Hard worker/ambitious
  - Wants to be charge nurse
  - Direct and abrupt
  - Feels she is "in charge"
- Barbara—less than 90 days
  - Still within the probation period
  - Previous experience with homebound patients
  - Good evaluation from preceptor
  - No other complaints
- Patient needed help going to bathroom
- Did not answer phone twice
- Refused order to stop bathing patient
- Talked back
- RN angry
- Barbara stated—trying to find solution
- Admonished for "not having her RN"
- Barbara liked her work

■ Was patient's first day after surgery
■ Family was visiting
■ Asked for "extra soaking"

She just quickly wrote down these facts as she remembered them. She didn't number them or use any other type of notation because she simply wanted to get them on paper without any special emphasis or meaning, without any premature judgment or any preconceived notions. Next, she turned to the JR pocket card to go through the items of Step 1 where she will be able to determine if she missed anything in her initial listing of the facts.

Item 1: Review the Record

The supervisor looked at both Sally's and Barbara's previous records in terms of performance, career, achievement, and so on. The facts she already listed for this item were: *Hard worker/ambitious, Wants to be charge nurse, Direct and abrupt,* and *Feels she is "in charge"* for Sally and *Still within probation period, Previous experience w/ homebound patients, Good evaluation from preceptor,* and *No other complaints* for Barbara. These facts all relate to things that had happened or been known prior to the problem and may or may not have been part of the written record. The supervisor included what she knew about Sally, in this case that Sally was ambitious and always acted as if she was in total charge of taking care of her patient's care, even if that meant being direct and abrupt. The supervisor looked at these facts and tried to see if these helped her to remember any similar facts concerning the record that she may have missed. After careful review, she felt that she had gotten them all.

Item 2: Find Out What Rules and Customs Apply

In reviewing the second item, the supervisor had already listed the following facts: *Refused order to stop bathing patient* and *Talked back.* In refusing to follow an assignment from her supervising RN, Barbara was breaking a written rule. Talking back to her superior was most likely breaking a custom set by precedent. While not necessarily written down in the rulebook, the custom had the same force as a rule. It was obviously not an accepted practice, so the supervisor put it down as a pertinent fact in this case. The supervisor reviewed the facts under this item and couldn't think of any others.

Items 3 and 4: Talk with Individuals Concerned and Get Opinions and Feelings

While the supervisor heard about the problem from Sally when she made her disciplinary report and knew she was angry about Barbara's behavior the day before, the most important individual in this problem was Barbara, and the supervisor got several important facts because she took the time to talk with Barbara and get her opinions and feelings: *Barbara liked her work, Was patient's first day after surgery, Family was visiting*, and *Asked for "extra soaking."* In particular, Barbara stated that she had been *trying to find a solution* showing her feelings about the situation she found herself in.

The final item under Step 1 is the caution point for the whole step: *Be sure you have the whole story.* By reviewing the record, rules and customs, and because she made the effort to talk with Barbara to get her opinions and feelings, the supervisor got all of the pertinent facts and felt she had the whole story.

Step 2: Weigh and Decide on the Barbara Problem

To *weigh* the facts in Barbara's problem and put some order and meaning to certain individual facts or groups of these facts, the supervisor used the first two items under Step 2. She began looking for gaps and contradictions and considering the relationships between the facts looking for cause-and-effect relationships.

Items 1 and 2: Fit the Facts Together and Consider Their Bearings on Each Other

The goal of the first two items of Step 2 is to take the raw facts and turn them into meaningful information that helps a supervisor understand a situation clearly in order to come up with good possible actions. The unit manager saw there was obviously a big "gap" in the facts between Barbara's refusal to carry out an assignment and her history of no complaints. There was also a "contradiction" between her refusal to answer her phone and her spotless record of excellent patient care. She also connected related facts to see what meaning she could draw from those relationships. The fact that her patient asked for "extra soaking" because the family was coming for a visit the first day after her surgery was the direct cause of why Barbara did not answer her phone. And Barbara's previous experience working independently with homebound patients was clearly related to her response to "find a solution" on her own.

While the focus of the problem is understandably on Barbara's alleged insubordination in refusing an assignment, the supervisor also considered Sally's own ambitions and her attitude toward the PCA who was assigned to assist her. She fit the facts together that Sally wanted to be a charge nurse, always acting direct and abrupt with co-workers, and her "pulling rank" and admonishing Barbara for "not having her RN." She began to see that the problem was not only Barbara's actions but Sally's pride and her attitude and behavior toward the people assigned to assist her.

Item 3: What Possible Actions Are There?

Weighing these facts carefully, the supervisor could come up with various possible actions to take. The unit manager got a feel for the personal friction between the two employees, Sally's more rigid approach to "being the boss" versus Barbara's history of working more independently on her own schedule. These are the personality traits that are not readily seen when you look only at the surface issues. Most tellingly, there were no signs that Barbara had any work issues at all and had even been praised by the patients, so the manager was cautious about a rush to judgment. She considered the following possible actions:

- Reprimand Barbara for insubordination
- Discuss and set priorities with group (e.g., going to bathroom vs. bathing)
- Review PCA job description with Barbara
- Coach Sally on leadership styles and skills

The supervisor was not yet ready to act. This was a brainstorming process during which she entertained *all possibilities* without judgment before drawing conclusions and taking action. The supervisor knew that the more possible actions she could list, the better the likelihood that she would come up with an effective solution.

Item 4: Check Practices and Policies

As previously noted, you may not be able to implement some of the possible actions because they break a practice or policy of the organization. In reprimanding Barbara for insubordination, while this would not go against any policies, she realized that she would have to check into the policy on insubordination before taking such a harsh action because certain conditions would have to be met first. The next possible action, discuss and set priorities with the group, was proper and good practice. Reviewing the PCA description with Barbara would certainly not go against any written policies and, finally, coaching Sally on leadership styles and skills would be something she could do without going against any hospital practices.

Item 5: Consider Objective and Effect on Individual, Group, and Patient Care

Applying this item to *each* of the possible actions helps determine which possible actions might give the best results for meeting the objective. The unit manager considered that *Reprimanding Barbara* would not get her to her objective of having Barbara "willingly follow instructions" and having Sally "manage in a motivating way that created good teamwork." If anything, a reprimand would demotivate Barbara who was obviously trying to do her best for the patient. On the other hand, a reprimand, if not outright dismissal, was just what Sally was recommending in her report and Sally would view this action in a very positive way. In spite of that, though, the unit manager thought this action would negatively affect the overall patient care since Barbara was doing a good job and killing her enthusiasm would be a loss to the whole team. In this way, the unit manager weighed the plusses and minuses and came to the decision not to take this action.

The next possible action of *Discuss and set priorities with group* could, the supervisor thought, get her to her objective. With mutual agreement across the team, she could help foster better teamwork while having Barbara willingly follow the guidelines, even if that meant interrupting a bath to help another patient go to the bathroom. This would have a positive effect on the group as well, she thought, and improve patient care, though Sally might still remain bitter about having her authority questioned. That is where the next two possible actions could help. By *Coach(ing) Sally on leadership styles and skill*, she could help Sally better develop a more effective approach to dealing with people. And by *Review(ing) PCA job description with Barbara*, she could help Barbara better understand that her role on a hospital team, where coordination of effort is critical, is different from working on your own and making decisions for yourself as she used to do in home patient care.

The supervisor had to question each of the possible actions while keeping in mind this step's caution point, *don't jump to conclusions*, and keep an open mind as she went through the entire Weigh and Decide process. It would certainly have been easy enough to jump to the conclusion, based solely on Sally's report, that Barbara was a troublemaker who would have to go. Questioning each item in this step would help her choose and pursue the best possible action(s). The supervisor looked at all of the facts and felt she had the complete story. She found out why Barbara refused to answer her phone and why she felt it necessary to have Sally, not her, help the other patient to the bathroom while she finished giving the bath. The story has an obvious moral: Sometimes the addition of just one more fact may suggest or preclude a possible action.

Step 3: Take Action on the Barbara Problem

The next day, the unit manager called Sally into her office and explained the facts she had learned about the situation in Sally's disciplinary report. In fact, in her patient rounds that morning she had talked to the patient in room 9 who expressed a desire to recognize Barbara for her compassion and kindness saying Barbara behaved quite professionally "when the nurse came charging into the room." The patient went on to say that the nurse was not very nice and never even acknowledged her or let her give her opinion after she burst in. The nurse had actually told Barbara to stop the bathing and go to another room and help someone else—"I mean, really!!!" She had heard the nurse yelling at Barbara just outside her door and apologized for any trouble she may have caused by delaying her. Sally's supervisor cautioned her on how her behavior not only influenced Barbara's morale and dedication but had a direct effect on patient perceptions and satisfaction.

While chastened, Sally said she would reflect on her own actions and accepted an invitation to take leadership training in Job Relations. The supervisor then went on to speak individually with Barbara thanking her for her dedication to the hospital patients but also reviewing the PCA job description emphasizing the need for teamwork and coordination. Barbara said she understood and agreed but would need some time to change her work habits based on years of working on her own with homebound patients. The supervisor also suggested that the whole team get together and come up with a list of priorities everyone could agree on and Barbara said she would love to be part of that effort.

Here are the action items:

- Counseled Sally on behavior
- Offered leadership training
- Thanked Barbara for dedication
- Reviewed PCA job description—teamwork and coordination
- Set priorities with group

These action items were all based on the facts that the supervisor got in Step 1 and weighed carefully in Step 2. In order to take these actions effectively, she had to apply the four items in Step 3. Let's see how she did this.

Item 1 is **Are you going to handle this yourself?** This was a simple decision. This was the supervisor's problem because Sally and Barbara worked in the area she was in charge of. Therefore, she had the *responsibility* to ensure Barbara followed her assignments and that there was good teamwork across the floor. Item 2 is **Do you need help in handling?** The supervisor felt she had the *ability* to carry out each part of her action plan and so did not need the help of specialists or other professionals. Item 3 is **Should you refer this to your supervisor?** The supervisor did not refer the problem to her own supervisor because she felt she had the *authority* to take these actions and did not need to bother her boss about it. At some appropriate time, though, she thought she would tell her boss about her work with Sally and future opportunities for her development.

The fourth item, **Watch the timing of your action**, is critical. The supervisor did not lose any time in acting and this made her action successful. Remember that *even a good action can be spoiled if the timing is missed.* In this case, the supervisor did a good job of listening to Barbara and was quick to understand her position. The effect of this quick response is easy to see. Barbara felt her supervisor understood her situation and took it seriously enough to respond right away. This would not only build trust in the relationship but would motivate Barbara to continue her dedication to the patients and not lose morale or entertain further ideas of changing departments or even quitting her job at the hospital. In addition, with clear priorities set among the team and improved leadership skills from Sally, patient care and satisfaction would continue to improve. The supervisor was also careful to avoid the mistake of ignoring the caution point for all of Step 3: ***Don't pass the buck***. She personally took strong and effective action.

Step 4: Check Results on the Barbara Problem

Although the Barbara Problem does not cover this, it is a good idea to look at the four items and determine how the supervisor should follow up with her action. The first of these is **How soon will you follow up?** Because of her concern for Barbara's morale and the possibility of poor patient care, the supervisor wanted to check right away. The second item is **How often will you need to check?** The supervisor will have to continue checking for some time because Barbara's work habits and Sally's leadership style will both take time to change. She will want to make sure that Barbara's situation has stabilized and that she is working effectively.

When the supervisor checks on her action, she will follow the third item on the JR pocket card: **Watch for changes in output, attitudes, and relationships**. In other words, she will look at Barbara's work to see if she is performing well; she will look at Barbara's attitude to ensure she is motivated and willing to follow orders and instructions as well as Sally's attitude when she directs the work of the PCAs; and she will look at the relationship between Barbara and Sally to see if they are getting along as well as their relationships with the other team members. There is a good chance that her action will help in all three of these, but she'll be sure of that when she reviews the caution point for all of Step 4: ***Did your action help patient care?*** Because she got to the root of the problem and kept a skilled and dedicated person on the job, there is no question that her action will help patient care.

The last item on the JR pocket card is **Did you accomplish your objective?** The supervisor wanted *to have Barbara willingly follow RN instructions without disrupting patient care and have Sally manage the workforce in a motivating way that created good teamwork.* Along with common sense and judgment, having this clear objective throughout the entire process helped the supervisor apply the JR four-step method to resolve the problem successfully and meet this objective. She was able to take action that kept Barbara motivated and on the job while taking some forward steps in helping Sally become the manager she aspired to be. You can clearly see how this situation could quickly and easily have gone bad had the supervisor simply reacted to the emotion of the moment when there was conflict between the two employees. Resolving these situations, and managing the personal relationships that exist largely unseen until they "blow up" in your face, is the skill of leadership following the four steps of Job Relations.

Chapter 9

JR's Foundations for Good Relations

Introduction

Chapter 8 illustrated how the JR four-step method guides supervisors down a systematic path of problem solving to arrive at actions that solve people-related problems. These are the kinds of problems that destroy motivation and cooperation and get in the way of creating and sustaining standard work processes. But what if you could prevent these problems from happening in the first place? Or address problems early, while they are still small? Many supervisors say that most of their big problems result from smaller problems that were neglected or poorly handled. This happens for a reason. In most cases, problems that are big and complicated right from the start tend to get immediate attention. Someone says, "This is a tough one. I'd better get all the facts and deal with it carefully." On the other hand, small problems often get ignored or mishandled. Because such problems seem insignificant, there is a tendency to jump to conclusions and make poor decisions by not taking the time to get the facts or think them through carefully. Before long, these minor problems grow into big headaches and what started as a small fire that could have been put out with a cup of water becomes a blaze that needs the fire department.

In Job Relations, as the old saying goes, "If you take care of the little things, the big things will take care of themselves" because *when it comes to people, the little things really are the big things.* Supervisors often complain

DOI: 10.4324/9781003035305-9

about people with "attitude problems" who disrupt the work of everyone around them. They are the "troublemakers" who turn every small issue into a crisis and try to convince anyone who will listen to them that their supervisor is "out to get them" or that there is a hospital conspiracy to take advantage of the workers. When you engage with these types, you can usually trace their bitterness back to some small episode that the supervisor or someone else handled poorly. Maybe they did not get recognition or thanks for a good or special effort they made. Maybe they believe they were unfairly criticized or punished for something that was not their fault. Maybe they resent or feel threatened by a recently implemented change in company policy or even a change that happened years ago. Maybe they feel they could be doing more in their job and are being held back by a supervisor who is not interested in their potential, a supervisor who only thinks about getting their own work done.

People with these feelings and attitudes can really cause trouble. Implementing techniques and methods for handling these "problem people" can be a long and difficult process but, on the other hand, it would be much smarter to learn how to handle all of your people correctly and effectively before they "go sour" and cause problems. In other words, a method that treats *everyone* fairly and equally can *prevent* problems or catch them *before* they become burning blazes. The purpose of this chapter is to illustrate how this "work smarter not harder" strategy for human relations works.

How to See Problems Coming

As defined in the last chapter, a problem is *anything the supervisor has to take action on*. When you understand how problems come up, you can learn to see them coming and take timely action on them. According to TWI, there are four ways in which problems come up:

1. *Sizing up before it happens.* Sometimes you may be aware of things about to occur that might disturb your people. For example, you know that management may be planning a change in policy, such as a promotion policy based on ability rather than seniority. You have the opportunity to do some preventive work and take action that can help minimize, if not eliminate, the potential problem.

2. *Being tipped off.* If you are attentive to people and on the watch in your department, you'll notice changes in people's work or attitudes. For example, suppose a normally pleasant person suddenly becomes quarrelsome. That is a problem in itself, but it is indicative of something else that, if not addressed, can grow into something more difficult to handle. Effective supervisors get into, and resolve, these kinds of issues early on. If you have good relations and know your people as individuals rather than just "workers," you are more likely to be "tipped off" when things change.

3. *Coming to you.* Some problems are presented directly to you—for example, someone asks for a raise or a transfer or someone comes to you with a concern or a question. Good supervisors keep an "open door" for their people to come to them with their issues, and it is your responsibility to listen and respond to them.

4. *Running into.* Finally, there are the problems that you just run right smack into you—for example, you tell an employee to do something and he or she refuses or an employee who has been warned about coming in late but keeps coming in late. On such problems, supervisors must act immediately.

The important thing to remember here is timing, including the timeline you have available for taking action. When you "size up a potential problem" or when you are attentive and "tipped off," the real trouble has not yet started, and you have time to deal with the situation before it breaks open. It is much easier to handle a problem in these early stages because you will be closer to the problem's root causes and there will be many "possible actions" available to you to resolve them. By the time a problem "comes to you," it is already serious enough for someone to bring it to your attention even though you don't see it. If you are "running into" a problem, it is probably in full blaze and has generated additional, new problems. This will make your job of finding an appropriate action even more difficult and time consuming.

People will swallow a lot of job-related frustration, anger, disappointment, and fear, but the container in which these negative emotions are stored does not have a safety valve. Sooner or later, the lid blows off or the whole container explodes. In the early stages of a problem, you may not notice that there is anything wrong because people are in the bottling-up-emotions stage. Your job as a good supervisor is to understand how problems emerge and escalate so you can recognize them at an early stage and use your skills to solve them right then and there.

The Mike Problem

In this case study, a supervisor had several opportunities to tackle a problem early but failed to do so at each stage. He then took a bad action with poor results. Reviewing this problem will help you understand the four ways problems come up and will also give you a chance to practice the JR four-step method. Pay particular attention to Step 2, **Weigh and Decide**, and refer to the Job Relations pocket card, Figure 8.1.

The Mike Problem

An office supervisor had received several complaints about Mike, who had been working in the office for about seven months. Mike evidently was not fully cooperative with other office members. For example, when the office had its weekly meetings to discuss the progress of current projects and to plan future projects, Mike frequently skipped these meetings. When he did attend, he did not participate.

Mike had been a scrub tech prior to being transferred to the office. Unfortunately, he had slipped in the OR and hurt his foot, so he wasn't able to walk or lift for six months. Mike was transferred to the office so he could get full pay instead of partial pay under Workman's Compensation. Mike had been uncooperative since being transferred into the office but ever since his foot had healed he made it known that he didn't like working in the office and that he wanted to return to the OR as soon as possible.

The office was quite busy, however, and needed the extra worker. While Mike was not enthusiastic about the work, he was capable. Moreover, Mike had recently been assigned to a critical two-month project to be done jointly with one of the other people in the office. Soon after, the team member complained that Mike wasn't putting any effort into the project and had refused to make a required report.

The office supervisor confronted Mike and told him to put more effort into his work. Mike replied that he "didn't give a crap"

about the current project or the office and just wanted to get back
in the OR again. The supervisor was pretty angry about his attitude. People in the department were watching to see what would
happen.

The office supervisor decided it was time to take action.

In the JR four-step method, the first thing to do is **Get the Objective**. What
did the supervisor want from Mike? Because the office was busy, it was
important for Mike to contribute to the work. At the same time, it was
also important for the supervisor to keep in mind the feelings of the other
employees in the department. Clearly, the supervisor's objective here was to
Get the job done without upsetting the department.

Step 1: Get the Facts on the Mike Problem

The task here is to list all of the facts you know right now, in no particular
order. The following list shows the facts that are currently available:

- In office 7 months
- Not cooperative in office
- Foot hurt
- In office for full pay
- Foot healed
- Asked to return to OR
- Office busy
- Two-month project
- Refused to make report
- Supervisor angry
- Department watching

Item 1 is to **Review the record** of Mike's previous performance, career,
achievement, and so on. This includes most of the facts on the list and com-
bines information from written sources (for example, *Foot hurt* and *In office
for full pay*) with information that came from observing Mike's behavior (for
example, *Not cooperative* and *Asked to return to OR*). The list also includes
facts about conditions in the office (for example, *In office 7 months* and
Office busy).

Item 2 is to **Find out what rules and customs apply**. In this case, the fact
that Mike *Refused to make a report* is a clear violation of the hospital rules

for doing work. The next two items are **Talk with individuals concerned** and **Get opinions and feelings**. The office supervisor did confront Mike to tell him to put more effort into his work. Whether he wanted to or not, he also heard Mike's feelings on the two-month project. Mike told him that he "didn't give a crap" about the project and just wanted to "get back in the OR again." Opinions and feelings are easy to see in this case. The *Supervisor is angry* about Mike's attitude toward his work; the *department is watching* shows that people have put up with Mike's negative attitude for some time and want to see some action taken to resolve the issue.

Now it is time to address the caution item under Step 1: ***Be sure you have the whole story***. Since Mike only came into the office seven months ago, there is virtually no information about his previous work in the OR. The whole story on Mike is not available, but because these were all the facts the office supervisor had when he took action, let's go forward with the method using just the known facts.

Step 2: Weigh and Decide on the Mike Problem

The first two items are **Fit the facts together** and **Consider their bearings on each other**.

Look over the facts listed above and try to see if you notice any gaps or contradictions between any of the facts. For example, there is a contradiction in the fact that Mike is not cooperative in the office, even though he was transferred there to maintain his full pay, clearly a benefit to him. By putting related facts together, you can look for any cause-and-effect relationships and see if you can find any meaning to the facts. Mike was moved into the office because his foot was hurt; now that it is healed, it would make sense for him to want to go back to the OR. It is especially important to analyze carefully all the facts you have because this will reveal various possible actions to solve the problem.

What possible actions are there? is the next item. Most participants in live TWI classes respond to this example by suggesting *Lay off* or *Transfer back to OR*. Almost always, someone will suggest "make a deal with Mike": If Mike works hard and completes the two-month project, then transfer him back to his OR position. In any case, you should always list all of the possible actions so that you can evaluate them one by one:

- Lay off
- Transfer back to OR
- Transfer after completion of project

In JR sessions, it is very common to have someone suggest "Talk to Mike" as a possible action. The question here is why? If the purpose of talking to Mike is to encourage him to do a better job, it is a possible action. However, if the purpose is to find out more about why he is not cooperating in the work, that is getting more facts and that means going back to Step 1, **Get the Facts**. It is always good to go back and get more facts, throughout the entire four-step process, when you feel or sense you do not have the whole story. However, be careful not to confuse this with a possible action, which is meant to solve the problem.

The next item is to **Check practices and policies** to make sure your possible actions do not break any rules. Laying off Mike might not go against any of this hospital's practices and policies, considering the fact that Mike has refused outright to do work assigned to him and that he has a history, albeit a short one, of being uncooperative in the workplace. Transferring him back to OR should not go against any practices and policies because he was transferred into the office from the OR in the first place. The same would be true for transferring him back to the OR after the successful completion of the special project.

You then want to evaluate each of your possible actions to help determine the best course of action. To do this, you use Step 2, Item 4, **Consider objective and effect on individual, group, and patient care**. Would the first possible action, *Lay off*, help the office supervisor to meet the objective to *"Get the job done without upsetting the department?"* The reason the office supervisor is keeping Mike, in spite of his uncooperative attitude, is that there is a lot of work to do on important projects, so laying him off won't get the job done and may actually upset the department. The effect on Mike would be negative since he wants to return to his OR position. The effect on the group might be mixed. Some people wouldn't mind seeing him go; others might be angry because laying Mike off would leave the department short-handed and would probably increase everyone's workload. The effect on patient care would be negative, at least until the supervisor could find someone else to train to do his work.

The second possible action, *Transfer back to OR*, would hardly meet the objective because the job cannot get done without Mike and the other employees would be upset that he got what he wanted at their expense. The effect on Mike would be extremely positive but that would be offset by the negative effect on the group and on patient care. The third possible action, *Transfer after completion of project*, seems like a good compromise. Mike can return to his OR position after he helps get the immediate two-month project completed. Both sides are giving ground and that seems fair to everyone. Furthermore, the effect on Mike, the group, and patient care will be positive. The office supervisor will need to prepare for Mike's departure in two months' time, but now has some lead time for this additional responsibility.

The caution point for all of Step 2 is ***Don't jump to conclusions***. You can avoid this if you do a good job of weighing the facts carefully and deciding on the best course of action from a variety of possible options. Now let's look at what actually happened.

The Mike Problem (contd.)

The office supervisor reported all this to his own manager and fired Mike. Mike complained to his former OR supervisor. The OR supervisor called up the office supervisor's boss and relayed the following facts, facts that the office supervisor could have obtained by using the caution item about knowing the whole story.

Mike had been with the hospital for almost 20 years and was an excellent scrub tech. He liked OR work, even though it meant being on his feet most of the time. He did not like office work and did not know he had been brought into the office to maintain full pay. The office supervisor had not even questioned Mike's former supervisor about his previous record before taking action. It was due to the former supervisor's intervention that these facts came to light. Eventually, Mike was reinstated in his old job with back pay.

As stated earlier, when initially hearing this problem, many people want to know more facts about Mike and his previous record. This instinct is correct—when you are not certain that you have the whole story, you should go back and get more facts. The facts that came up from Mike's former supervisor were:

- With hospital 20 years
- Excellent scrub tech
- Liked OR work on his feet
- Not advised why in the office—pay

Many people question how it was that Mike did not know why he was transferred into the office—so he wouldn't lose money under Workman's Compensation. Knowing this, Mike would probably have been more cooperative, and his attitude would have been more positive. However, in many hospitals and organizations, certain changes are implemented "automatically" with no one questioning the purpose or the duration. In addition, throughout the hustle and bustle of every working day, the intent and timeline are not necessarily communicated clearly or properly to the employee. It is easy to see that Mike's attitude was affected by what he did not know and just as easy to see that the supervisor had never talked to Mike about why he had been transferred and how long he was expected to be there. Let's now look at Steps 3 and 4.

Steps 3 and 4: Take Action and Check Results on the Mike Problem

The office supervisor chose to fire Mike. What facts do you suppose the office supervisor used to come to this decision? Probably *Not cooperative in office* and *Refused to make report.* More importantly, what are the facts the supervisor did *not* consider or use when making this decision? Probably all the facts about why Mike was in the office in the first place—*Foot hurt, In office for full pay, Foot healed.* In addition, the supervisor ignored the fact that Mike *Asked to return to the OR.* It is instructive to note that even though the supervisor did not have the whole story, especially on Mike's work history with the hospital, if he had weighed all the facts that he did have more diligently and more carefully, he probably would not have fired Mike. In our TWI classes, we do not tell trainees the second half of the story but, by using the JR method effectively and completely, they are still able to come up with better solutions like having Mike finish the report and then go back to the OR. As it was, this supervisor made a bad decision and got bad results. Let's wrap up this problem by reviewing the items and caution points for Steps 3 and 4.

Step 3 is to **Take Action** with four subheads, which are listed below with remarks about the supervisor's handling of each.

1. **Are you going to handle this yourself?** This was his problem.
2. **Do you need help in handling?** He didn't ask anyone for help.
3. **Should you refer this to your supervisor?** He referred it to his boss in order to fire Mike and his boss went with his recommendation.
4. **Watch the timing of your action.** Was this the time to take action? Even though the people in the department were watching, Mike was still needed because the office was busy.

Don't pass the buck. On this caution point for the whole of Step 3, the supervisor did not pass the buck.

Step 4 is to **Check Results** with three subheads:

1. **How soon will you follow up?** The supervisor did not check up at all on the results of his action because he evidently thought that when he fired Mike the problem was solved.
2. **How often will you need to check?** Same as the first subhead.
3. **Watch for changes in output, attitudes, and relationships.** Because of the action he took and the subsequent bad results, it's pretty clear that this supervisor lost standing with the individual, the group, and management.

Did your action help patient care? Without a doubt, this action did nothing to help patient care. Obviously, this supervisor did not achieve his objective.

The Four Ways the Mike Problem Came Up

Let's look at how Mike's problem came up and what might have happened had the supervisor recognized and handled the problem sooner.

The supervisor had ample opportunity to "size up the problem before it happened." He might have considered Mike's transfer from the OR to the office as a potential source of trouble, especially because of the unusual circumstances that led to the transfer (Mike's foot being hurt). He might also have considered the differences between OR and office work, being on your feet all day long and participating in surgeries as opposed to sitting at a desk and participating in meetings. Most changes have the potential to create problems. When you know from past records or experience that a new directive or order has the potential to cause problems, then you must use your position to take preventive action that counters or minimizes that possibility.

Mike's supervisor also failed to act when he was "tipped off" about the problem. If he had taken up this problem when he first got reports of Mike being uncooperative, especially at planning meetings, things might have turned out differently. In Mike's mind, he had no intention of staying in the office after his foot healed so was not interested in future planning with the office team. As it was, the supervisor ignored the first signs of trouble, perhaps wishfully thinking it would go away by itself, and the problem continued to escalate.

The supervisor also failed to act when the problem "came to him," when Mike stated after his foot had healed that he did not like working in the office and wanted to go back to the OR. With the office being busy, the supervisor didn't take the time to address Mike's protestations and only focused on his own issues. Neglecting problems at this stage is inviting bigger troubles because people will feel that you are ignoring and not listening to them. They may feel they have no choice but to resort to stronger ways of getting your attention.

At any rate, Mike's supervisor waited until the problem "blew up in his face" and regrettable words were exchanged—Mike refused to do a required report and rebuffed his supervisor's request to put more effort into the work. As a result, we can say the problem came up when he "ran into" it. It had evolved into something he could no longer ignore. A good supervisor would have handled this problem before it got to the point where Mike overtly broke organizational rules and was openly insubordinate. Because of the severity of the offense, the supervisor felt justified in resolving the matter through strict disciplinary procedures. Knowing the background of the case, the missed opportunities, and the end results, you can see how poorly this situation was handled.

Foundations for Good Relations

Through practice, you can gain the skills to see problems coming and engage them when they are small and easily handled. An even more important issue to address is what you can do to prevent problems from occurring in the first place. Because people are at the center of everything a supervisor does, a key principle in the JR leadership model is that *a supervisor gets results through people*. Experience shows that successful supervisors have learned to use specific foundations for good relations to maintain good job relations and *prevent* problems. You can compare this to preventive medicine. The key is to understand common-sense rules for working collaboratively with your people and then make up your mind to use them routinely and conscientiously. When it comes to relationships with people, as we've said, the simple things are often the most important things. When you neglect these, you miss important opportunities to maintain strong relationships that can prevent problems down the line.

Figure 9.1, the front side of the JR pocket card, lists the *Foundations for Good Relations*. Ideally, you use these foundations to prevent problems

```
JOB RELATIONS

A SUPERVISOR GETS RESULTS THROUGH
PEOPLE
_____

FOUNDATIONS FOR GOOD RELATIONS

Let Each Worker Know How He/She is Doing
     Figure out what you expect of the person
     Point out ways to improve

Give Credit When Due
     Look for extra or unusual performance
     Tell the person while it's "hot"

Tell People in Advance About Changes
That Will Affect Them
     Tell them why if possible
     Work with them to accept the change

Make Best Use of Each Person's Ability
     Look for abilities not now being used
     Never stand in a person's way
_____

PEOPLE MUST BE TREATED
AS INDIVIDUALS
```

Figure 9.1   JR four-step method pocket card: front side.

before they surface. Keep in mind, however, that while these foundations will help you reduce the number of problems that might occur, they will not prevent all problems. If problems surface in spite of your efforts to prevent them, you handle them using the JR four-step method.

Let Each Worker Know How He or She Is Doing

Strong job relations mean telling people on an ongoing basis how they are doing in their work. Imagine for example, that someone asks one of your employees, "How are you doing at work?" or "How is your job going?" and all he or she has to say in reply is, "I don't know—no one says anything." What this answer really means is that you don't have good job relations with that employee. People's jobs are important to them. They want to know how they are performing. But too often, supervisors are so focused on schedules and deadlines in the course of day-to-day work that they forget to give their people the feedback they want and need. Some supervisors, in fact, give feedback only when the organization requires them to do so in yearly evaluations or reviews. The problem with leaving feedback for annual reviews is that many things about work performance are long forgotten by this time. In most cases, the evaluation process is seen as a management tool for salary increases or promotions rather than a tool to provide guidance and support. Maintaining good job relations means regular communication that lets the employee know, on an ongoing basis, what is going well or not so well.

Figure Out What You Expect of the Person

Before you can tell someone how well he or she is doing in performing their work, it is important to know beforehand what the person is supposed to be doing and how. Indeed, this is the whole premise of standard work as we described in Section I. When people know what is expected of them, they usually do it. In addition, knowing what the job entails inspires confidence. Setting a standard and clearly communicating up front what you expect of someone to do has two benefits. First, it reduces the number of problems. Secondly, if things do go wrong, you can focus your problem-solving effort on the job itself, and the set standard for doing that job, instead of blaming the person involved. Our Job Instruction skill, which we learned in Section II, is invaluable here.

Point Out Ways to Improve

It doesn't do much good to say, "That's all wrong!" if the worker is not doing what you expect. This is confusing as well as offensive. A better way to handle this situation is to point out *exactly* what is not being done correctly (chances are it's not *all* wrong) and then suggest how this specific thing can be improved. Again, pay attention to the work and what needs to be done differently to improve performance instead of blaming the worker. By creating a "no-blame" environment, you motivate the person doing the job to become your partner in getting the job done well.

Give Credit When Due

Maintaining good job relations also requires giving people credit when they do something well. It is human nature to want recognition for special efforts and everyone responds well to positive acknowledgments. When people are not recognized for their outstanding efforts, they may feel their efforts and contributions are not appreciated. This can lead to frustration and even bitterness. In fact, it is a well-known fact that the number one reason people leave their jobs, or are dissatisfied with their work, is that they feel they are not appreciated. Companies who value their people recognize this and have a variety of creative ways to make employees know their work is appreciated (for example, an Employee-of-the-Month program, or a "Caught You Doing Something Good" award). Even a handshake with a heartfelt "Thank you very much!" can go a long way to building a bond and strengthening the job relationship.

Look for Extra or Unusual Performance

It is easy to give appreciation to people who hit a homerun and go beyond normal business expectations. But it is important not to forget the person who contributes by being steadfastly and quietly diligent and reliable. Supervisors often tend to overlook such people and this is a mistake because it is these people who contribute in an extra and unusual way to the overall stability of a department or hospital. Maintaining standards is no easy feat and recognizing those who keep up this steady performance is a good way to help prevent problems and help supervisors maintain good job relations. Because they do not usually broadcast their efforts, their special contributions may go unnoticed. We must be conscious about seeking them out and showing appreciation for what they do.

Tell the Person While "It's Hot"

One of the reasons end-of-the-year evaluations are not effective as motivating tools is because they describe a performance that may have occurred some time ago. Expressing your appreciation for something performed long in the past renders it an afterthought or insincere. Giving thanks when it is due is essential. If you miss the timing on this, you may miss an opportunity for strengthening a relationship.

Tell People in Advance about Changes That Will Affect Them

It is important to let people know in advance about any change that will affect them. Suppose, for example, your desk or locker is moved to a different place without any prior notice. Chances are, you will not be very happy about this. Now consider something more important, for example, a big lay-off, that will affect employees. In organizations where this has occurred with little or no prior notice, employees are justifiably upset. A typical reaction is, "It's not *what* they did, but *how* they did it." Most people can accept a layoff; it is never pleasant, but it happens. What causes more distress is when management springs the announcement on employees out of nowhere, leaving them out of the process with no say and no clear understanding of what happened. When you make *any* change that affects your people, it is best to let them know in advance and let them express their opinions about it. A change that is made without prior notice can make your people feel betrayed or even humiliated—strong emotions that will do real damage to overall job relations.

Tell Them Why If Possible

Many supervisors feel that people do not need to know or should not know the reasons for certain decisions and should simply follow directions without question. The problem with this is that people tend to resist changes they do not understand. When you give people reasons, and not just arbitrary decisions, about a change, it is easier for them to accept that change, even when they don't agree with it. It also helps to address the concerns they have about what those changes will mean for them.

Work with Them to Accept the Change

Giving people an explanation of what is going on and why will help them understand the changes you are going to make. Working with them means giving them some of your time, whether you spend that time answering their questions and concerns or just letting them vent their frustrations. Change can be like a death in the family where people go through a grieving process: denial, anger, bargaining, depression, and acceptance. Letting go of the old way can be like saying good-bye to a loved one. Understanding the emotions people go through and helping them work through those emotions while not giving in to their demands is a real skill. Everyone has to adjust to change, but it is the supervisor's job to make the adjustment easier.

Make Best Use of Each Person's Ability

The last item under the Foundations for Good Relations is to make the best use of the ability of all of your people. Every supervisor knows people who lost interest in a job simply because they felt they could do much more than they were asked or allowed to do. Most people want to make the best of their own abilities and look for work in hospitals and health care organizations that promote learning and growth. Good supervisors challenge their workers with jobs that fully utilize and maximize their abilities and potential. When you don't get the most out of each person every day, you are failing to manage the organization's most important resource.

Look for Ability Not Now Being Used

Most people have untapped potential, and good supervisors look for it and try to put it to good use. Do you know today exactly what skills exist in your department? Do you look at the possibility of cross training your people so that they have more than one skill? Do any of your people have skills from a hobby, sport, or some other special interest, that you could make use of in the work? These are the kinds of questions you should ask yourself when looking to maximize the abilities and talents of the people in your department.

Never Stand in a Person's Way

One of the reasons supervisors do not challenge their people with new tasks is because they get comfortable having a skilled person at every station and want to maintain this status quo. But failing to provide skills development may prove to be a costly mistake. It won't be long before your best people master their jobs and want to move on to something more challenging. If you don't find that challenging job for them, they will either find it for themselves by moving to another hospital, or they will lose interest in the jobs they currently hold in your organization.

These basic rules, or foundations, for good relations are important to everyone and using them will smooth job relations and help supervisors meet their responsibilities. They are the groundwork upon which good relations are built. But they will help prevent problems and strengthen job relations only if you put them to use on a regular basis. Are they the only things that help build strong job relations? Of course, there are other important things. For example, these foundations must be used with good common sense and judgment. But if used correctly and consistently, on a regular basis, they will go a long way to making your job more manageable and rewarding preventing problems from happening in the future.

People Must Be Treated as Individuals

The word "people" has appeared quite a few times in this section, but it is important to remember that no two people are alike. Obvious as this may seem, the JR pocket card reminds supervisors that *people must be treated as individuals*. So what makes one employee different from another? When you look at the people at the center of your responsibilities and try to understand this, you will find similarities and differences. One thing your people have in common is the need to work or making a living. Look beyond that, however, and you will see there are a number of factors that make each of your people unique. Your employees can be married or single, have children, or be a caregiver for a parent or family member. They may come from a rural community or a big city. Some are well educated, some are not. One person is strong or athletic while another is weak or prone to illnesses or maybe has a disability. These factors concerning their family, background and health, and many others, make each person unique. They also affect an individual's performance on the job.

Most people do not leave personal concerns or problems at the door when they enter the workplace, even if they conscientiously try to do so. One thing or another concerning that person's family, background, health, etc., comes through the door with them each day. And because individual circumstances change constantly, they may not bring the same things through that door from day to day. For this reason, supervisors must maintain a steady relationship with each individual to keep up with his or her changing life and attitudes. This may seem daunting and difficult, but when it comes to building strong relationships with people, this effort is necessary and worthwhile. Strong relationships help you make good decisions that take individual differences into account. The goal and purpose here is not about "changing" people—that is impossible. The goal is to recognize each person's uniqueness and how this affects performance and to act wisely based on this understanding when you apply the Foundations for Good Relations and the four-step method of Job Relations problem solving.

Some supervisors question whether it is right, or even legal, to pry into an employee's personal business. This is a delicate issue. There are many areas of a person's life that are off limits, such as medical history, religion, ethnic background, age, etc. It is never polite or advisable to intrude on anyone's privacy. You can, however, in the normal course of daily interaction and friendly conversation, learn many things about the people who work with you. People generally share information about themselves, especially if they trust you, and trust is something that you are trying to build. They may, for example, tell stories about children, trips, school, relatives, health issues, their house or car, or sports. Take the time to listen and show an interest. This will help you understand them and relate to them as individuals.

Conclusion

The TWI developers built the Job Relations method on simple, common-sense principles of human interaction that are easy to understand and apply. Their focus was on treating people as individuals, building strong relationships of trust through good communication and understanding, and maintaining good relations with *all* people on a regular basis. They did not try to invent new terminology for old concepts. Nor did they place their focus solely on only *handling* people problems. Instead, they made JR easy to master by using the same scientific four-step methodology as we saw in Job Instruction while providing insights and techniques on *preventing* problems before they occur.

In order to get to standard work in health care it is imperative that we obtain and maintain the dedication and cooperation of the people we call upon to carry out that work day in and day out. This takes real skill that can be learned and practiced. When we implement this skill in good Job Relations, we will be able to obtain better and better results in our ultimate goal of perfect patient care.

IMPLEMENTING TWI INTO THE CULTURE

Chapter 10

Starting Out Strong with a Pilot Project

Introduction

You will remember from the Preface that this Job Instruction method was developed during World War II by the Training Within Industry Service, the first emergency group set up to respond to the wartime needs for increased production, as a means of training millions of new workers going into the workforce replacing all of the men who went off to fight in the war. A large portion of those people were women, the famous Rosie the Riveters, who had never worked in manufacturing jobs before, and the program also was used in health care to train new workers replacing doctors and nurses who also went to war. The success of this program came from the inspired principle that continues to this day to be the key to a successful rollout: the Multiplier Effect. As Walter Dietz, one of the TWI founders, explained it in his 1970 book, *Learning by Doing: The Story of Training Within Industry* (self-published), that means to "develop a standard method, then train people who will train other people who will train groups of people to use the method." For the multiplier effect to work, the training had to be designed as a standardized method that could be successfully taught in all situations in a variety of industries. Once taught, stringent quality control would be needed to sustain the multiplier effect of the training. This combination of standardized training and follow-through was established with Job Instruction (JI) and then successfully repeated for the other two TWI courses that followed: Job Methods Improvement (JM) and Job Relations (JR).

DOI: 10.4324/9781003035305-10

To illustrate how the multiplier effect worked, 1,305,570 supervisors had been certified to teach jobs using the JI method in the 10-hour training sessions. These people, in turn, trained over 10 million workers, one sixth of the entire workforce of 64 million when the TWI Service ceased operations in 1945.* However, this multiplier effect was triggered only when the training of the 10-hour JI course was properly delivered by a qualified instructor who had been trained to deliver the program following the trainer manual that had been developed by the TWI Service.† This strict adherence to standard delivery locked in the quality of the content that spread rapidly through the workforce by those teaching it.

A Plan for Continuing Results

The very large volume of people in need of the training during the war provided the TWI Service with feedback from trainers and from companies throughout the United States. That led C. R. Dooley, head of the Service, to issue a national policy on *How to Get Continuing Results in a Plant from Training Within Industry* in June 1944, near the end of the war, to all TWI staff members. "This plan for getting 'continuing use' of TWI programs," he wrote, "is the out-growth of two years of practical experimentation and experience. You will recognize many features of the plan as your own. It is another splendid example of the combined efforts of many TWI people."

Dooley's Statement of Policy separated the implementation of TWI into two phases.‡

Phase 1: *Basic Training*: The initial introduction and follow-through efforts with JI, JM, and JR. The Detroit VA hospital is a good example today of an organization in this initial phase, giving people the skills to improve in the 10-hour sessions of JI.

Phase 2: *Continuing Use*: All of the things companies do to see that supervisors make continued application of the principles given them in the TWI 10-hour sessions. The advancement of all three TWI modules at

---

* A. G. Robinson and D. M. Schroeder, "Training, Continuous Improvement, and Human Relations: The U.S. TWI Programs and the Japanese Management Style," *California Management Review*, 1993, 35: 40.

† P. Graupp and R. J. Wrona, *The TWI Workbook* (New York: Productivity Press, 2002).

‡ C. R. Dooley, Director, *How to Get Continuing Results in a Plant from Training Within Industry Program* (Washington, D.C.: Training Within Industry Service Statement Policy, July 1944).

Baptist Memorial Health Care is a good example of how one organization with multiple hospitals has moved beyond the initial introduction phase to keep their line organization focused on using TWI to continually improve.

Applying what is learned in the 10-hour sessions may differ between organizations or even between hospitals within the same organization. However, the same positive results will be generated when each hospital or facility conforms to a fundamental plan. The planning process developed in 1944 for introducing TWI and for getting continuing use of the TWI method is a good place to start our review of how an effective TWI rollout can be managed:

Phase 1: A plan of action to suit each facility.
Commitment from top management to:

a. Sponsor the program
b. Assume the function of a coordinator or to designate someone in that role
c. Approve a detailed plan for basic training and continuing use
d. Check results

Phase 2: Plan for getting continuous results.

a. Assign responsibility for getting continuing results. Each executive and supervisor must:
   i. Use the plan himself/herself
   ii. Provide assistance to those who report to him/her
   iii. Require results of those who report to him/her
b. Get adequate coverage
   i. The 10-hour course is not just for first-line supervisors. Third and fourth line management, and perhaps people at all levels, should get the training to know what the program is about.
c. Provide for coaching of supervisors
   i. Provided to each supervisor by their own boss, or
   ii. The person best able to influence them
d. Report results to management
   i. The appropriate executives should be regularly informed as to results in order to have some continuing connection with the program and some incentive for continuing interest.

ii. The purpose of the report is to show the relative improvement accomplished by the use of the method.
   e. Give credit for results
      i. Prompt and proper recognition by the appropriate executive is necessary to obtain continuing interest and, hence, continuing use.

Unfortunately, in spite of the phenomenal success of TWI during the war, when this plan was put out at the end of the TWI Service's life, the timing to blaze new trails could not have been worse. Manufacturers in 1944 were already shutting down the production of war materiel in order to ramp up the production of consumer goods now that an Allied victory was no longer in doubt. Management had come to view TWI as a wartime program, so taking the TWI training to another level to get continuing results from the methods was not on their list of priorities. TWI also had provided grassroots attention to how people were treated in the workplace, which was especially necessary with so many new people coming into the workforce for the first time, and this made management uncomfortable at this time in history.

After the war finally did end, TWI soon traveled to Japan, along with the quality control teachings of Juran and Deming, at which time the Japanese Labor Ministry set up a small TWI working group. This group sent one member abroad to a JI Institute directed by the International Labor Organization that had obtained copies of the TWI manuals. This person returned to train 10 of its members as TWI Institute Conductors (Master Trainers) who trained approximately 500 people in JI and 70 people in JM, but this effort did not trigger the multiplier effect as was done in the United States.* Realizing the failure, the Japanese Labor Ministry then contracted with TWI, Inc., a company set up by former TWI administrators after the war to continue expanding TWI's usage, to introduce TWI into Japan. In 1951, a specialist for each "J" program was selected to travel to Japan from the United States to deliver the programs along with a fourth specialist, an expert in "plant installation" of TWI programs. This person was charged with selling the value of TWI programs to top management. According to the newly arrived TWI specialists, the failed efforts that preceded them had lacked the rigid quality control and attention to detail in the delivery of the 10-hour programs to trigger the multiplier effect.†

---

* Robinson and Schroeder, "Training, Continuous Improvement, and Human Relations," pp. 40, 47.
† Ibid.

The TWI specialists simply applied in Japan what they had learned while training TWI in the United States throughout the war.*

- They publicized their arrival and the "J" programs they were to install through the press and government and military authorities.
- They helped to select trainees from a wide variety of industry groups.
- Unions were invited to participate to learn that TWI was to train people to become better supervisors, not to make laborers work harder.
- The TWI plant installation specialist worked with Japanese partners to sell the value of TWI programs to top management.
- JI, JM, and JR trainers delivered the standardized TWI training to groups of 10 people.
- TWI, Inc. selected and prepared Follow-Through Trainers, Quality Control Specialists, Installation Specialists, and a core of Institute Conductors (TWI Master Trainers) to train instructors.

According to Dr Alan G. Robinson, in his groundbreaking research that reintroduced TWI to the Western World in 1993:

> When the TWI, Inc. specialists departed from Japan, they left behind seeds of change in the form of 35 certified Institute Conductors (Master Trainers), the beginning of a large multiplier effect, which would extend to over 1 million Japanese managers and supervisors by 1966, and to many millions more by 1992.†

The purpose of going through this history is to show how the TWI programs were designed to support quick and effective expansion of training to literally millions of people and how the discipline of delivery was so central to these successes. As we will see later in this chapter, the approach to effectively introducing TWI to organizations today follows this same sequence of events. Although we are not dealing with a national rollout of TWI anymore, the fundamental concepts learned by the TWI Service in the 1940s still apply on a narrower scale to individual health care organizations that are using these concepts today to make TWI a central part of how they get work done correctly, safely, and efficiently.

* Ibid.
† ibid. 47–48.

Getting Started on the Right Foot

As you can tell from the above discussion, we lean almost exclusively on the wisdom of the TWI founders to show us how to do TWI today. The fact of the matter is that what they taught us really works. What we are looking at in this chapter, then, is how to roll out the TWI programs so they become part of the everyday culture of an organization. This was successfully done during World War II in the United States and after the war in Japan, as we have described above. What is left for us to consider is how we can do it again today. Here, let's sum up what we have learned from our current endeavors at implementing TWI in hospitals, companies, and organizations in various industries across the country and around the world, always mindful of the history of TWI, which has guided us to this point.

Form a TWI Working Group Responsible to Lead the Way

Interest in TWI is typically initiated by one or two people who, one way or another, come to TWI as the answer to pressing problems within their organization. For them to then select the right person to lead the implementation is a critical step to ensuring success. Linda Hebish of Virginia Mason "discovered" TWI at a TWI Institute workshop conducted at an AME (Association of Manufacturing Excellence) conference, but it took a person like Martha Purrier to drive the initial pilot projects and then to lead the expanded use of TWI as a certified trainer. Lili Bacon of St. Joseph Health System had heard about TWI from consultants helping her in her role leading Lean implementation throughout the St. Joseph Health System (SJHS). One of their 14 facilities had actually run a JI pilot and gotten outstanding results. So she set up an initial JI introduction at a combined seminar of all their Lean staff, and the positive reception she got led her to then run several 10-hour classes for select members to begin piloting TWI. Skip Steward of Baptist Memorial Health Care was hired by Dr Paul DePriest to lead the continuous improvement effort at this 22-hospital system headquartered in Memphis and immediately began by inviting two members each from five of the main hospitals to take an initial class in Job Instruction and Job Relations. From there, Skip engineered TWI rollouts of all three modules starting with JI and then proceeding to JR and finally JM. He began with the larger facilities but did not leave any of the more rural smaller hospitals behind. Today there are embedded trainers of each of the three TWI programs in each hospital.

These people are passionate about TWI because they see how the training changes the way people think about themselves, about others, and about their work. This passion rubs off on other employees as they too begin to see the value of TWI. Nevertheless, it takes a cross-functional working group to move TWI from talk to action. Practicing the TWI skills is an activity that must take place across the entire organization and no one person alone can achieve this big a transformation. The initial TWI leaders must put together a team of people, a TWI Work Group, who can assist them in getting TWI to take a firm hold. The strong team of trainers that introduced the new RF identification equipment at St. Joseph Health System is a good example of the importance of teamwork in this effort (see Chapter 4). Interestingly, it is quite common for people to come forward and, without solicitation, volunteer to be on the TWI team once they are introduced to the method saying things like, "I was born to do this!" They inherently see the value in the program and want to be part of the transformation.

Once formed, this TWI Work Group must first attain a fundamental understanding of the TWI program before they try to sell it to the organization. Fortunately, there is a wealth of information available on the subject. Here are a few pointers to get a team started:

1. Numerous books and articles have been published about TWI and its connection with Lean and the Toyota Production System. Visit www. twi-institute.com for a list of recommended books and articles to start down that path.
2. Contact the TWI Institute to find out which health care organizations are using TWI so you can visit and/or benchmark with them.
3. Attend webinars and workshops that educate people about the TWI programs.
4. Attend the annual TWI Summit Conference (www.twisummit.com).

Select a Pilot Project to Show the Need for Standard Work

Organizations that have standard work, but are unable to train their people on how to perform jobs in conformance with these standards, are the same as organizations that have no standard work at all. There is no better place to begin introducing TWI than where there is a compelling need for standard work. As we discussed in Section I, the need for standard work in health care is pervasive and there is no shortage of opportunities for improvement in this area. If performed well, the TWI effort will show almost immediate results because, by stabilizing an unstable process, variation will be removed and problems will go away or rise up to the surface where they can be spotted and taken care of. With quick results, the TWI implementation will begin to gain momentum as people throughout the organization see what can be done with good skills training.

Select a small project to showcase JI and "grow" the implementation. This does not necessarily mean that the amount of training will be small, but the target of the training itself should be limited in scope. For example, you may want to select one task, or one specific process or set of processes, or one area that is causing problems or holding back the entire process. This target should be well known as being a trouble spot or an area of great opportunity so that, when corrected, people will notice the difference. The selection of hand hygiene as a pilot task to teach is a good example of just such a focused approach (see Chapter 3). And even though the trainers at Virginia Mason cut down their pilot to just three tasks, the effort was not small in scale—they trained 467 people over a nine-week period. Even then, take good data before and after the training so that the results can be broadcast to show how TWI helped make an improvement. Also, while the pilot is running, follow the instruction activities closely to ensure they are being carried out faithfully and energetically by those who have taken the 10-hour classes.

If you picked the correct area to run the pilot and if you shepherded the process meticulously to ensure that the instruction method was properly installed as described in the next section, then before long everyone should be able to see positive change coming out of the effort. This will create "pull" from the entire organization for JI training as executives as well as supervisors begin asking for the training to be given in other areas outside of the pilot site. As we always tell our new trainers, "You will know your efforts are succeeding when supervisors come up to you and ask to be put into a 10-hour training class."

Initial Delivery of TWI Training

By maintaining a limited scope to pilot the initial TWI effort, you will be able to avoid the big mistake many organizations make when they become enamored with the TWI program—to try and break down and reteach every job in the facility. As tempting as that may sound, it is doomed to failure because the training activity is so dispersed that, while some good results may happen, the training cannot be monitored and controlled and will soon

get watered down and lose momentum. Even after the program has stabilized beyond the pilot, as we discussed in Chapter 7, you still do not want
or need to teach every single job in the facility. The smarter course is to start
small and *build momentum*.

No two organizations are alike and no two hospitals even within the
same organization have the same culture, so there is no set plan to begin JI
training. The TWI Institute can assist hospitals and health care organizations
with making a training plan and provide trainers for the classes. But some
considerations for the initial training classes can be as follows:

■ The first class(es) of trainers should be a select group of people who will
be responsible for implementing JI in the pilot area. The group could
include nurses, assistant nurses, staff, "informal floor leaders," and other
support staff. The class can also include trainer candidates (who will go
on later to become 10-hour class trainers) so that they will be ready to
take the trainer development program in the next phase of the rollout.

■ The JI classes should be delivered to groups of 10 participants in each
class.

■ Training must be scheduled to make the best use of the participants'
time. The TWI class is designed to be given 2 hours per day over a
5-day period, for a total of 10 hours. The best way to learn a skill, just
like learning to play the piano, is to practice a little each day, but when
you try to cram the 10 hours of training into a day and a half or two
days, people just don't "get it." On the other hand, it is not possible
to pull a nurse off the floor for just two hours out of a day when she
has been assigned a group of patients. So, in this case the training for
frontline staff could be delivered offline for five days: two hours/day of
class, one to two hours/day of individual preparation and practice, and
the remaining time spent on other projects on the unit including extra
practice making breakdowns and, toward the end of the week, more
practice giving instruction as described in the last bullet point below.

■ If they are not actual participants in the class, key people, such as
management and support staff, may and should observe the training
to understand the content. Only then will they be able to support the
people being trained when they move on to implementing their new JI
skills. However, they should remain observers and not interrupt or take
part in the class activities.

■ TWI trainers should give one-on-one guidance to help participants
select a good JI practice demonstration for the class. Typically, trainees

select practice jobs that are too large in scope and complexity for the training. The purpose of the training is to learn and practice the method, not to break down and teach the most difficult job in the department. What they learn, though, with this guidance, is that when we neglect the "easy" jobs, that failure leads to many, if not most, of our "difficult" problems.

■ To a limited degree, TWI trainers also give, in the participants' workplaces, additional instruction and guidance with making JI breakdowns for the practice demonstrations. But they should never tell them how to do it. That would take away from the learning experience.

■ While *all* the practice demonstrations take place in a classroom setting where people can hear and there are few distractions, we have found it very effective, if time permits, to do one *last* application practice in the facility and at an actual working space using a real worker who has not taken the JI class to act as a learner. This allows the class to get a taste of what JI is like in actual practice now that they have learned how to do it in the classroom.

The people who take these initial classes should then begin applying their new TWI skills to the jobs in the designated pilot area. The TWI Working Group leading the project should be completely engaged in this process so that questions are answered and stumbling blocks overcome. For example, there will inevitably be much difficulty making the initial JI breakdowns for training as this skill takes a lot of practice and perseverance to master. As we saw in both the hand hygiene (Chapter 3) and the RF identification equipment introduction (Chapter 4) case studies, the teams of trainers spent a lot of time and effort up front developing the breakdowns and making sure they were "just right" with trial deliveries before taking them out to the hospital floors and ORs to train. This investment will pay great dividends when it comes to successfully training the jobs and this will, in turn, help them to develop strong skills in making good job breakdowns for future training.

Having made sure that the JI method was actively applied to the pilot area, positive results will follow as the targeted jobs begin to stabilize. Because we have picked a pilot area that is well known for troubles or opportunities, everyone in the organization will see the improvements made through the TWI intervention or, if they don't see them, you should broadcast these results using the before and after data you meticulously collected during the pilot period. It won't be long, if it hasn't happened already, before other areas begin asking for the TWI training to be given to them so that they, too, can benefit from the method and get the same kind of good results. This is a typical pattern we have seen in countless rollouts in all industries including health care.

Based on this feedback from the organization and your strategy for wider implementation, you can begin to plan the next area(s) to apply TWI. Keep in mind, as you move forward from the pilot, that it will still be wise to "go slow to go fast." Resist the temptation to apply the method everywhere but, taking it one step at a time, continue to build on the "pull" you have created from the overall organization. The moral of Aesop's tale of "The Tortoise and the Hare" applies especially well here—slow but steady always wins.

Create In-House Trainers

Once the pilot has had time to show results and nears completion, it is time to think about the next step which is to have more people outside of the initial pilot group take the 10-hour training and begin practicing the JI skills. You could have certified TWI trainers come back and deliver more sessions, but the best way of proceeding is to develop in-house trainers who take a trainer development program, sometimes called a "train-the-trainer" class, in which they learn to deliver the 10-hour sessions following the TWI Trainer Delivery Manual. This is how the program was designed to spread and the key to engaging what we called the "multiplier effect."

There are many reasons why this is the best approach, but perhaps the most important one is that these in-house trainers can act as the "TWI experts" for the facility in the JI method. Taking the trainer development course not only allows the person to be able to teach the 10-hour class, but it helps her or him to get much deeper into the material and to understand the nuances of the method. Once they begin training others and help them begin practicing the skills for themselves, then the trainer's mastery of the method grows. As the saying goes, the person who learns the most in the class is the teacher. The TWI trainer who works inside the organization and knows the many details of the work of the health care facility is in an excellent position now to guide the effort as it grows from department to department. An outside trainer will not be as familiar with that work and will not be as available on a constant and consistent basis.

The next question that comes up is "Who is best qualified to teach TWI?" The TWI Trainer Delivery Manuals were designed and written so that even a person who had little or no experience in training could learn how to put on the courses. They literally tell the trainer what to say and do every step of the way. However, it is a big mistake to think that one can simply pick up the manual, study it, and then begin teaching classes successfully. We saw how the Japanese Labor Ministry, in their first attempt to get TWI started in Japan, failed to trigger the multiplier effect because they thought that a single person could go learn it and bring it back. Fortunately for everyone, the Japanese wound up starting over by hiring qualified instructors who were able to train trainers properly based on their vast experience developing and promoting TWI during the war. There is an incredible amount of wisdom and technique embedded in the TWI manuals and it takes an experienced TWI professional, what we call the master trainer, to guide a new trainer to finding out how to deliver the courses correctly using this invaluable resource.

People with no training background, then, when put into a trainer development program directed by a qualified master trainer, can learn to teach the TWI classes effectively getting the same great results literally millions of trainers have been getting for over seven decades. In fact, our experience has been that the best trainers are those who have little or no training experience, but a deep background in the industry and jobs in which they are working. This is not a coincidence. On the one hand, consultants and professional trainers tend to want to put their own "flavor" or "spin" on the training they give by injecting their unique personalities and perspectives. This goes directly against the "standard delivery" approach of the TWI formula and these people have a difficult time when they are told to "follow the manual." On the other hand, because the bulk of the TWI 10-hour class is spent on actual jobs brought in from the work site, the trainer must be familiar with the work being done in the facility to effectively lead the group in applying the JI method in this "learn by doing" approach. Understanding the jobs, then, is a more important qualification than experience as an instructor.

Typically, the Clinical Education Department would be where a health care instructor would live in the training organization. But, with the TWI model, we can see how the person delivering the JI 10-hour class could be a part of the education department, the process improvement department, human resources, frontline staff departments, or any number of other possibilities. Everyone has a stake in good training and understanding the Job Instruction method and incorporating its principles, but each organization will have to find the right place for these JI instructors that fits into its model of care delivery. The key is that these JI instructors have some firsthand knowledge of the jobs as well as ample time to interact with the people they are training to deliver the JI method.

With in-house trainers on board, the organization can put on JI sessions at will and develop this essential skill of job instruction where needed throughout the workforce. These trainers also will be able to serve as coaches and consultants for the ongoing TWI implementation as it spreads throughout the organization.

Create a Rollout Plan and Spread the Training

We started out this chapter showing how C. R. Dooley of the TWI Service instructed companies on *How to Get Continuing Results in a Plant from Training Within Industry* in June 1944. As he said so eloquently, "It is another splendid example of the combined efforts of many TWI people." While there is no cookie-cutter approach to rolling out TWI, we feel that the best plan that provides the foundation for companies to build a long-term successful TWI program is just the Phase 1 and Phase 2 approach Dooley gave us as outlined at the beginning of this chapter. When companies deviate from this standard, but basic, approach is when they tend to fail.

The key to this plan is to have everyone on board, from top management to floor supervisors. Notice how the plan suggests giving the JI training to management personnel even though they may never actually teach a person how to do a job. What is so unique about the TWI training is that it gives a hands-on experience that is invaluable to truly understanding the method and, once that is accomplished, management can see for themselves the true need for good training because they have actually done it. Remember how, after completing the hand hygiene pilot, Virginia Mason's medical director, Donna Smith, actually took the 10-hour JI training and became a true believer in the method after she saw how easy it was to teach a person to properly take a throat culture, which was her practice job in the class. Also, when the head of nursing at Virginia Mason, Charleen Tachibana, saw the power of the training method, she herself became a JI trainer teaching nurses and nursing aides during the pilot and this sent a clear message to her staff that this was a method everyone needed to learn and to use.

Another key aspect to the plan is its focus on supporting and coaching supervisors and others responsible for doing the training. By having leaders who are assigned responsibility for creating continuing results, these leaders not only assist trainers in getting the training done, but also require results and stay in touch with the effort through continuous and active reporting. As the plan states: The purpose of the report is to show the relative improvement accomplished by the use of the methods. And by highlighting the need to give "prompt and proper" credit for those results, we can maintain continued interest in and use of the methods.

As we noted earlier, the "detailed plan for basic training and continuing use" should start small and gradually build in breadth and depth. It bears repeating that a common mistake is to try and do too much training right up front because we see so much need for it. But keep in mind that the hospital or health care facility is already up and running and functioning and that most of the people know and do their jobs pretty well on a continuing basis. When we select the critical areas that need our attention and focus on these one by one, we get the "biggest bang for our buck" and then can move on to the next priority.

Introduce JR and, Later, JM

From a logical perspective, if you studied Section III of this book carefully you might be thinking Job Relations should have been introduced and promoted before Job Instruction because, first, we have to *lead* people if we want them to *follow* our instructions. For some organizations that understand this basic principle, they do begin with JR but, honestly, they are few and very far between. And this is not a mistake. Job Instruction was the first TWI program developed and it is still to this day the most popular and a very good place to start. As we have been describing throughout this chapter, an organization needs to see quick and dynamic results if it wants to move the culture to change, and having a focused pilot project rollout with Job Instruction accomplishes this quite effectively. Changing people's behavior with Job Relations, on the other hand, is a slower and not so visible process despite the deep and lasting results it eventually brings. Beginning with JR, then, runs the risk of having the initiative "die on the vine" as people lose initial enthusiasm waiting for the promised change to occur.

When an organization begins moving forward with Job Instruction, however, it will quickly see, in spite of the great results quickly obtained in job stability and work standardization, that something is still missing. Not everyone is reacting to the good and better instruction as expected and the effect is clearly not at 100 percent. This is when the need for Job Relations skill reveals itself. Most organizations that implement Job Instruction quickly come around to seeing this need, like the LEGO corporation that had a truly excellent culture of progressive human resource practice where they initially felt they didn't need JR. But after starting a world-wide JI implementation they realized that the JR method was not only something they needed, but a skill that could quickly be adopted because their supervisors were already trained in JI and were familiar and comfortable with the TWI style of 10-hour courses and four-step methods.* What is more, the JR method helped them leverage and fully utilize other "soft-skill" programs they had been previously training like listening skills, constructive feedback, change management, and problem solving.

There is one big difference, though, in the way we recommend rolling out Job Relations. Whereas with Job Instruction we went through a meticulous process of starting on the ground level with a limited pilot project and then letting the program evolve and mature one step at a time throughout the organization, Job Relations should start at the top of the organization and intentionally flow down, one level of management at a time. When we teach JR directly to frontline supervisors, the persistent comment we hear is, "I love this method and want to use it with my people; but my boss doesn't treat me this way and I'll be darned if I do it." People treat others the way they are treated and if we want to change their behavior we must first set a good example for them and model the JR method and foundations.

Without exception, the best results we have seen for an organization-wide rollout of JR is when training is started at the very top, with the CEO of the hospital and her staff, so they can begin utilizing the four-step method and foundations on the people who report to them. Once they see, and experience, the difference in how they are being treated in this more effective and respectful manner, this next level can then learn the method and repeat the cycle for the people who report to them. Continue the process until you get to your frontline supervisors who, by this time, perhaps many months, have begun to recognize that management is "walking the talk" and is serious about a change in how the organization should be treating its people. By building strong relationships, these frontline supervisors will now be in a stronger position to influence how work is done on a regular basis and

---

* Patrick Graupp, Gitte Jakobsen, and John Vellema, *Building a Global Learning Organization: Using TWI to Succeed with Strategic Workforce Expansion in the LEGO Group* (Boca Raton, FL: CRC Press, 2014).

skillfully lead people in their own departments to implement the standard work we are trying to establish.

Finally, now that a strong basis of leadership and instruction has been established that can promote and sustain standard work practices, your organization can move on to improving those standards. This is the *kaizen* process and is covered by the TWI Job Methods Improvement plan which will be described in the next chapter. Continuous improvement is a big topic that is covered in countless books and we will not try to recommend any specific implementation methodology. However, we can say that, from our experience, there is no rush to move to JM once you have established JI and JR. In fact, most of our clients regularly say, when we recommend JM to them, that they are getting so much benefit and value from JI alone that they do not want to distract from that effort by introducing a new method. In fact, there is an improvement component to the JI activity because, when we standardize a job around "the one best way," it means that the "not so best ways" go away. Nevertheless, most organizations have some kind of improvement activity going on, whether it be a simple suggestion box or a well-organized idea management system, and it is not that they are ignoring improvement. But there is so much benefit to be gained in the immediate term just by focusing on creating and sustaining standard work that the attention should remain here and not be rushed to "the next best thing" until standard work is well established. As we will see in the next chapter, the stability in the process created by standard work will be a condition for starting the improvement journey.

Conclusion

Figure 10.1 sums up our recommended implementation steps. By getting passionate people in place to lead a TWI implementation, by creating a good plan to start training, by being sure management's strong support of the TWI skills is firmly in place, by creating in-house trainers who will continue to spread the program and follow up directly with implementation, and by supporting training and TWI activities on the floor, you can be sure to have TWI fulfill its promise of creating a strong foundation for the highest quality health care services.

TWI Implementation Steps	
Form TWI Working Group	Select strong leader Form cross-functional team Study TWI fundamentals
Create Pilot Project	Limited in scope Process/Area/Task in need of Standard Work Obtain current metrics
Initial JI Training	10-hour Job Instruction classes A select group who will work in pilot area Include TWI Trainer candidates
Carry Out Pilot Project	Break down and train pilot area jobs Close guidance and support from TWI Working Group Obtain after training metrics
Publicize Pilot & Plan Next Steps	Create "pull" from other parts of organization Plan for next areas to push out training
Develop In-house Trainers	Key members learn to teach JI 10-hour class Training for supervisors/trainers outside of pilot area
Roll-out JI to Entire Organization	Slow but steady — not everywhere at once Ensure top management commitment Provide adequate coverage Continued coaching for supervisors Reports to management Give credit for results
Introduce JR and, later, JM	Roll-out JR from top to bottom When ready, introduce and promote JM Create system for handling improvement proposals

Figure 10.1 TWI implementation steps. (From P. Graupp and R. J. Wrona. 2011. *Implementing TWI: Creating and Managing a Skills-Based Culture.* **Boca Raton, FL: Taylor & Francis Group/CRC Press. With permission.)**

Chapter 11

Four Steps of Job Methods Improvement

Introduction

As discussed throughout this book, the foundation of quality care is to provide patients with the best practices available that are performed correctly and consistently by each worker delivering health care. We have called these best practices "standard work" because they are defined and performed based on a standard that has been proven to be effective when learned and practiced in the standard way. However, as we noted right from the start in Chapter 2, these standards are not written in stone. In fact, the PDSA cycle of continuous improvement defines a never-ending process of bettering that standard as we move to "better practice" from the "current practice" where our standard work is the wedge that locks in our progress at the next higher level (see Figure 2.2). The TWI founders recognized this potential and the need to add to our skill set the ability to improve our current methods. Specifically, Job Methods Improvement is a four-step method that helps supervisors develop an improvement plan *to deliver higher quality patient care more efficiently by making the best use of the people, equipment and supplies **now** available.*

Note that in defining the objective for JM, the TWI developers stated we must make "the best use of the people, equipment and supplies *now* available" which means JM is *not* about investing large amounts of money in new technologies, infrastructure, and so on. It is about what you can do better with what you have right now. Of course, there is an important role

DOI: 10.4324/9781003035305-11

for specialized staff to work on broader scale improvements, for example, automated dispensing cabinets for drug storage and disbursement or even robots for surgery like the Da Vinci surgical system. As supervisors, though, you don't have to wait for these big and expensive investments to start making real improvements to your jobs right now.

While there are many ways to increase health care efficiency, the most effective way is through improving job methods. If you stop to think about it, most of the affordable products that consumers enjoy today are a result of improvements in production methods. For example, it did not take long for the first cell phones, with few makes and models costing several hundreds of dollars, to be replaced by smart phones and a myriad of options with the cheapest ones practically being given away. This kind of rapid progress comes from countless improvements and the same effect can be had in health care as we shall see demonstrated in this chapter. JM is a practical method that accomplishes this quickly and easily.

Example of TWI Job Methods Practice

A frontline manager in charge of perioperative care at a large hospital was taking the Job Methods training class, two hours per day over a five-day period, when a big problem arose on Wednesday of that week. Perioperative care is the treatment given to a patient before and after they go into surgery, and blood was drawn by a phlebotomist* from the lab on a patient who was getting ready for surgery. Here it was imperative that blood be drawn from the opposite, non-operative, side of the body so as not to jeopardize the ability to perform the surgery, but the phlebotomist mistakenly drew blood from the operative side. What made matters worse, the same mistake had occurred just two weeks prior to this and the surgeon was frustrated and angry at these unnecessary delays.

When she heard about it, the manager's first inclination was to call up the lab and give them a piece of her mind. How could this have happened again?! And why didn't your lab tech follow the procedure of drawing blood from the arm that did *not* have the patient's arm band attached, the standard practice that was designed to prevent this mistake from happening? Obviously, relationships between the Operating Room and the Lab were being strained here as the standards for the work were not being upheld.

---

* A specialist who draws and prepares blood for medical testing, transfusions or donation.

But Kelly, the manager in charge, thought to herself, "I'm taking this JM class, so why don't I try and use it to see if I can make this better. What do I have to lose?"

In the current method of the Date of Surgery Blood Draw procedure, after placing an arm band on the non-operative side of the patient, the perioperative nurse then went to the computer to release the orders in the EMR (Electronic Medical Records) system which automatically assigned the blood draw procedure as a "Lab Draw," rather than a "Nurse Draw." This meant that once the orders were entered into the system the lab was automatically scheduled to come to the surgery holding room to collect the blood before surgery. The lab tech would then print labels in the lab and take them with her to the pre-op area, some 200 feet distance from the lab. At the nurses' station, the lab tech would check the white board to confirm the location of her patient and then walk another 50 feet to the patient. After verifying the patient's name and date of birth with the arm band on the patient, she would draw the blood from the non-operative side of the patient's body, label the specimens at the bedside, and then take them back 250 feet to the lab for processing. This was the current method.

After using her new skills in the JM method, Kelly came up with following new method based on ideas she got from using the method. The perioperative nurses, who were directly preparing the patient for surgery, would now do the blood draw themselves since, as RNs, they were qualified to draw blood and were already setting up an IV for the patient, so they knew very clearly which side of the patient's body to draw from. Since they could draw the blood samples directly from this IV port they had already inserted, there would no longer be a need to "stick" the patient twice. A printer was placed in the holding area so the labels could be printed right there instead of in the lab. A pneumatic tube transport system was already in place and the samples could then be sent directly to lab using the canisters that already sent X-rays, patient results, drugs, and test results throughout the hospital.

The results of Kelly's proposed method included the elimination of the walking by the lab tech and, more significantly, the interruption of that lab tech's daily round in the hospital to walk over to the OR holding rooms when orders came through for a surgery that was previously scheduled. The new method greatly reduced the risk of error and also eliminated the patient's discomfort of having to get two needle sticks by combining the blood draw with the IV start, significantly reducing the total amount of work. Moreover, the perioperative manager had the opportunity to improve

HOW TO IMPROVE
JOB METHODS

A practical plan to help you deliver *higher quality patient care more efficiently* by making the **best use** of the **people, equipment and supplies now available**.

STEP 1 – BREAK DOWN THE JOB

1. List **all** details of the job **exactly** as done in the **Current Method**.
2. Be sure details include everything:
   — Material Handling
   — Machine Work
   — Hand Work

STEP 2 – QUESTION EVERY DETAIL

1. Use these types of questions:
   WHY is it necessary?
   WHAT is its purpose?
   WHERE should it be done?
   WHEN should it be done?
   WHO is best qualified to do it?
   HOW is the 'best way' to do it?
2. Question the following at the same time:
   Supplies, Instruments, Equipment, Tools, Workplace Layout, Movement, Safety, Housekeeping

STEP 3 – DEVELOP THE NEW METHOD

1. **ELIMINATE** unnecessary details
2. **COMBINE** details when practical
3. **REARRANGE** details for better sequence
4. **SIMPLIFY** all necessary details
   To make the job easier and safer to do:
   - Put supplies, instruments & equipment into the **best position** and **within convenient reach** for the worker
   - Use **gravity feed hoppers** or **drop delivery chutes** whenever possible
   - Make effective use of **both hands**
   - Use **holders or devices** instead of hands
5. Work out your ideas WITH OTHERS
6. WRITE UP the proposed new method

STEP 4 – APPLY THE NEW METHOD

1. SELL your proposal to the *boss*
2. SELL the new method to the *staff*
3. Get FINAL APPROVAL of all concerned on Safety, Quality, Delivery, Cost, etc.
4. PUT the new method TO WORK. Use it until a **better** way is developed.
5 Give CREDIT where credit is due

Figure 11.1   JM four-step method pocket card.

the relationship between her department and the Lab by making the work they needed to coordinate together more efficient and error free.

To understand the Job Methods Improvement plan, you need to learn and follow the JM four-step method, which is on the JM pocket card (see Figure 11.1). These four steps were all that Kelly used to improve the Date of Surgery Blood Draw. Let's take a look at just how she used the JM four-step method to get these great results.

Step 1: Break Down the Job

The starting point of all JM improvements is making a job breakdown listing all the details of how a job is currently performed. A job breakdown creates a complete record and an accurate picture of how a job is executed. It gives the supervisor the opportunity to review forgotten details or details so familiar they are performed almost unconsciously. Inevitably, it also lets the supervisor see if something needs to be improved. The more detailed and accurate the breakdown is, the more complete and effective the improvements will be. *Details* mean, quite literally, *every single movement that is done in the job* including inspections or even delays.

Applying Step 1 to Date of Surgery (DOS) Blood Draw

Let's take a look at the DOS Blood Draw job and make a breakdown for the Current Method (CM) of doing the work, the way the job was done before Kelly made any improvements. What happened first? The process begins when the nurse places an armband on the patient's non-operative side arm. The first detail is *Place armband on pt.—On non-operative side.* She then turns to her computer, which is on a wheeled stand next to the patient, and releases the order to EPIC, the hospital's computer system, making sure to include the bay number so the lab knows where the patient is waiting. The second detail is *Release orders in EPIC—Include Bay #.* What happened next? The job continues in the lab where the orders are sent automatically by the computer. The third detail is *Lab receives order—Automatic setting: Lab, not Nurse Draw.* If the lab tech is doing rounds, she must return to the lab first in order to retrieve the orders and print labels. The fourth detail is *Return to lab— up to 1,000 ft.* and the fifth detail is *Print labels.* Continuing in this way, you can capture everything that is done in the job, detail by detail. Figure 11.2 shows a breakdown of the entire job in the three main columns on the left side of the form.

Job Breakdown Sheet

PROCESS: Date of Surgery (DOS) Blood Draw   MADE BY: Kelly T.   DATE: Aug. 16, 20xx
OPERATIONS: ID check, blood draw, label specimen   DEPARTMENT: Peri-Op

	CURRENT METHOD DETAILS	Distance traveled in feet	REMARKS TIME/TOLERANCE/ REJECTS/SAFETY	WHY-WHAT	WHERE	WHEN	WHO	HOW	IDEAS Write them down, don't try to remember.	Eliminate	Combine	Rearrange	Simplify
1	Place arm band on patient (pt)		On non-operative side										
2	Release orders in EPIC		Include Bay #										
3	Lab receives orders		Automatic setting: Lab, not Nurse Draw										
4	Lab tech walks back to Lab	~1,000 ft.	During daily rounds										
5	Print labels												
6	Lab tech walks to Pre-op	200 ft.											
7	Check white board at nurses' station												
8	Walk to holding area	50 ft.											
9	Verify pt's name & DOB		Looking at armband										
10	Draw blood		From non-operative side										
11	Label specimens												
12	Transport to lab	250 ft.											
13	Run lab test												

Figure 11.2   Current method JM breakdown sheet for Step 1.

Now consider how long it would take you to think of the first five details as outlined above? Probably not more than a few minutes. At that pace, you can do a breakdown for the entire job in 10 to 15 minutes. This is not usually a favorite part of the method, especially for busy nurses and staff who find it excruciating to dwell on small details like how far it takes to walk from one point of the hospital to another. But it is time well invested because it lets you see what can be improved.

Notice that Figure 11.2 includes a column for remarks. This space is used for recording anything that might be useful to know about any particular detail: distances, specifications, waste, errors, safety, time taken, etc. It can also be used for comments about actions that are important but are not details. For example, when the lab received the orders in detail #3, the computer system was set up to automatically classify it as a "lab draw" and not a "nurse draw" which sent the order directly to the lab for processing. Kelly noted this in the remark's column rather than in the details column because this was not something performed by the people doing the procedure but was a critical point in this detail.

This JM breakdown is very different from the breakdowns for Job Instruction we looked at in Chapter 6. In JI, we listed only the Important Steps which were "logical segments" of the operation which served to *advance the work*; anything that is "common sense" or clear to the operator is not included. In Job Methods, on the contrary, each Important Step may include quite a number of details. For JM, *you must list all details because you cannot omit anything in the search for improvement.*

The best place to do a job breakdown is at the job site. Don't rely on your memory. Make sure you actually "go and see" the details. Get complete and accurate facts. At the worksite, if you are observing other people performing the job, tell them what you are doing and why you are doing it. Show them your job breakdown sheet and ask for their help. Tell them about the JM program and show them the JM four-step method pocket card so they can work with you as you go through the method. In most cases, when staff understand the purpose and technique of JM, they become very enthusiastic about participating.

Step 2: Question Every Detail

Your success in improving an operation will depend on your ability to question everything about that operation. In Step 2, question every detail of the job that you broke down in Step 1. Use the "Five W's and One H" presented below.

	Five W's and One H
1.	*Why* is it necessary?
2.	*What* is its purpose?
3.	*Where* should it be done?
4.	*When* should it be done?
5.	*Who* is best qualified to do it?
6.	*How* is the "best way" to do it?

The answers to these six questions have taught us practically all we know now about the world around us and are very useful for JM and improvement. They are most useful when they are asked in the order presented. There is a very good reason for this. When you ask "*How* should we improve this detail?" before you ask "*Why* is it necessary?" you may waste time improving something only to find out later that the detail was not necessary.

It is important *not* to act on any answer in this sequence prematurely. When an answer gives you an idea for improvement, it is often tempting to go and put that idea into effect immediately. Resist the temptation and continue the questioning process because you may find another idea later that supersedes or eliminates the need for a previous idea. When you do get a good idea for something, just *write it down* on the breakdown sheet. Ask all of the questions, in the right order, for each detail before proceeding to the next detail. Do not act until you have questioned all of the details so that your improvement plan is complete and well thought through.

Asking the Five W's and One H

Let's look at each of these questions individually. "*Why* is it necessary?" is the most important question. Asking this question first, for each detail, helps you distinguish between necessary and unnecessary details. "*What* is its purpose?" is a check question for "*Why* is it necessary?" It lets you see if the detail has any useful purpose or if it adds quality or value to patient care. In other words, it confirms that a detail is necessary or allows you to see that it is not.

If you decide that a detail is necessary, continue asking questions. "*Where* should it be done?" helps determine the *best place* to do each detail: In which department? In which work area? On which equipment or work station? "*When* should it be done?" helps determine the *best time* to do the detail: First or last? In what order? Before or after some other detail(s)? When will the necessary people, instruments, supplies, equipment, or tools, be available? "*Who* is best qualified to do it?" determines the *best person* for this detail in terms of knowledge, skill level, licensure, experience, physical strength, or availability. "*How* is the 'best way' to do it?" is the last question in the sequence because it should only be addressed when the answers to all the other questions are covered. Usually there is a better way when we think about it.

Questioning Other Important Items Regarding the Overall Job

In addition to questioning every detail of the job process in Step 2, you must take into consideration and question a list of important items for the overall job. This list is shown on item 2 of Step 2 on the JM pocket card (Figure 11.1) and includes *supplies, instruments, equipment, tools, workplace layout, movement, safety,* and *housekeeping*. Questioning these items at the same time you question the details of the job helps you develop a complete improvement plan. For example, *supplies, instruments, equipment,* and *tools* can be expensive and hard to get, so improving their usage can make a dramatic improvement in efficiency. Even minor changes in the *movement* or in the *layout* of the area or the workplace can save on unnecessary effort and floor or working space. Because poor *safety* and *housekeeping* habits can lead to injuries or inefficient work, you must consider them when analyzing the details of the job procedure itself.

Applying Step 2 to DOS Blood Draw

Now that you understand what questions to ask, why to ask them, and in what order to ask them, let's review how Kelly applied these questions to the details of the DOS Blood Draw. For this process, Kelly continued using the breakdown sheet presented in Figure 11.3. The left-hand columns of the table show the details and remarks obtained in Step 1. To the right of these are columns for the questions. Notice that "Why?" and "What?" are combined in one column since they address the same question of necessity. To the right

Job Breakdown Sheet

PROCESS: Date of Surgery (DOS) Blood Draw   MADE BY: Kelly T.   DATE: Aug. 16, 20xx
OPERATIONS: ID check, blood draw, label specimen   DEPARTMENT: Peri-Op

	CURRENT METHOD DETAILS	Distance traveled in feet	REMARKS TIME/TOLERANCE/ REJECTS/SAFETY	WHY-WHAT	WHERE	WHEN	WHO	HOW	IDEAS Write them down, don't try to remember.	Eliminate	Combine	Rearrange	Simplify
1	Place arm band on patient (pt)		On non-operative side										
2	Release orders in EPIC		Include Bay #										
3	Lab receives orders		Automatic setting: Lab, not Nurse Draw	X					Find out why. Nurse can draw if able to print labels				
4	Lab tech walks back to Lab	~1,000 ft.	During daily rounds	X					No need if nurse draw				
5	Print labels				X		X		Place label printer in holding area				
6	Lab tech walks to Pre-op	200 ft.		X					Same as #4				
7	Check white board at nurses' station			X					Same as #4				
8	Walk to holding area	50 ft.		X					Same as #4				
9	Verify pt's name & DOB		Looking at armband			X	X		Already done by nurse on entry to room				
10	Draw blood		From non-operative side			X	X	X	When nurse starts IV, Draw blood from IV				
11	Label specimens				X		X		Print in holding area				
12	Transport to lab	250 ft.						X	Use tube system				
13	Run lab test												

Figure 11.3 Current method JM breakdown sheet for Step 2.

of the question columns is a column for Ideas. (The columns at the far right are used in Step 3 of the process and are discussed later in this chapter).

Because the answers to the questions stimulate new ideas and suggest improvements, Kelly questioned each of the details, one by one. For the first two details, *Place arm band on patient* and *Release orders in EPIC*, she questioned these details by asking each question for each detail and determined that the current method was good as is and didn't have any ideas for improvement. It was from detail #3 that she began to get ideas. Let's take a look at her thinking process as she used the questioning pattern of Step 2 to come up with ideas and to record them on the breakdown sheet. Follow along with Figure 11.3 as we review the comments illustrating her thinking process for each detail.

Details 3 and 4: Lab receives orders and Lab tech walks back to lab

Why is it necessary?
"To ensure that the blood draw process is started. But is it necessary for the lab to come and draw the blood?"
What is its purpose?
"This is questionable. Why does the system automatically assign a lab draw when our nurses are qualified to do it? Let's find out why."

The system was set up to have an automatic lab draw. In cases like this, supervisors are tempted to think, "This is the way it is supposed to be." This is when the check question *"What* is its purpose?" comes into good use. You cannot simply accept the current method. You have to find the purpose for the work. Kelly wondered if the lab coming to take the blood added value to patient care. Furthermore, she thought, her pre-op nurses were qualified to draw blood and they knew the surgery being performed and which side of the patient's body was the non-operative side. She wrote, "Find out why" in the "Ideas" column along with a note that "Nurse can draw if able to print labels" and put a checkmark in the "Why" column. She put a checkmark in the "Why" column because the idea she got for this detail came from answering the question "Why?" Since she thought she could eliminate the detail, she didn't bother asking the remaining questions and moved on to the next detail. She questioned Detail 4 in the same way and came up with the same ideas. See Figure 11.3 to see how Kelly recorded her ideas on the breakdown sheet for the questions for these two details.

Detail 5: Print labels

Why is it necessary?
   "Necessary to track blood with the correct patient."
What is its purpose?
   "We have to make sure we don't mix up blood specimens. So this detail is necessary." Since Kelly determined that this detail was necessary, she continued with the questioning.
Where should it be done?
   "How about printing the labels right in the holding area?" If the nurse could draw the blood, then she would have to be able to print the labels as well. "Since all the printers are connected to the EMR," Kelly thought, "what difference does it make where they are printed?"
When should it be done?
   "Any time before the blood draw. This is the same as in the current method."
Who is the best person?
   "The nurse. This is different and follows the same idea in detail #3."
How should it be done?
   "This is pretty straight forward. The same way as in the current method."

In the current method, the lab tech printed the labels in the lab before leaving to go to the pre-op area. But if a printer were made available in the holding area, the nurse could print them just before drawing the blood herself, instead of waiting for the lab tech to come and collect it. Kelly wrote, "Place label printer in holding area" in the "Ideas" column and put a checkmark in the "Where" and "Who" columns.

Detail 6: Lab tech walks to pre-op

Why is it necessary?
"If it's not necessary for the lab tech to draw the blood, then it's not necessary for her to walk to pre-op."

Kelly felt that by having a nurse in the perioperative area do the blood draw there would be no need to have a lab person come to the area. She wrote, "No, if nurse draws when starting IV" in the "Ideas" column and put a checkmark in the "Why" column.

Detail 7: Check white board at nurses' station

Why is it necessary?
"Not necessary since the attending nurse is already with the patient."

Kelly felt that the only reason for checking the patient's location was because the lab tech would not be familiar with where patients were assigned in the holding area. If the nurse did the blood draw, then she doesn't have the need to find out where the patient is because she is with them already. She wrote, "Same as #4" in the "Ideas" column and put a checkmark in the "Why" column for this detail.

Detail 8: Walk to holding area

Why is it necessary?
"More walking! There is no need for the nurse to walk since she is already with the patient." She wrote, "Same as #4" in the "Ideas" column and put a checkmark in the "Why" column for this detail.

Detail 9: Verify pt's name and DOB

Why is it necessary?
"Necessary to maintain safety and quality of patient care."

What is its purpose?

"We have to make sure we don't mix up the correct patient with the correct treatment." This detail was obviously necessary, so she continued with the questioning.

Where should it be done?

"At bedside. This is the same as the current method."

When should it be done?

"Since the nurse has already verified the patient's name and date of birth on entry into the room, this detail will be done earlier in the process. This is different from the current method."

Who is the best person?

"The nurse. This is different and follows the same idea as in detail #3."

How should it be done?

"The same way as in the current method."

She wrote, "Already done by nurse on entry into room" in the "Ideas" column and put a checkmark in the "When" and "Who" columns for this detail.

Detail 10: Draw blood

Why is it necessary?

"Necessary to prepare for surgery."

What is its purpose?

"To have lab results ready for the procedure." This detail is necessary, indeed the whole reason for doing the job in the first place.

Where should it be done?

"At bedside. This is the same as the current method."

When should it be done?

"Can be done at the same time as the IV is set up earlier. This is different from the current method and makes the overall work more efficient."

Who is the best person?

"The nurse. This is different and follows the same idea as in detail #3."

How should it be done?

"The blood specimens can be taken directly from the IV port. This is a better way because it will eliminate the need to stick the patient twice."

She wrote, "When nurse starts IV" in the "Ideas" column and put a checkmark in the "When" and "Who" column for this detail. She also wrote "Draw blood from IV" in the "Ideas" column and put a checkmark in the "How" column for this detail.

Details 11 and 12: Label specimens and Transport to lab

Kelly questioned *Details 10 and 11* in the same way. For "Label specimens" she wrote, "Nurse labels in holding area" in the "Ideas" column and put checkmarks in the "Where" and "Who" columns. For "Transport to lab" she noted that we could "use tube system" to transport the specimens to the lab and made a checkmark in the "How" column.

While Kelly was questioning each of these details and getting definitive answers, she wrote down her ideas and did not take any immediate actions. In this way, she was able to generate a thorough and complete analysis of the entire job. As a result, she discovered that certain ideas opened up the door to additional, complimentary ideas. She was now ready to move on to Step 3, Develop the New Method.

Step 3: Develop the New Method

In the last step, you learned to apply a questioning process to each detail of a job to discover ideas that can help improve a procedure. The next step is to formulate those ideas into a clear development plan for the new method. Step 3 of the Job Methods program provides tools that will easily and quickly lead you to a better way to do the work.

Health care organizations deliver higher quality patient care when they begin to *eliminate, combine, rearrange,* and *simplify* the details of each job. When you find opportunities to accomplish these four things, there is no question that you will improve the efficiency of your care delivery. This step will show you how questioning each detail in Step 2 leads directly to the development of the new method, which becomes your new and improved standard, using these four elements of improvement.

Four Improvement Elements

1. *Eliminate* unnecessary details.
2. *Combine* details when practical.
3. *Rearrange* details for better sequence.
4. *Simplify* all necessary details.

Job Breakdown Sheet

PROCESS: Date of Surgery (DOS) Blood Draw   MADE BY: Kelly T.   DATE: Aug. 16, 20xx
OPERATIONS: ID check, blood draw, label specimen   DEPARTMENT: Peri-Op

	CURRENT METHOD DETAILS	Distance traveled in feet	REMARKS TIME/TOLERANCE/ REJECTS/SAFETY	WHY-WHAT	WHERE	WHEN	WHO	HOW	IDEAS Write them down, don't try to remember.	Eliminate	Combine	Rearrange	Simplify
1	Place arm band on patient (pt)		On non-operative side										
2	Release orders in EPIC		Include Bay #										
3	Lab receives orders		Automatic setting: Lab, not Nurse Draw	X					Find out why. Nurse can draw if able to print labels	X			
4	Lab tech walks back to Lab	~1,000 ft.	During daily rounds	X					No need if nurse draw	X			
5	Print labels				X		X		Place label printer in holding area			X	X
6	Lab tech walks to Pre-op	200 ft.		X					Same as #4	X			
7	Check white board at nurses' station			X					Same as #4	X			
8	Walk to holding area	50 ft.		X					Same as #4	X			
9	Verify pt's name & DOB		Looking at armband			X	X		Already done by nurse on entry to room		X		
10	Draw blood		From non-operative side			X	X	X	When nurse starts IV, Draw blood from IV		X		X
11	Label specimens				X		X		In holding area		X		
12	Transport to lab	250 ft.						X	Use tube system				X
13	Run lab test												

Figure 11.4   Current method JM breakdown sheet for Step 3.

Notice that there is a definite order to these four items. If you eliminate a detail after spending time and effort to simplify it, you've wasted your time. Likewise, before you rearrange a set of details into a better sequence, check to see if there are any opportunities to combine those details and do them all at the same time. Eliminating is a 100 percent improvement because you don't have to do the detail at all. Combining two or more details is a 50 percent or more improvement. Although you still have to do all of these operations, you can do them at the same time instead of separately. Rearranging the order of several details produces less dramatic results, but if doing so reduces back-tracking and repetition, it is more efficient than what you are doing now. Simplifying an operation to make it easier and safer, only after you are sure it cannot be eliminated, combined, or rearranged, is an incremental improvement that fine-tunes the way the work is done. Let's look at these items individually, using Kelly's breakdown sheet for Step 3 (Figure 11.4).

Improvement Element 1: Eliminate Unnecessary Details

The goal is to eliminate details to avoid the unnecessary use of people, equipment, and supplies. If you have determined, by asking the question "Why?" in Step 2, that a detail serves no useful purpose, there is a good chance you can eliminate it without losing any added value to the job or patient care.

Kelly's notes on Figure 11.4 showed that she decided that details 3, 5, 6, and 7 could all be eliminated. All of these details have to do with the lab tech receiving the orders and walking to the pre-op area and can be eliminated if the pre-op nurse draws the blood instead of the lab tech. By making this one change, Kelly was able to eliminate four details of the job. As you can see on the breakdown sheet, she put a checkmark in the "Eliminate" column for each of these details.

Kelly found out that detail 3, the lab receiving the orders, was indeed unnecessary. Before making this decision, she consulted with the IT department. When she asked why the automatic setting for lab draw instead of nurse draw was necessary, the response was, "Are you guys still doing that?!" She learned that when the EMR system was put into place three years earlier the staff had been unsure how the new computer system would behave. To play it safe, they set it up as an automatic lab draw since the lab staff were specialists and could better adapt to any unusual or difficult circumstances created by the new system which they were unfamiliar with at the time. The EMR system had now been in place for several years and that concern was no longer valid. But the automatic settings remained and they had been doing the lab draw for several years for no good reason. It is very common for a practice to continue long after the reason for that task has gone away, such as when a temporary countermeasure is put in place when a problem is being addressed. The countermeasure continues even after the problem has been resolved. This is the reason why it is so important to ask "Why?" for every detail of a job.

Improvement Element 2: Combine Details When Practical

The answers to the questions "Where?" "When?" and "Who?" can help you find details that may be combined or done simultaneously. In the DOS Blood Draw improvement plan, Kelly found she could combine details 9 and 10, verifying the patient's name and DOB and drawing blood, with the setup of the IV which was taking place before the blood draw. With this change, the nurse, not the lab tech, would perform these details. Asking "Where?" and "When?" and "by Whom?" the blood should be drawn, she decided that the best person for this activity was the nurse who was already setting up the IV and could draw the blood directly from the IV port. Needless to say, the nurse would have already confirmed the patient's name and DOB before inserting the IV. The nurse could do all these details at one time and Kelly was able to improve the efficiency of the overall operation by combining these details.

Improvement Element 3: Rearrange Details for Better Sequence

Rearrange, the third improvement element in Step 3, is a good option to consider if it is impossible or unpractical to eliminate or combine details. Here again, the answers to the questions "Where?" "When?" and "Who?" suggest details that can be rearranged into a better sequence. Rearranging the order of details can help you save unnecessary movement of equipment or supplies and reduces backtracking and picking up and putting down motions.

Let's look at the details that Kelly rearranged. Because the blood would be drawn in the pre-op area and not in the lab, she had to set up a printer and rearrange the printing of the labels to be done in the holding area (detail 5). She would also rearrange this detail to be done before the IV setup, which had been done before the blood draw in the current method. Furthermore, the labels would be applied to the specimens directly after the blood draw and that also was rearranged to be done in the holding area, not the lab (detail 11). These details still had to be performed but would now be done by the nurse in the holding area before and after the IV setup. A common error in Step 3 is to think you have eliminated a detail because you don't have to do it anymore. But if it has been moved to another area or person, it still has to be done by someone and has not been eliminated.

Improvement Element 4: Simplify All Necessary Details

The fourth improvement element of Step 3 is to simplify details to make them *safer* and *easier* to do. It is facilitated by the question "How?" The JM pocket card (Figure 11.1) lists some specific principles that can help you find ideas for simplifying work details in Step 3. Let's look at how Kelly applied these principles to the sample job.

The first principle under simplify is *put supplies, instruments and equipment into the best position and within a convenient reach for the worker.* Everything the person needs to use is easy to pick up, within arm's reach, and placed at the worksite ahead of time on shelves or holders or racks. Keep in mind that this space is a semicircle radiating from the center of the body and varies according to a person's arm length. The second principle is *use gravity feed hoppers and drop delivery chutes whenever possible.* Coffee bean or candy dispensers at the supermarket and mail or laundry chutes are common examples of this principle. The third principle is to *make effective use of both hands,* a commonly overlooked common-sense improvement just like when you are typing on a keyboard.

Finally, the last principle for simplifying the work is to *use holders and devices instead of hands*. A holder is a *movable* mechanical holding device such as a clamp, a template, or a guide. A device is a *fixed* mechanical device usually used in connection with a piece of equipment. The terms are often used interchangeably because both holders and devices are made to hold supplies, parts, or instruments in place, freeing the hands to move. Without them, staff have to hold supplies in one hand and use the other hand to do a procedure. It is difficult, unwieldy, and often unsafe to do work this way.

Kelly applied these principles to details 5, 10, and 12. Following the first principle (*put equipment into the best position*), she had a printer placed directly in the holding area and within reach of the computer used for releasing the orders. She also used the principle *put supplies within a convenient reach for the worker* and had the blood draw supplies placed alongside the IV supplies directly at each bedside for easy collection. Kelly applied the principle of *using holders and devices instead of hands* and used the IV port to draw the blood for the specimens. This idea actually came from one of her nurses who suggested this was possible and would eliminate the need for the nurses to have to insert another needle to draw the blood. With this new arrangement, she also applied the principle *make effective use of both hands*—the nurse could now pick up and hold the tubes in each hand without having to hold on to and manage the syringe.

Kelly found a way of applying the principle of *use drop delivery chutes*. Though not necessarily using gravity to move the object, the tube system was a "chute" mechanism by which samples and other items could be transported without having to physically carry them to another place or location. The blood specimens still had to be delivered to the lab, but this made it much easier than having to walk 250 feet to make the delivery.

In making these improvements, Kelly applied all but one of principles (using *gravity feed hoppers*). In each case, she was able to simplify the details of the job.

Step 2 leads us directly to the development of the new method in Step 3. The answers to the questions "Why?" and "What?" identify unnecessary details that we can *eliminate*. The answers to the questions "Where?", "When?", and "Who?" lead us to areas we can *combine* or *rearrange*. And the answers to the question "How?" give us hints for developing the "one best way" to do the job when we *simplify* the details. Steps 2 and 3, then, are like two sides of the same coin because they work together as one. The model in Figure 11.5 shows the relationship between them and is

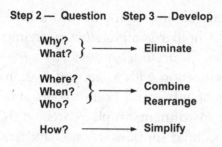

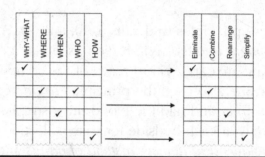

Figure 11.5 Relationship between Steps 2 and 3.

incorporated into the breakdown sheet as a tool for moving quickly and decisively from Step 2 to Step 3.

Work Out Your Ideas with Others

The last two items in Step 3 are critical to developing the new method. The fifth item, *work out your ideas with others*, means that you have to get other people involved in your improvement activity. Recognize that you can get good ideas from others (your boss, fellow supervisors, or staff). In the sample job, Kelly got important ideas from her nurses.

Getting the people involved in improving their own jobs may be the most significant thing that affects the success of your improvement plan because it is the worker, after all, who will be implementing the new and improved methods you are developing. Involving workers in the improvement process motivates them to use the new method when it is completed. A wise adage for leadership is "No involvement, no commitment." People involved in developing a new idea will commit themselves to making it work. This, in the long run, may be more important than the idea itself.

In training JM across the United States and around the world, we have found that many supervisors have been hesitant to work with their people on improvement. They are anxious about resistance to change, concerned that workers may question their methods, and wary about damaging relationships they have built. Almost without fail, these supervisors are surprised to find that their people are eager to get involved, once they see the purpose and the mechanics of JM. In some cases, trainees have actually complained that the staff get *too excited* about the process and suggest more ideas than they could handle at one time.

Write Up the Proposed New Method

The last item in Step 3 is to *write up the proposed new method*. Many ideas are never put into action because supervisors have failed to write them down. You need an accurate written record explaining what the new method will do and how it will work. A complete, written summary of your ideas and proposed improvements will be a useful tool to help you explain the improvement to your boss and can be used to sell your ideas to management. They will also go a long way to help in getting approvals from other departments or agencies that have a stake in the changes you are proposing. If your proposals are written down, other people in separate departments can look at them and use them and it will be a useful tool for implementing your work changes.

It is very important that the proposal explain concretely how people, equipment, and supplies will be better used compared with the current method. The proposal should also include improvements made to quality, layout, safety, housekeeping, etc. In other words, we must first accurately record the improvement method and its results and this can be done by including copies of your before and after breakdown sheets to show your thinking and where your ideas for improvement came from. Attach any diagrams, drawings, photos, data, etc., that will help explain and confirm the content of the proposal. Names of the persons submitting and receiving the report should be clearly written and always be sure to follow the rules of your workplace for correctly filling out and submitting reports. Finally, don't forget to include the names of those who should receive credit for cooperating and helping make the improvement.

Figure 11.6 shows the proposal sheet made by Kelly for her improvement of the Date of Surgery Blood Draw.

STEP 4: Apply the New Method

Needless to say, improvements are of no value unless you put them into use. Step 4, *apply the new method*, insures the success of improvements because

Submitted to: Brad P., Director	
Made by: Kelly T., Manager	Dept.: Peri-Op
Procedure: Date of Surgery (DOS) Blood Draw	Date: Aug 17, 20xx
Operations: ID check, blood draw, label specimen	

The following are proposed improvements on the above operations.

1. Summary

We worked on improving the date of surgery blood draw in Peri-Op. Our analysis shows that there is too much walking and handling by lab staff that led to wasted time and effort as well as the high risk of errors. By rearranging the sequence of the work and allowing peri-op nurses to do the blood draw, we were able to make dramatic improvements.

2. Results

	Before Improvement	After Improvement
Output (one worker per day)		No change
Distance walked	1,500 feet	30 feet
Error Rate	2 errors in last month	Zero errors
Number of Staff	1 nurse, 1 lab tech	1 nurse, 0 lab techs
Other—Patient needle sticks	2 sticks	1 stick

3. Content

1. By changing the EPIC settings to Nurse Draw, from Lab Draw, and having the peri-op nurse draw the blood, Lab techs will no longer have to interrupt their morning rounds and walk to the OR.
2. Drawing blood from the IV port will eliminate the need for a second needle stick and reduce the risk of error in drawing blood from the non-operative side of pt. body. This will also reduce the total amount of work.
3. Placing a printer and printing labels in the holding area will expedite drawing blood by the peri-op nurse.
4. Having supplies placed directly at the point of use will allow nurse to set up IV and draw blood efficiently in one location.
5. Using the pneumatic tube transport system will make it easier to transport specimen to lab. (Refer to the attached breakdown and layout sheets.)

This proposal was made with the cooperation of Jane B. and Bob R.

NOTE: Explain exactly how this improvement was made. If necessary, attach current and proposed breakdown sheets, diagrams, and any other related items.

Figure 11.6 Improvement proposal sheet submitted by Kelly T.

it turns ideas into action. Many a frustrated supervisor has been heard saying, "Nobody listens to my ideas!" These supervisors saw their improvement plans and ideas go nowhere because they failed to apply Step 4 of JM, which places the responsibility squarely and unequivocally on the supervisor to implement their improvement plans. The five vital elements of Step 4 are outlined below.

Item 1: *Sell Your Proposal to the Boss*

Whether you call the person who approves your work your boss, your superior, or your manager, this is the person who will (or will not) approve any changes that you want to make. For this reason, you will need to *sell* your ideas to this person. The best way to do this is to give him or her a short but complete summary of the plan, with supporting facts, in writing. The proposal should contain breakdown sheets, samples, data, sketches, and pictures along with anything else that will aid in illustrating your improvement plan. This written record, which you made in Step 3, will give the reader confidence that you have "done your homework" and understand the process in question well enough to know how to make it better. Figure 11.7 shows the proposed method breakdown sheet for the DOS Blood Draw process using the improvements Kelly developed following the JM four-step method.

Compare this breakdown sheet with the current method breakdown (Figure 11.2) and you will recognize that the proposed method suggests a much better way to do the work. So will the boss. The presentation in this format is clear and compelling and makes it quite easy to sell your ideas. When you explain in your written proposals the increases and better uses of people, equipment, supplies, space, quality, safety, etc., the point is already made.

Job Breakdown Sheet

PROCESS: Date of Surgery (DOS) Blood Draw   MADE BY: Tracy B.   DATE: Aug. 16, 20xx
OPERATIONS: ID check, blood draw, label specimen   DEPARTMENT: Peri-Op

	PROPOSED METHOD DETAILS	Distance traveled in feet	REMARKS TIME/TOLERANCE/ REJECTS/SAFETY
1	Place armband on patient		On non-operative arm
2	Release orders in EPIC		
3	Print labels		
4	Verify patient name & DOB	5-10 ft.	At bedside
5	Collect IV & blood draw supplies		Available in holding area at each bed
6	Start IV and draw blood		
7	Label/Collect at bedside		
8	Transport to lab through tube system	20 ft.	

Figure 11.7 Proposed method breakdown sheet for "Date of Surgery Blood Draw."

Item 2: Sell the New Method to the Staff

To get the full benefit of the improvement, you need the support and coop-eration of the staff who will actually be using the new method. Sometimes, people resist change. Your people may become defensive, especially if they perceive your ideas as criticism of their work. For these reasons, it is vital to take the time to gain the support and cooperation of the staff who will be putting the plan into action. The best way to get this support is to involve workers at an early stage, just as Kelly did when she worked with her nurses. When you get people to take part in the process of putting the new method together, they take ownership and commit themselves to carrying out the new method properly.

With staff who do not take part in the Job Methods Improvement exer-cise, be sure to explain that the purpose of the improvement is *to construc-tively seek better ways to improve patient care*. You can explain how the new method makes the work easier and safer to do, emphasizing that it is not a form of "speeding up" the process. Point out the areas of waste that you are eliminating and explain the principles you are using to streamline and sim-plify the procedure. Knowing that you have their best interest in mind will make it easier for them to trust the new method.

Whenever you instruct the new method to a worker, follow the Job Instruction four-step method we studied in Section II being sure to "Get the person interested in learning the job." Remember that using proper JI technique helps workers learn the new method quickly, conscientiously, and correctly.

Item 3: Get Final Approval of All Concerned on Safety, Quality, Quantity, and Cost

Remember that other related departments have a stake in how the work is done in your department and may need to *approve* any changes you make in methods for a job. Quality Assurance needs to be sure that the work is being done in a way that satisfies patient care. The Patient Safety as well as Infection Control and Prevention people need to be sure that no one is being injured or hurt in the process. The Cost Accounting department needs to be sure that you are doing the work within budget. And the Planning Department needs to be sure that the work you do fits into the overall plans for the hospital or organization. In some cases, even the patients that you serve may need to approve new work procedures. Getting approval from everyone beforehand will prevent trouble and misunderstandings.

It is a big part of the supervisor's responsibility to know what authority or function will be needed to approve the improvement plan, either in full or in part. Different proposals will need different approval depending on the content. Be sure to follow your organizational procedures and policies. Your best asset will be your written proposal because this can be copied, passed around, reviewed, marked up, revised, and signed by any and all interested parties.

Item 4: Put the New Method to Work—Use It until a Better Way Is Developed

Amazingly, even with full approval and support, supervisors sometimes place improvement plans in a drawer and quickly forget them while they deal with the pressing problems of the day that need immediate attention. Don't wait. Put your plan into action as quickly as possible. Your plan is an investment in the future. It will pay for itself with interest. You cannot afford to be "too busy" when your improvement plan can solve the very problems that are eating up so much of your time. And remember that this new method has become the new and updated standard for how we do the work, so be sure that it is integrated into the standard work processes we have been talking about throughout this book.

Never allow yourself to think that this is the end of your improvement activity for this job. Use your improved process *until a better way is developed*. Never assume that all of the improvements have already been found. Always remember that improvement is a continuous process.

Item 5: Give Credit Where Credit Is Due

As suggested throughout the process of developing your improvement plan, you should get ideas or advice from other people and incorporate these into your final proposal. Do not forget to give these people credit and show your sincere appreciation for their contributions. Not doing so can provoke resentment and one "stolen" or unacknowledged idea will stop all others. Showing gratitude is not difficult and can take many forms like asking your own boss to say a word of appreciation to the person who helped with or made the improvement. At the very least, you should include the names of the people who assisted you in your final proposal. The more credit you give, the more people will contribute ideas.

Closing

As you saw with the Date of Surgery Blood Draw example, the principles of Job Methods Improvement are all that you need to make substantial and vital improvements to your work. People from around the world have used these principles to make countless improvements in the many decades since their development. Today, in health care facilities and organizations around the world, the Job Methods Improvement plan is used as a simple but effective method to introduce and sustain the process of continuous improvement which will raise our standards of patient care.

Chapter 12

Integrating TWI into the Culture to Sustain Results

Introduction

Every organization is unique with its own quirks and culture that will have an impact on the application of any program it tries to implement and make its own. If the new program is not aligned with these unique aspects of the organization's culture it may, in the end, be doomed to failure. Countless "flavors of the month" have come and gone as the strength of the culture ultimately won out over whatever enthusiasm and drive there was for the change. In Chapter 10, we learned that there is experience from the past that can help guide us in making a plan, starting with a good pilot project, to make Training Within Industry (TWI) a lasting and integral part of any health organization's culture. These lessons include:

- Start small
- Stay true to the method
- Advertise results
- Create pull for more training and follow that demand.

Much thought should be given, and plans should be made, to *how* TWI will be engineered into the culture of any organization. Because every organization is structured differently, there is no single correct pathway to implementation. In fact, each implementation must find its own course while following

DOI: 10.4324/9781003035305-12

basic guidelines, like those outlined in this section. Still, we can learn from the experiences of other organizations when it comes to how to integrate a program into the organizational culture in order to sustain it. While each organization will have its own structures, champions and skeptics, our experience has taught us to focus initially on these three areas:

1. Inclusion and involvement from all departments currently responsible for training
2. Utilizing TWI tools alongside and in conjunction with other Lean tools
3. Engineering TWI principles into the Leader Standard Work including *gemba* rounds

TWI as a Common Language

Work is currently being done in health care to restructure how training is done. What we have found is that the key is to work within the existing structure. It may seem counterintuitive, but in order to change a culture you have to work within it—from the inside.

In many health care organizations, training is both centralized and decentralized as described in Section I. Jobs and tasks that are common to all areas and unique to a specifically licensed staff member, for example, a nurse, are taught centrally by a skilled instructor working for the clinical education department. Other jobs are learned "on the job" or at the place where patient care occurs, usually with the oversight of a trained peer or preceptor as a guide. Many organizations are now moving beyond this model of specific training departments and are seeking to integrate aspects of Human Resources and Organizational Talent Management into their training. These new departments incorporate traditional Organizational Development principles with the focus on Process Improvement and Human Resources' Performance Management so there is a broader focus on effectiveness and results.

The objective of the new structure design is to have effective teaching and training leading to effective and measurable patient outcomes and effective succession planning and retention of good people. All of the various departments, then, with their various missions and charters, are now invested in the proper training of the organization's people and play a role in the implementation of effective training programs. Therefore, for the TWI methods to take hold, it must become a familiar tool to *all* of the leaders in *all* of these related departments. This is an opportunity here for TWI to become the common language; the common method that crosses the natural barriers that tend to exist between multiple departments. Because the TWI methods are so fundamental, by placing them within this new organizational structure, they can permeate the efforts of everyone involved and become the foundation for common modes of behavior that, in the end, make up what we call "culture."

With all of these departments being separated and reporting to different leaders and directors, perhaps an oversight council or advisory group can guide the implementation and application priorities. In that way, communication is strengthened and there is assurance that each group is integrating the methods into their training. An example of this type of integration might be found in the case of training a new leader. Using the Training Timetable in their orientation might be a perfect way to get a new leader to know his or her new department. By identifying the specific skilled jobs of their new staff and noting who has been trained for which job, the new leader can quickly assess the needs of the department. As discussed in Chapter 7, having a well thought out plan for who needs to be trained for which job and by when is an excellent antidote to "firefighting," saving the new leader operational time that is better spent elsewhere.

This is only one vision of how TWI might be integrated into the daily work of an organization as it tries to improve its ability to provide perfect care for its patients. When each organization looks at its own priorities and direction and captures clearly the role of effective training in reaching its goals, it may find other structures or avenues for how it can use the TWI methods in a way that they become a part of the organization's DNA. However, as we have stressed throughout, providing effective training that creates standard work in how things get done is the foundation of just about anything we must do to improve our current performance. Therefore, we must know our own organizations intimately and think long and hard about the best way to anchor TWI into the culture in a way that it grows organically and, little by little, begins to create the performance results we want and need.

Some of the key factors that need to be considered in integrating TWI into an organization's training culture would be

- Identify all of the people/departments that are involved in training.
- Invite key leaders of these areas to participate in JI, JR, and JM training and encourage them to go on to become leaders in the implementation efforts.

■ Designate a "primary" home department for the purpose of providing logistical infrastructure (training classes, tracking results, manpower for coaching, etc.).

■ Enforce a strong auditing process for both the trainers (how they instruct) and the trainees (how they perform the standard work).

■ Provide strong and consistent follow-up coaching for JR practice.

■ Capture experiences and consolidate expertise.

■ Engage in improvement activities and lead/coach JM practice.

The goal here is to make TWI the "common language" by which everyone communicates when it comes to passing on and developing skills. You will know this cultural change is occurring when you hear people, when they run into a problem, say things like: "Do we have a job breakdown on this task?" or "What's the Key Point here to doing this correctly?" Instead of blaming someone when something goes wrong, the first question should be "How was the training?" When a problem with people is holding back needed performance, you will hear questions like: "What is our objective here?" and "Have we gotten the facts?" and "What possible actions can we consider?" Instead of rushing to "get rid of the bad apples," the question is whether we have built strong relationships of trust using the Foundations for Good Relations. And when finding needed improvement on a difficult or unwieldy procedure or practice, you will hear questions like: "Have we broken down the task and questioned the details?" or "Can we eliminate these motions?" When we have a common language for analyzing our work and sure methods for teaching it, motivating people to follow it, and working together to improve it, we can zero in on the real culprit to our problems—our ability to perform the work correctly and safely each time it is done.

In this book, we have tried to show how creating and maintaining standard work is the foundation for what we need to do to make health care better. Having a sure and dependable method of instructing people on these standards is a requirement. Having a solid leadership method of getting the cooperation of the people we lead is a necessity. TWI's Job Instruction and Job Relations methods give us that common language around which we can embed the discipline into our culture in order to ensure continuing results long after the pilot project is finished and people understand its value. And TWI's Job Methods Improvement plan will help us continue improving those methods in a continuous cycle of *kaizen*.

Using the Tools of Lean with TWI

If you are fortunate enough to work with an organization that has adopted Lean principles as the method for improving processes, then matching these with TWI will be quite natural. "Lean" is the name that has come to be associated with a school of principles and practices that seeks to find continuous improvement by eliminating waste in the process, thus, the name *lean*.* Multiple publications show how these principles and practices can be applied in the health care industry, such as Mark Graban's *Lean Hospitals* (CRC Press, 2016, 3rd edition) and *Transforming Health Care: Virginia Mason Medical Center's Pursuit of the Perfect Patient Experience* by Charles Kenney (CRC Press, 2010), but what is significant to note here is how the TWI methods formed the foundation for these Lean tools that came after it. Just as you need to know how to do basic math and algebra before you can do calculus, you need to have basic skills like TWI before you can succeed in doing Lean. This makes sense because many of the Lean tools like "Just-in-Time" were developed, for the most part, in Japan directly from and based on TWI and other programs that were introduced there after WWII.

Hospitals and health care facilities across the country and around the world are discovering how Lean can improve quality, patient safety, and employee satisfaction just as it did for our manufacturing counterparts over the past few decades. Just think about any product that you own today and, in almost every case, it will be of better quality and cheaper than the same thing you owned many years ago. Computers and cell phones are good examples. We can credit the use of Lean principles for these results and the same thing can be done in health care.

Beyond the basic need for having good skills and creating standard work, which has been the central theme of this book, when these fundamental TWI skills are used in the broader context of continuous improvement, they further can become a foundation for how an organization gets things done—the culture of excellence. Because the TWI methods of Job Instruction (JI), Job Relations (JR), and Job Methods (JM) are essential elements to the success of the Lean tools, an organization applying Lean will more readily see the value of the methods and be able to get strong and

---

* Many have found the name "Lean" to be unfortunate because it gives the impression that its purpose is simply to reduce people. This is not the case. The goal is to create added value in the work that people do.

immediate results from their use. On the other hand, most organizations trying to apply Lean struggle to "sustain the gains" they initially get from their efforts because they do not have strong instruction and leadership skills like JI and JR in place, and they lack a method by which to practice and refine their standard work like JM. Without proper leadership and instruction, improvements they make are not securely planted in the organization because they haven't been "learned" correctly and, thus, fall away as people slip back to their old ways. So, the combination of TWI and Lean make for a strong program of culture change that can give continuing results.

Typically, Lean concepts are taught through one department by a small number of staff members so that the rigor of the implementation remains intact. In the same way, the TWI material could be taught centrally by a small number of people, and then applied broadly. Our suggestion of finding a primary home department for TWI applies here so expertise can be consolidated for TWI training, coaching can be provided for continued skill development, and guidance given on effective rollout strategies. This group could then inform the Lean advisory group regarding which staff should be selected to attend training and what types of successes and setbacks are being discovered. By having this "home base," the probability that the method will become embedded in the culture can be raised.

The opportunity to combine Lean tools with TWI enhances any effort at improvement and can take advantage of the organization's new "common language" around its processes. The tools of Lean, such as PDSA Cycles, Value Stream Maps, Standard Work Sheets, Standard Work, Target Sheets, Cycle Time, Takt Time, and Root Cause Analysis, can all be integrated seamlessly. Let's take a quick look at some of these tools to see how they can be applied with TWI to enhance our work in health care.

PDSA (Plan–Do–Study–Act) Cycles

As discussed in Chapter 2, *PDSA Cycles* (see Figure 2.1) are plans for testing interventions or countermeasures for improvement purposes. Using this framework method, we carefully observe a process and identify possible solutions that we think might lead to an improvement. We make a plan to roll out the new process and then study the results. If the expected good results are not what we see in reality, we assume that the idea or intervention was flawed. This is where a common problem occurs, though. The idea or intervention might actually have been brilliant, but it was the rollout that was flawed, and by flawed we mean incomplete. Instead of moving directly to studying the results, we suggest studying the rollout. Was everyone fully trained in the new process and was the process in place long enough to give us good data to review? If yes, *then* you can move on to study and take action upon the results or the identified outcome metrics. TWI's sure and effective method of training is a perfect fit with the PDSA Cycle, right after "Plan" and as part of "Do." The "Doing" step involves training everyone on the new process and establishing reliability. If you wish to improve a process, your intervention trial should be stable so that you can rely upon the results. In order to achieve that stability, you have to train staff effectively.

Value Stream Maps

A *Value Stream Map* (VSM) is a visual depiction of the steps in a process, quantifying the amount of time utilized for each step and tabulating the wait time between steps. VSMs often show the flow of materials, information, and people and, in health care, the VSM depicts the experience flow of the patient. VSMs are created by observing the process many times, writing down each step, and timing each step using a stopwatch. The more reliable a process becomes, the easier it is to map. The main contribution of this tool is the opportunity to involve the workers and to have a common, agreed-upon written depiction of the process as it is currently done. The VSM provides easy-to-see areas for improvement such as long wait times between cycles of work, redundant steps, or areas where mistakes occur. As improvement efforts begin, the team can review these "blueprints" of the process and understand when and why the process will be changing. Figure 12.1 is an example of a VSM depicting the process flow for a patient receiving chemotherapy in the hospital. This VSM became the basis for improvement efforts for the next two years.

Standard Work Sheet

A *Standard Work Sheet* is a simple grid tool used to diagram the flow of a process, usually depicting the physical layout of the place where the work is done. Figure 12.2 is a Standard Work Sheet that was utilized in the creation of the Job Instruction breakdown for hourly rounding (see Chapter 6) to support the identification of the right sequence of steps as the staff member moves through the room. Figure 12.3 is the same Standard Work Sheet tool, this time being utilized to support the two preparatory elements of JI: Get Everything Ready and Arrange the Worksite. This tool depicts how

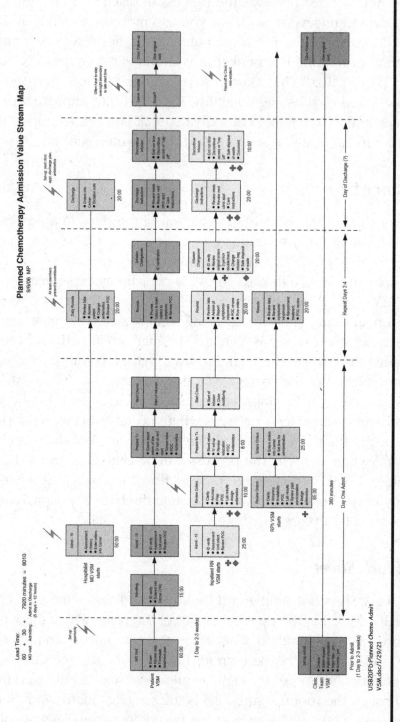

Figure 12.1   Value Stream Map of process flow for a patient receiving chemotherapy. (2011 Virginia Mason Medical Center. All rights reserved.)

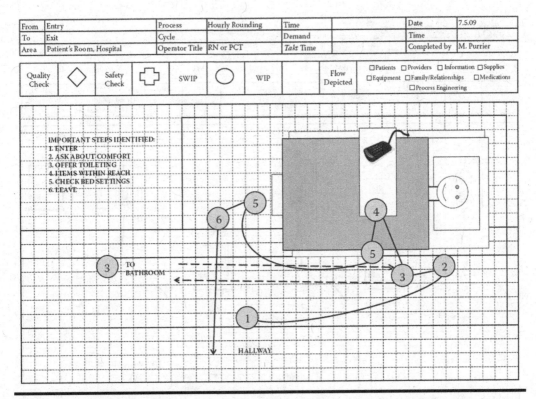

From	Entry		Process	Hourly Rounding	Time			Date	7.5.09
To	Exit		Cycle		Demand			Time	
Area	Patient's Room, Hospital		Operator Title	RN or PCT	*Takt* Time			Completed by	M. Purrier

| Quality Check | ◇ | Safety Check | ✚ | SWIP | ◯ | WIP | | Flow Depicted | ☐Patients ☐Providers ☐Information ☐Supplies ☐Equipment ☐Family/Relationships ☐Medications ☐Process Engineering |

IMPORTANT STEPS IDENTIFIED:
1. ENTER
2. ASK ABOUT COMFORT
3. OFFER TOILETING
4. ITEMS WITHIN REACH
5. CHECK BED SETTINGS
6. LEAVE

TO BATHROOM

HALLWAY

Figure 12.2   Standard Work Sheet for Hourly Rounding. (2011 Virginia Mason Medical Center. All rights reserved.)

equipment and people are best positioned to optimize the learning for the High Risk Medication Double Check job.

Standard Work

Standard Work is developed once the intervention or idea has proved itself to be a reliable improvement to the previous way of working. Training is needed again at this point to assure that every single worker is trained in the new process and that there is a means by which future staff will be trained upon their arrival. A standard work document (see Figure 12.4) differs from a Job Instruction breakdown in that the standard work document is intended to give full and specific instructions in the steps of a job as it relates to time—the time it takes to perform each step is noted and assigned based on time available and demand. Often posted at the location of the work, a standard work document is a reference for the worker of the entire cycle of work. A Job Instruction breakdown, on the other hand, is a document created to assist the instructor—brief notes identifying the Important

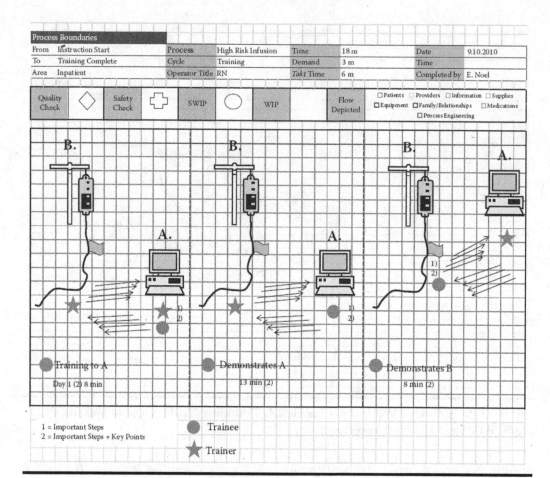

Figure 12.3 Standard Work Sheet for High-Risk Medication. (2011 Virginia Mason Medical Center. All rights reserved.)

Steps and the Key Points of how to do a particular job (see Chapter 6)—and not meant to be used or reviewed by the worker.

Target Progress Reports

Target Progress Reports are utilized to track progress in any number of metrics. They show the current state or baseline being measured, the goal that is set to be reached, and the actual observed and measured results over time. A Target Progress Report is a great tool to track the results you get applying TWI to processes. Figure 12.5 depicts one such document used during a project to reduce the rate of hemolysis of samples obtained from the staff of one emergency department. Training for the actual process of collecting the blood specimen was the focus of the improvement effort.

Quality Check	Safety Precaution	Standard WIP
◇	✚	⬤

Purpose:
To Assure Quality Process Flow Assurance of Proper Meal Provision RCP MEAL

Related Policies or Evidence:
(X4) ID Prefix Tag F241, in conjunction with Text; Assisted Dining: The Role and Skills of Feeding Assistants, 2003.

Roles/Work Units Who Must Adopt This Process:	Takt Time: 120"
RN	

STEP	OPERATOR role responsible for each task	TASK DESCRIPTION	TOOLS/SUPPLIES REQUIRED	CYCLE TIME
1. -75	RN	Meet with Charge. Finalize all patient assignments.	Assignment sheet RN Meal Plan Grid	3"
2. -60	RN	Obtain blood glucose results. Review RN Meal Plan Grid with PCT. Make plans for anticipated care needs of patients.	RN Meal Plan Grid	15"
3. -45	RN	Room Rounding to assure Pt Readiness: (Medications, toileting, washing, transfers/positioning. sequence by: 1) Group, 2)Eating in room independently, 3)those pt's with Assigned Assistants	Hygiene needs, medications, transport devices	30"
5. -15	RN	Review compiled meal plan. Assess for defects. Assure transportation of residents to Dining Room. Anticipate availability for Meal delivery.		15"
6. 0 ◇	RN	Deliver Meals Room by Room, Assure Set up with meal items off trays, accessible, lids off per pt preference, & correct. relay defects	Delivered meal cart	10"
7 +15 to +45	RN	Circulate, assuring proper process flow, patient dignity, Service Provision & timely defect resolution. Cue residents PRN, remove tray when finished.		
8. +45- +60	RN	Transport Residents as needed & provide post meal care	Briefs, clothing changes, toiletries, needed medications, Transfer & transport devices	

Figure 12.4   Standard Work Sheet for Proper Meal Provision by RN. (2011 Virginia Mason Medical Center. All rights reserved.)

When the JI method was utilized, they could know for sure that there was real improvement because the correct metrics had been identified to signify the health of the process and they had a baseline to measure them against. Once the new training was put into place, they were able to quickly identify results because the volume of lab draws was high and they could show reliability in the new process proving it was working.

Target Progress Report

Team Name: Reducing Hemolysis in the ED						Date: November 16-17, 2010					
Department: Emergency Room						TAKT Time: (include calculation) Peak hours takt time=11:00-14:00 180 min/18 avg patients per day=10 minutes					
Product/Process Summary: Gathers supplies->Tourniquet on->palpates->Cleans with cholorprep->Poke->Connects transfer device>Draws blood tubes->Tourniquet off->Flushes->Secures IV						Team Leader: Karen Process Owner: Jane					
Metric (units of measurement)	Baseline	Target	Day 2	Day 3	Day 4	Final	30 days 12/16/2010	60 days 01/16/2011	90 days 02/11/2011	% Change
Space (square feet)	NA	(>= 50%)	NA	NA	NA	NA				
Inventory (dollars)	NA	(>= 90%)	NA	NA	NA	NA				
Staff Walking Distance (feet)	NA	(>= 50%)	NA	NA	NA	NA				
Parts Travel Distance:										
Lead Time:										
Work in Process (WIP):										
Standard Work In Process (SWIP)										
Quality (defects)(%)										
1. % of time blood sample is hemolyzed in the ED	1. 5%					1. 0%	**			1. **
2. % of time tourniquet left on for greater than 2 minutes**	2. 92%	0%				2. 0%	**60%			2. 34.8%
3. % of time chloroprep dry time is less than 30 seconds	3. 55%					3. 0%	60%			3. -9.1%

Figure 12.5 Target Progress Report for reducing the hemolysis in the emergency department (ED). (2011 Virginia Mason Medical Center. All rights reserved.)

Cycle Time

Cycle Time is the actual time it takes to complete one step in a process. While the Value Stream Map depicts the entire process at a glance, there is a need to watch and time each individual cycle (or step) of the process when looking for ways to make the work safer, easier, and more efficient. This is where we get "down to the hand motions" of the job itself. In addition, this tool is extremely useful in planning a training rollout of any kind. First, time yourself or another trainer giving the training to a real learner. Do this several times to establish a fair representation of multiple learners and identify how long the training takes to complete. Next, time the follow-up of the training in the same way. Identify the number of people to be trained and you will have a good idea of the amount of resources needed to complete the training rollout.

Takt Time

Takt Time is a formula for describing the pace of the work needed to meet the demand at any given time. It is calculated by identifying the amount of time available and dividing it by the demand. This is another helpful tool in planning a successful training rollout and staying on a projected timeline. Let's review a practical example:

Five hundred eighty people need to be trained in a particular job within the next two months. The clinic offices are open on weekdays only, giving you Monday through Friday to train. Our original two months is now calculated out to be eight weeks, or, more precisely, 40 days. To calculate the takt time for training, reverse the formula and divide 580 (demand) by the 40 days (time available). Now we know that to meet the deadline we must set a pace of training of 14.5 people per day. If you have already established that the cycle time for teaching one job is 12 minutes, you can get a sense of the number of trainers you might need to carry this plan forward. Further building on our case study, if three weeks (15 days) go by and we have trained 160 staff, what is the new pace, or takt time, for training if we still intend to keep to the timeline? So, 160 subtracted from the original staff number of 580 is 420, and 420 divided by the 25 remaining training days equals 16.8, or 17, people who need to be trained every day. Therefore, we must increase our efforts by adding more time to the trainer's schedule or provide more trainers.

Root Cause Analysis (RCA)

Root Cause Analysis will be the last example of Lean tools we will look at, but there are others. RCA is the process of attempting to sort out the true cause(s) contributing to poor results. Without understanding the true cause of a problem, you will have great difficulty identifying appropriate interventions; it would be no better than guessing. Therefore, a great deal of effort should be put forth to identify the root or true cause of the poor results that you are seeing. This review is done in a variety of ways. One method is to continue to ask "why" repeatedly for each answer to the previous "why" and diagram out the answers until the trail of information is exhausted. Another method for discovering root cause is to categorize the types of errors or reasons for the errors and the frequency with which they occur. Once identified, they can be displayed in a pareto chart, such as the one in Figure 12.6. This chart depicts the frequency and types of errors and near misses for a medication process. It also shows where in the process an error occurred.

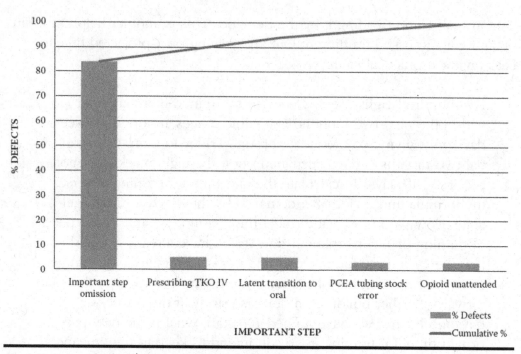

Figure 12.6 Pareto Chart for Medication Errors.

By understanding these reasons, appropriate countermeasures can be put into place. In this case, one countermeasure was to provide training for the actual process. Once a reliable sequence and process was agreed upon, Job Instruction was utilized to train those involved in the new process. But an important lesson from this case is that not every single cause can be mitigated by the new process and the training. Other countermeasures would need to be implemented to achieve zero defects. Figure 12.7 depicts a simple version of asking questions about failures for standard work whereby the different identified barriers would require different approaches for resolution.

The key for integration of Lean and TWI is to engineer the fit into the organizational structure by involving the right people in the process as stakeholders. For that, you need to create shared, matrixed accountability. Any opportunity to utilize the tools of Lean will only enhance your efforts by making your intention and progress clear and visible in the shared language of process improvement. Remember, standard work creates reliability. Reliability allows us to measure and quantify the process as it currently exists. These measurements can provide the common language amongst diverse groups so that an agreed upon plan and priority might be set for the next steps. In this way, you can share your good results. And, in the meantime, the TWI methods become a fundamental part of how things get

Failure of Standard Work Root Cause Analysis

Title:

Problem Statement:

Last known metrics:

Barriers to Standard Work (check all that apply)	Plan to Return to Standards – (corresponding countermeasure to each item listed)
☐ 1. Can't find it	
☐ 2. No longer relevant	
☐ 3. Not enough detail or incomplete	
☐ 4. No accountability after training	
☐ 5. Training incomplete or	
☐ 6. Staff issues/crisis mode	
☐ 7. Leadership changes	
☐ 8. Can't be done as designed	
☐ 9. Process Owner unprepared	
☐ 10. Lack of enthusiasm to continue or improve	
☐ 11. Mutiny	
☐ 12. Relaxed after training – drift	
☐ 13. Other – be specific	

Figure 12.7 Example of tool used by author to analyze failure. Each "barrier" identified would require a different approach to overcome that barrier.

done. In other words, they become part of the culture. Figure 12.8 is an example of a visual depiction of how one organization imagined the tools of TWI integrating with their Lean tools in the larger context of Process Improvement. Notice how this diagram resembles the PDSA Cycle process.

Sustaining Improvement by Engineering TWI into Leader Standard Work

The key to sustaining improvement over the long term is to lock in standard work practices that can then be improved upon and, in turn, locked in as higher-level standards. Like climbing up a hill, you have to make sure your footing is secure before you take the next step or you may find yourself tumbling back down to the bottom. Without a solid foundation

Developing Standard Work

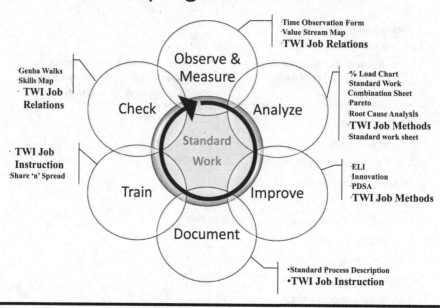

Figure 12.8   Example of one organization's standard work development process. Notice how it resembles the PDSA Cycle.

of standard work in our daily performance, anything we try to improve or change will just be, as we have stated, one more way of many, many ways things get done. We won't be able to assure that the "best practice" gets performed each and every time by each and every person doing it and, therefore, we won't be able to lock in the improvement and sustain the best results possible. We have seen how the TWI methods give us skill that we can utilize in locking in these best practices so that we can sustain high performance and achieve outstanding results. We can't expect things to get better on their own; we have to apply ourselves using proven skills that get the job done.

In order to sustain the results of a TWI introduction, then, it is imperative that it becomes part of the culture. We defined culture as being "the way most of the people behave most of the time." When they get to know and feel, and enjoy, what it is like being a well-trained and motivated workforce performing consistently at high levels, they will begin behaving in those ways on a regular basis. What is more, they will always be thinking of better ways to do the work and have a method that helps them actualize their ideas. Getting them to that stage is a heavy lift, but well worth the effort. Essential to any change management effort is the need for the leader to assure that the process *can* be performed as designed and that it *is* being performed as designed.

There is a need then for the supervisor to *go to the gemba*, the place where the real work is done, and check for themself that things are going as planned. Mr Cho, former Chairman of the Toyota Motor Company, used to say, "Go and see. Ask questions. Show respect." This good advice is the foundation for what has become known as "*gemba* rounds" and the practice by which the leader goes to the *gemba* daily, observes the work, and continually makes improvements is known as Leader Standard Work. Much more can be learned on this topic in other publications such as David Mann's *Creating a Lean Culture* (CRC Press, 2015, 3rd edition).

One practical element of Leader Standard Work is to audit the process. In this way, the leader can observe the process design and the effectiveness of the training as well as the attitude of the worker to the job. Further, the presence of a person in a position of authority sends a clear message that it is expected that the work be completed as designed, every time, until the team improves it further and audits should be aligned with the metrics that are being targeted for improvement. Some examples of great points to observe in an audit include:

- The correct sequence of Important Steps in a job (wet hands *before* applying soap)
- Conscientious application of the job's Key Points (enough to cover *all* surfaces)
- Specific aspects of a recent improvement effort (*label* identifying a hazardous medication is placed onto medication by pharmacy)
- A sticking point for change of routine (*by 0900*, the Charge Nurse has sent the requests for late breakfasts to the kitchen).

Another helpful aspect of auditing is to think through *how* the data being observed is collected and reported. Having pre-printed data collection sheets with actual instructions for auditors assures the continuity of the data being collected. This allows the collection to be delegated to more people which allows for observations at various times of the day and days of the week. Resist the tendency to make the audit comprehensive or too long. By creating short, simple audits of the points that matter to a process, the auditor is not overburdened and is more likely to "work it into" her existing process. If the audit uncovers unwanted results, it serves as a signal for a more comprehensive review and analysis for diagnosing barriers. Figure 12.9 shows a

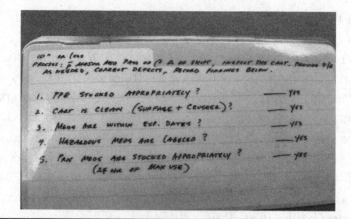

Figure 12.9 Sample of an audit card for the Medication Cart Audit. Cards are laminated so that results can be documented with a dry-erase pen directly onto the card and then reused. Directions for the auditor are listed first.

simple 3 × 5 note card that has been laminated so auditors can use it again and again with a dry-erase pen to record their observations right onto the card.

Exactly who, besides the leader, should conduct *gemba* audits is the next question and the answer is that it depends upon the results that you are trying to influence. The table below shows different team member roles and the differing results/influence that having them as an auditor might illicit:

Team Member	Impact to Culture
Leader/Charge Nurse	• Sets expectations that the work is done as designed • Ability to see, ask questions, show support, and engage
Peer of same discipline	• Signals alignment with the standard • Expectation of others to follow similarly • Engagement
Other discipline impacted by change	• More formal review practice • Opportunity for team development as we make processes transparent

There is a benefit in recruiting as many auditors/observers as possible in order to be able to see the process from differing angles and viewpoints. By having instructions on how to conduct a good audit as well as references to the standard work or job breakdown sheet, data inputs can be collected that give a more realistic picture of what is really happening on a regular basis and not behavior that only occurs when "the Boss" is on site and watching. This view will be more aligned with the true definition of standard work: the way in which the workers do the work *all* the time.

The next question for the leader is to determine *when* the audit should be done. The audit should be completed at the same time the job being audited is being done. When auditing a meal tray line build, the audit time is during the meal preparation times. Auditing different mealtimes on different days of the week, including weekends, would give you a much clearer picture of the standard process and its training results than if you only audited a "convenience sample" of lunch times on weekdays.

Figure 12.10 is an example of a modification of the Training Timetable that we learned about in Chapter 7. Instead of jobs to be trained, this board displays *who* will be auditing *what process* and *when*. The distribution of the audits allows coverage for a unit operating on a 24/7 schedule and the jobs scheduled to be audited might easily change depending upon the need. For example, the leader might audit a new process more frequently early on in

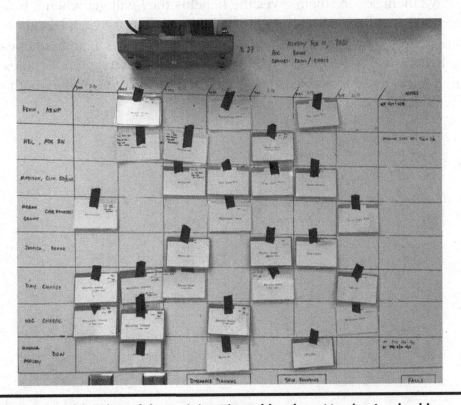

Figure 12.10 Adaptation of the Training Timetable where Nursing Leadership Team are assigned different audits throughout the week. Completed audit cards are re-taped to the wall and tallied at the end of the week.

the week until reliability has been established over multiple shifts. Then that job might only be audited monthly to assure that the work is still in place. If there was less reliability on the weekends or on nightshift, more attention might be given to conducting audits during those times. If there was a particular problem arising that needed further review, more focus might be given to that job by a variety of auditors bringing different skills to the observations.

Conclusion

Just because the need for good leadership and training seems so straightforward and logical, don't assume that your organization will immediately embrace a method like TWI wholeheartedly. Any time we put an additional burden on an already harried workforce, there will naturally be strong resistance. In the end, the only real way to get people to want to use a tool is to have them see for themselves the benefits they will get when it is used properly. That is the path each organization must find for itself based on its own unique history and structure. How we get them to see and experience those benefits is the secret to effective change. Moving a culture is no easy thing, but it is not impossible. And, if we don't change the people, nothing else will change. This is the way.

Conclusion
A Call to Action

Health care is dangerous. The opportunities to improve the care that patients receive are seemingly endless. We discussed in Chapter 1 the gap between what we know to be clinical best practices and our actual performance, pointing out the astounding costs in dollars and suffering that accrue when we do not perform at the highest levels possible. Poor outcomes are well documented and waste is rampant, so it is our responsibility to mitigate these dangers. This is our purpose.

While the challenge before us is great, the work has begun. Cultural shifts away from faultfinding and finger-pointing to collaborative problem solving are already pervasive and it is our duty to promote and expand on these efforts using the best of our abilities. We must continue to learn and improve. Tools from Lean help us to systematically identify and track our incremental improvements. The very belief that it is possible to be successful in this improvement effort is a phenomenal new addition to our way of thinking. There is momentum here and we must nurture this movement and carry it forward.

TWI is a program that provides a sure and reliable method to leadership, training, and improvement which is foundational to this effort. It is only through good leadership that we can realize the true power of standard work—every worker doing the job in the same, best way every time. This gives us reliability. Reliability gives us visibility to see where our problems and opportunities lie. And visibility gives us new targets to address. This is the path to improvement.

Thank you for all of your hard work in making health care better. Please continue to do your best.

DOI: 10.4324/9781003035305-102

Index

Printed in the United States
by Baker & Taylor Publisher Services

Printed in the United States
by Baker & Taylor Publisher Services